CW00346914

This is Not a Book About
Charles Darwin

This is Not a Book About Charles Darwin

About

Charles Darwin

A writer's journey through my family

Emma Darwin

For Caroline
best wishes
Emma Darwin

HH
Holland House

www.hhousebooks.com

Hardback ISBN: 978-1-910688-64-9
Kindle ISBN: 978-1-910688-76-2

Cover design by Liam Relph
Typeset by Polgarus Studio
Published in the UK

Holland House Books
Holland House
47 Greenham Road
Newbury, Berkshire RG14 7HY
United Kingdom

For my sisters, Sophia Katharine Darwin and Carola Frances Darwin

Contents

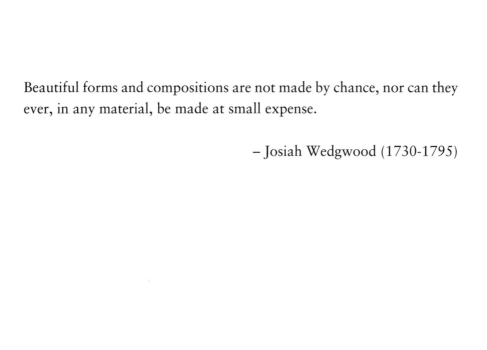

Beautiful forms and compositions are not made by chance, nor can they ever, in any material, be made at small expense.

– Josiah Wedgwood (1730-1795)

I think

case must be that one
generation then should be
as many living as now.
To do this & to have
many species in same
genus (as is) requires
extinction.

①

B C D A

Then between A & B. immens[e]
gap of relation. C & B. the
finest gradation, B & D
rather greater distinction
Thus genera would be
formed. — bearing relation

PREFACE

The University of Valencia's Darwin Day dinner has been cooked from my great-great-grandmother's recipe book, which is digitised and available to all on the internet. We eat – it's delicious – and discuss what, exactly, my great-great-grandfather meant when he wrote 'I think' before the most famous mind-map in human history.

One of the biggest literary bloggers striding through the nascent internet jungle writes that 'Emma Darwin may have smart genes, but she doesn't use them well in her novel *The Mathematics of Love*'.

Brisbane Zoo's Galapagos tortoise Harriet *may* have been ridden by Charles Darwin: if only I could be photographed riding her in my turn, says the *Australian*'s photographer at the Brisbane Writers Festival. But Harriet died a month ago, so these equally primaeval-looking trees will have to do.

Publishing News writes that 'There were genuine grumbles at the book fair about the shortage of toilets, and the director recognises that the book fair has to evolve. Talking of evolution, Headline Review author Emma Darwin, descendant of you-know-who, was among those fêted at Headline's 20th birthday party on the river, for her *Mathematics of Love*. Mathematics of queuing, more like.'

I am a very ordinary, unknown person, and I was a very ordinary, unknown debut novelist. The only thing which made me different from the next debut novelist in the struggle for life on the bookshop tables is that my great-great-grandfather, Charles Darwin, wrote the book which changed forever how the human race conceived of itself and the universe. And I was named after his wife.

That Emma Darwin, Charles's wife and my great-great-grandmother, is why the Wikipedia entry that a friend surprised me with has to be labelled 'Emma Darwin (Novelist)'. She was born Emma Wedgwood, the youngest child of the potter Josiah Wedgwood II, and had known her first cousin Charles all her life.

I have been Emma Darwin all my life, and although I'm sorry I missed Harriet the tortoise – Galapagos tortoises are venerable, endearing and a top-quality demonstration of evolution-in-action – from the day I was named until well into this century, and despite the upsurge of the global Darwin industry in the 1980s, all I encountered was the occasional question asked at a party, on a course, or across the counter of the dry cleaners when I gave my name. In all cases, my answer to the 'Any relation?' question was the one my sisters and I had grown up observing our parents give: a smile, a quiet, 'Well, yes, actually,' with or without an amplification for the curious which, in our case, was, 'He was my grandfather's grandfather.' And that was usually that.

True, when the *The Mathematics of Love* was published I was disconcerted by how every single newspaper or blog review, every press-release, column, comment or interview – even the briefest New Books listing – mentioned You Know Who. But although sometimes it was fun, and sometimes it was irritating, it still wasn't *important*.

Then I decided to write novel about my family.

We are a weakly, pedestrian species which, to compensate, has evolved a big brain, and when it comes to creating new human beings that's a combination which is survival-giving for the species, but death-dealing for child and mother. My idea to create a novel out of my family's history very nearly didn't survive conception, but at the end, the novel I did create nearly killed me.

But what you don't die of, you learn from. The novel that came to be called *Black Shadow and Bone* taught me a lot about how fiction works and how it gets written, by showing me, over and over again (which is the only way a novel has of telling you something) that it wasn't working. And in allowing the novel to mutate into the book you are holding, something of it has survived.

This is Not a Book About Charles Darwin is about my family, and it's also about my personal entanglement in a particular set of creative and writerly circumstances. But this is not a biography or autobiography, because it's not a fully-realised narrative of even a part of anyone's life, and since a better label for the research one does for a novel is poet Philip Gross's 'freesearch', it doesn't observe the biographer's boundaries of structure and academic rigour.[1] Nor is it a novel – although one way and another it has quite a bit of fiction in it – because it's about something that happened to people who actually existed, and to some people, including me, who still do; it also has footnotes and other non-novelish things. It's certainly not a how-to-write book, not least because it's about how I failed to write a book.

Of course, I don't have total recall. The writer revising a first draft, or re-building it totally, is always chiefly concerned with the best-adapted to the *new* environment: not with what isn't useful, but with what is. The no-longer-useful disappears, unheeded, into the mud, so comparing the first, second, or umpteenth drafts would only show the traces, not the process, of how each evolved into the next. And if the essential work of murdering our darlings involves cutting away the traits that would show the finished novel's relationship to its origins, then we get out the knife and do the deed, so that a liberating amnesia leaves us free to imagine new things.

It's for the literary palaeontologists of posterity to dig in the mud-turned-rock, and puzzle out the evolutionary stages from such fossilised corpses as they can find. Yes, some of the ideas I started the novel with still showed in the final version: some central and essential, others – like the python's pelvis or nipples on men – mere vestiges which had no function by then, but were not enough of a disadvantage that they were

---

[1] However, out of respect for my fellows I have always named the author of any writing I'm referring to.

selected against by the ruthless evolutionary processes of re-drafting.

On the other hand, where things I wrote during those years make what I'm trying to evoke here clearer than any second-order writing *about* that writing would, I've put them in: notes, fiction, non-fiction, work-in-progress and thinking aloud. Not all of these are writing that I'm proud of, but they are true to what, as part of a progress which was frequently a regress, I did write.

So where *Black Shadow and Bone* was strung painfully on the tension-line between the responsibilities of the storyteller and the responsibilities of the historian, *This is Not a Book About Charles Darwin* whizzes as cheerfully and irresponsibly to and fro along the same line as a ten-year-old in an adventure playground. It is a lens formed by the creative process which seems the best lens for observing the stories of creative work and creative thinking that run through my family like Potteries clay. In other words, when I say 'Trust me: I'm telling stories,' the first act of trust has to be my own, in accepting my memories for what they are, no more, no less. 'Writing a novel is like remembering something which never happened', Siri Hustvedt says in her essay 'Yonder'. I have to accept that in *This is Not a Book About Charles Darwin,* writing what I remember is halfway to writing a novel: like remembering something which sort-of happened.

This book is about my not-writing the family in another way, too. Each of my sisters Sophy and Carola, each of my twelve Darwin first cousins, each of my many more second, third and fourth cousins (some of whom are both third and fourth cousins) has their own relationship to the family tree, and their own context, experience and understanding of it. This story is one refracted, diffracted version of one part of *my* life, and I wouldn't dream of suggesting that it in any way speaks for the other 151 great-great-grandchildren of Charles and Emma Darwin.

Photo

1

Emma

The story of *Black Shadow and Bone* starts with my agent and me having lunch.

Getting published is a difficult business of learning to fit what you can write to what an agent can persuade a publisher will make money. Eventually one of those agents – let's call her Catriona – did take me on as a client, and sold *The Mathematics of Love* and then *A Secret Alchemy*. Since then, as for most writers, my agent has also become an adviser, facilitator and advocate in the even more difficult business of staying published. In the last month I've read all the way through my new manuscript – let's call it *Novel Three* – and there is no way to heal the central flaw that we both acknowledge: it is incurable. Lunch is to discuss what I should write next.

While I grappled with *Novel Three* plenty of new ideas floated in, washed in, or muscled in, and I've condensed the best of them into a place, a character, a beginning, a dance of themes. I talk about them.

'But where's the story?' asks Catriona.

I've resorted to ordering chips. I talk about the places: Malta, Suffolk, Salonika. I talk about the characters: a First World War Red Cross nurse – or an ambulance driver might be more fun – coming home to the house she shares with her brother. I've had her in my mind for a couple of years, since a walk on Boxing Day when I was in the thick of *A Secret Alchemy* and saw an old farmhouse, muted by mist, which clearly held a different story. But now it's 2010, or thereabouts, and there's *just* time to write it, sell it and have it on the shelves in time for 2014. I talk about the themes: men and women; brothers and sisters;[2] war giving women chances at the men's jobs; coming home and finding nothing is different and everything is – and is it you, or home, which has changed?

'But where's the story?' asks Catriona.

I do my best.

'But where's the *story*?' asks Catriona.

We establish, definitively, that I have no story.

And to the book trade – which means the people who earn their living by finding enough people to like a book, and persuading them to buy it – story is king. True, by those standards, and for a debut 'book-group' novel by an unknown writer (unknown, that is, but for my 'household name', as the *Daily Telegraph* titled a piece I wrote for them) *The Mathematics of Love* did very well. It was widely reviewed and was long- and short-listed for prizes; it sold in the US, sold in translation, sold round the world. Everyone was happy. But it's two years since my second novel, *A Secret Alchemy*, followed in its footsteps, and in commercial publishing two years is getting on for a

---

[2] I have no brothers, but I have a son and a daughter: I've always been curious about siblinghood across the genders.

lifetime, though not quite a death-time. In literary publishing it's not so terminal, but then for 'literary', battle-weary book-trade insiders would say, read 'doesn't sell'.

In that not-quite-a-lifetime, writing hard, I have, in fact, done quite a lot. The whole of *A Secret Alchemy* was only part of my PhD in Creative Writing – the first to be awarded by Goldsmiths, University of London – and since then I've become an Associate Lecturer in Creative Writing for the Open University, as well as doing other teaching, lecturing, workshopping and mentoring. I've had several short stories and some scraps of journalism published, and a story broadcast on BBC Radio Four. My blog about creative writing, This Itch of Writing, is in its third year, and as well as being read by individual writers, gets linked to by more and more creative writing MAs and other courses.

So, what am I going to write now?

Catriona says, 'I'm going to start with the idea you're going to hate most.'

I know what she's going to say. There's no escape. And she says it.

'How about the story of Emma Darwin, and her marriage to Charles?'

It's a question I've been asked many times by journalists, festival audiences and Darwin enthusiasts – some of whom are very, very enthusiastic. So of course I've asked it of myself, and, since one of an agent's functions is to interpret the market in ways which mean their author understands it, of course Catriona had to ask it: would I, should I, *could* I write the novel of Emma Darwin?

My resistance was intuitive and physical: somatic, like all real, deep, hard-wired resistances, fizzing across my skin and cramping deep in my solar plexus.

But I had good reasons for resisting too, because *A Secret Alchemy* was published – by sheer good luck – in the Darwin Bicentenary, during which I learnt a lot more about my great-great-grandparents. 2009 was my great-great-grandfather's 200th birthday and at the same time the 150th birthday of *On the Origin of Species by Means of Natural*

Selection, or the Preservation of Favoured Races in the Struggle for Life.
I read Edna Healey's biography of Emma and enjoyed it very much; I warmed to Emma herself, and loved discovering her mother's family, the Allens of Cresselly in Pembrokeshire. I was convinced, too, by Healey's argument that it was Emma's calm and relaxed take on marriage, child-rearing and housekeeping which meant Charles's life didn't go down the same neurotic, hypochondriac road as his brother Erasmus and others in the family tree. Since then I'd been asked to read and endorse a new Emma biography by Loy and Loy; and I'd read Desmond and Moore's biography of Charles, and more recently Janet Browne's.

So the lunch conversation went something like this:

Catriona: Emma would sell, of course.

Emma: I know, but she's *so* well-documented. Two biographies, as well as all the stuff about him. Two volumes of her letters.[3] There's no space for imagination – creativity – fiction. There's no story-space for me.

Catriona: So where might there be story-space?

Emma: I don't think there is any. They got married – they lived in London for a few years – they moved to Down House in Kent. And they stayed there, pretty much, for the rest of their lives.

Catriona: How about a pudding? What about his voyages?

Emma: [while weighing up her need for more comfort food] The voyages were all before they married. He was a bit in love with someone else when he left on the *Beagle*, but by the time he got back five years later, she'd got married.

Catriona: What about his and Emma's courtship?

Emma: Short and amicable. They'd known each other all their lives, he wanted a wife, she wanted a husband, their families were intimate friends[4] and they were first cousins. They set about very consciously and deliberately making a happy marriage, and they succeeded.

---

[3] They live by the bed I was born in, as it happens. That's why I'm named Emma.

[4] For example, it was Emma's father, Josiah II, who had persuaded Charles's father to let Charles take up the offer of the *Beagle* voyage. And one of Charles's best friends was Emma's brother Hensleigh, while another brother, also Charles, later married our Charles's sister Caroline.

Catriona: And they sorted out the religious problem. About him being an aetheist.

Emma: Though he never said he was more than agnostic. But yes, exactly, right at the beginning of the marriage. They found a way to differ – to not-talk about it and still love each other. And they left it at that.

Catriona: Yes. And their daughter dying – Randal Keynes did it in *Annie's Box*.[5]

Emma: Yes. Non-fiction, but still … No space for me.

Catriona: No.

Emma: She was very calm and relaxed. They had a comfortable life. Of course they were technically Victorians, but with those un-brutal, liberal, eighteenth-century Whig values. Anti-slavery, ethical behaviour, compassion, tolerance, helping the villagers, tactfully supporting friends and colleagues less well off than them, kind, sensitive and liberal parenting, financial prudence, and plenty of finance to be prudent with.

Catriona: Happy marriages don't make novels.

Emma: No … There are enough *little* white spaces – and some of them are really fun. Her uncle-by-marriage was a fantastic Swiss diplomat called Sismondi. Emma spent time in Geneva with the Sismondis, and she *may* have studied the piano with Chopin. I could do linked shorts. [Emma knows what the industry thinks of short story collections. Even a big-name writer's story collection will sell perhaps 10% of what their novel would sell.]

Catriona: [doesn't have to say anything].

Emma: No, I know.

Catriona: No, there's no novel there.

No.

I'm frustrated: I'd love to write a novel about one of the nicest people I've ever not met, while also knowing that it was nearly certain to sell.

---

[5] *Annie's Box* was the original title, but it's since been re-titled *Darwin, His Daughter, and Human Evolution*, presumably because the battle for life has shifted onto social media, and search-engine algorithms are king. Catriona's agency also represents Randal Keynes, and not long before they had signed the deal for the film *Creation*, based on his book. It stars Paul Bettany and Jennifer Connelly, and it's rather good.

And I'm relieved: I *don't* have to try to write a novel that every cell of my body is refusing to write.

* * *

Notebook fragment dated 4th January 2012

M. Chopin regretted that he would not, as it turned out, be able to give Mlle Wedgwood her lesson, as he was indisposed and gone into the country for a cure. However, his friend, M. Lavallière, whom he could recommend wholeheartedly as a teacher, would be delighted to instruct Mlle Wedgwood, if she cared to make the arrangement.

'What do you think?' said Emma to the top of Fanny's head, where Fanny was kneeling to stitch up a flounce that Emma had trodden on in going upstairs. 'Is it bad?'

'No, merely a couple of inches. And if M. Chopin has confidence in him, he must be good, mustn't he?'

M. Lavallière was not, however, someone in whom – at least at first glance – one felt much confidence. He was very tall and thin, the room was dusty and small, the piano out of tune, and his manner seemed at once diffident and agitated. Emma played her best piece: a Haydn sonata.

'You—' He stopped. 'I – you should ... '

'I should what, monsieur?' Emma asked after a moment. It was true that, since they had left Geneva and the Sismondis, she had not been able to practise for want of a piano in any of the inns in which they had stayed. But had her performance really been so faulty as to deprive him of speech?

'I – I don't ... forgive me. I am unwell.' He pressed the heels of his hands to his eyes, and Emma could feel as directly as if she had put her own hands over them how great was his effort to pull himself together. 'You must think me very feeble.'

'Not at all. No one can help being unwell. I am sorry for it. Can I help in any way? Fetch your landlady? A doctor?'

At which M. Lavallière burst into tears and confessed that what he most needed was food. 'I have not eaten for nearly three days,' he whispered. 'And still I have no idea where I shall find next week's rent.'

2

Where's the story?

But if not Emma, then who, and what? Catriona and I go back to picking over my original ideas: Malta in the First World War – because we both loved that part of *Testament of Youth* – and the aftermath. I fly a few kites from other bits of the family history: Revolutionary Paris, Waterloo if I can track down that particular Wedgwood, London between-the-wars.

There's my other family tree, I suggest. My mother's mother was born Lucie LeFanu, in an Irish family of Huguenot origin. Like all Huguenots she was brought up on the stories of persecution in Louis XIV's Catholic France: stories of their heretical Calvinist, vernacular bibles and prayerbooks being hidden in secret compartments or baked into loaves of bread; of secret tokens, tiny lanterns, coded messages, and flat-pack pulpits disguised as chairs; of escapes hidden in apple barrels; of bayonets thrust through the hay in the cart; of babies suffocated because they were crying as the dragoons boarded to search the ship. As you might (or perhaps might not) expect, the LeFanus became for the most part passionate, Protestant supporters of Irish independence from England.

What's more, the LeFanus – with or without that capital F – are a parallel dynasty of sorts. Granny's great-uncle was Dublin's 'Prince of Darkness', the mystery-writer Joseph Sheridan Lefanu,[6] whose best-known work is *Uncle Silas*: an excellent, shiveringly scary novel. Uncle Joe's great-grandmother was the successful novelist Frances Sheridan, his grandmother the playwright Alicia Lefanu, née Sheridan, while Alicia's brother, Richard Brinsley Sheridan, was the owner of the Theatre Royal Drury Lane and author of *The Rivals* and *The School for Scandal*. When my parents got engaged, my mother undertook to read *The Origin* if my father read *Uncle Silas*.

I think I'm making a good case for them. 'Drama is character in action', as Aristotle says in the *Poetics*, and here in the Irish part of the same academic-professional-intellectual middle class that the Darwin-Wedgwoods inhabited, there are also refugee dramas, theatre dramas, religious dramas, psychological dramas.

'Yes,' says Catriona patiently, as agents do when their authors ramble on, 'but they're not Darwins.'

My LeFanu granny swore that the Darwin-Wedgwoods were the only English family she knew who were as clannish as the Irish are, and I think of the club suggested by my great-uncles-by-marriage, Jacques Raverat and Geoffrey Keynes, who were also not Darwins. The Anti-Darwin League they founded was 'for people who inadvertently marry Darwins': i.e. those who thought they were marrying a person whose surname happened to be Darwin, and find they have married into a

---

[6] This might have remained no more than a curiosity to me, until it was J S Lefanu's turn for a Bicentenary, in 2014. I've been known to say that I don't 'do' horror stories, or speculative fiction, but I had a lovely time writing 'A Cold Vehicle for the Marvellous', for the anthology *Dreams of Shadow and Smoke: stories for J S Lefanu*, which was published by Swan River Press.

clan.[7] My mother considers herself a member, and my then husband and my two brothers-in-law would have joined, no doubt.

I seem to have been born into something inescapable, but I want so much to escape.

I knew that some of my rage at that blogger's catty comment about my writing and my genes was justified, because it broke Number Six of John Updike's classic rules of reviewing: 'Review the book, not the reputation'. This rule should be applied even more stringently, I argued crossly to anyone who was still listening, if the reputation you're measuring this book by is not even the writer's own, but her great-great-grandfather's.

But my rage was also the reflex of hurt: someone with serious critical credentials had said, and in public, that I had written a worse book than I 'ought' to have been capable of writing. If I grew a novel directly from those darned genes, how much more of that kind of comment would be tossed at me? How many others would measure me and mine against their idea of my clever ancestors, and find me wanting? How much more time and energy – energy so much better spent on writing or laughing or sleeping or, frankly, on picking one's nose – would I have to spend on the rage and the calming of the rage, on the hurt and the healing of the hurt?

Of course, it makes a good story for an event platform or a blog interview. And yet, every now and then, instead of a friendly wince flickering through my audience, I sense an acid draught of *count yourself lucky*. Many debut authors and aspiring writers would give their eye teeth to have been noticed by that blog – to have an agent – a very-nice-thank-you book contract or two – a big publisher celebrating their book – an ISBN number or fifteen to their name – a name that gets talked about.

A name. My name. Ah, yes.

Your publisher needs to sell your book to more people than your

---

[7] On the other hand, Geoffrey Keynes proposed to Gwen Darwin, unsucessfully, before he proposed to Gwen's younger sister Margaret, and that chapter in his memoir *The Gates of Memory* is titled 'Marrying into the Darwins'. Perhaps 'inadvertently', in his case, is a little disingenuous.

family and friends, so you and the publicity department have to catch those more-people's attention – in marketing-speak, to 'disrupt' what they were doing and thinking – and hook them in, first to notice your book, and then to buy it. The big hook is what the book's about, but these days there are too many hooks, too many books, too many non-book disruptors and disruptions, and too many other ways that those more-people might spend their leisure time and leisure money. So publishers reckon that with fiction you need a second, 'non-fiction', hook, as my American editor calls it: something which makes you and your book more intriguing than the next ordinary, unknown person who's written a novel that Waterstones and Tesco might choose to have taking up expensive real estate on the front table or the back shelves ... or might not.

What I've been born into is also inescapable because the only non-fiction hook I have *is* You-Know-Who, whose surname is so conveniently unusual, and therefore noticeable.

Even Emma's first name – my first name – has turned out to have a certain noticeability. A couple of years after *The Mathematics of Love* was published, I woke one morning and found that, overnight, several hundred times more people had looked at my fledgling blog *This Itch of Writing* than I would have expected on a very good day. I clicked through from my stats, and found that a Nebraskan geneticist blogger, with the vast reach that the pioneer bloggers could achieve, had recommended it to his readers. This Emma Darwin wrote well and interestingly, he said, and he'd checked, and yes, she was a direct descendant.

In a mere twelve hours, half the geneticists in the world, it seemed to my sleep-smeared eyes, had piled over to This Itch of Writing to have a look. Someone commented that, as a great-great-grandchild, this Emma Darwin only shared 2% of her genome with Charles Darwin. A bit further down, someone remarked that it's strange how in the Darwin-Wedgwood-Galton genealogy the same first names crop up over and over again, and how in such families the women's first names are the linguistic equivalent of mitochondrial DNA: transmitted through the mother, as surnames may be transmitted, like other DNA, through the father. Further down again, a third someone pointed out that those two of this Emma Darwin's great-great-grandparents were first cousins. So, since Charles's mother was the older sister of that Emma's father, this Emma's genome had more like 3% of theirs[8] ... but only if *that* Emma wasn't playing away when the relevant son was conceived. That made me laugh out loud, because even though I can very confidently say that Emma wasn't doing anything of the kind, I do love a geek.

As it happens, I look startlingly like my entirely non-Darwin mother, so I have no idea *which* 3% of Charles and Emma you could discern in me with a mirror, a microscope or a psychological assessment. Never mind: it's fun and useful, and it's taken me to places like Mexico, Brisbane, the *Daily Telegraph*, and the Hay Festival. Besides, yet another someone on that Nebraskan blog did say that my novel, *The Mathematics of Love*, looked interesting, while since then I've heard from other readers who picked my books up because of the surname, and bought them.

So complaining about this freakish chance of genealogy and names would be like complaining about how much tax you're paying now that your income is so large: bad manners, bad taste, showing-off, stealth-bragging. Anyway, I haven't the slightest urge to complain; at worst I endure the occasional irritatingly irrelevant review, and get bored with the more predictable questions, but so does any author about their work, and answering cheerfully as if it's the first time of asking is part of the job.

But, I thought uneasily as Catriona and I finished our lunch, if I wrote a novel about the family I'd be doing the exact opposite of how we were brought up: no longer just answering modestly when questioned, but standing in the marketplace and shouting; not only meeting the questioner's gaze but trying to tell them a whole lot more; no longer politely acknowledging people's interest, but arguing that the

---

[8] Recently, in a Twitter conversation Professor Graham Coop went into more detail: 'So you've on average inherited 6% of your genome directly from CD, including the fact that you can't share on the X chr. There's 95% prob. you've directly inherited 2-11% due to the randomness of Mendelian transmission down the male Darwin line leading to you.'

family is even more interesting than they thought. I would be doing exactly what we were not supposed to do.

Nor was I keen to put my Darwin head above the parapet and so into the flak of the 'science versus religion' debate. Of course I've been asked what I think (or, worse, 'believe') at parties, on Facebook and by Tweet, and that's fair enough, you could say. But although the debate is entirely irrelevant to my writing and teaching, I've also been asked about it in workshops, as questions from the literary festival floor, in interviews on air and in print, and at press conferences – and by some distinctly persistent interviewers.

I don't join the debate because it never gets anywhere, since so few participants are open to reconsidering their own convictions, or to trying to enter imaginatively into those of others. And I loathe the aggressive rhetoric and narrow-minded, knee-jerk responses of the fundamentalists at both ends of the spectrum of debate; they drown out the genuinely fascinating exploration which could take place in the middle, about psychology, philosophy, human nature and the evolution of knowledge. So the only time I've deliberately commented on the question was in that piece for the *Daily Telegraph* about my household name, in an honest and exact expression of what I feel about it all:

> I have difficulty imagining that any sentient modern adult could not accept the principle of evolution by natural selection, but a book-trade website [in the US] suggests a bookshop display to court the controversialists. Alas, the American book-buyer who moves on from *The Origin of Species* to *The Mathematics of Love*, expecting another tome of world-altering scientific genius, is going to be a bit disappointed.

That was lightheartedly put, although of course easy reading is hard writing and it took me ages to get the tone just right. And, yes, it was honest, although I have to plead guilty to deliberately trailing my coat in saying it. My coat-trailing worked, mind you: the following week, on the Letters page, the hem was firmly trodden on by a reader who patronisingly compared my 'unquestioning acceptance' of my ancestor's theory to his own greater sophistication in doubting it, and the week after that another reader leapt to my defence. So that was three weeks running that *Telegraph* readers were reminded that someone called Emma Darwin – and yes, she is a descendant – had written a novel. As I said, it's useful.

Still, in the context of *this* book, maybe we should just clear the topic up for good and all.

Frequently Asked Questions

Q: Are you obliged to believe in evolution? A: I'm not obliged to believe in anything. If my family has any tradition at all, it's that no belief is immune from investigation. But evolution happens, as provably as it's provable that the earth is round and the tides[9] are controlled by the moon. The scientific theories that have been developed to frame and explain these observable processes are the only ones that fit all the available facts, have accurately predicted facts which have later been confirmed by observation, and have never yet been shown to be false. So, if 'believe' is an appropriate verb for things which have been proved beyond all reasonable doubt, then I believe in all those observable processes and the theories which explain them.

Q: But it's only a theory. A: In science, a fully tested and explained theory is the goal of all research: a statement of our best understanding, to date, of the reason why a certain observable process happens as it does happen. It is, of course, always subject to revision if different data comes along, but there's certainly no 'only' about it.

Q: But Wallace did it really. A: Alfred Wallace and Charles Darwin shared their knowledge and insights, and their separately conceived papers on Natural Selection were presented jointly at the Linnean Society in 1858, without having much impact until *The Origin* was

---

[9] Coincidentally, one of the first major works on the geophysics of tides was written by my great-grandfather, Charles's second son Sir George Darwin.

published in 1859. For the rest of their lives the scientific community acknowledged their shared precedence but Wallace himself said that, although he and Darwin had both, separately, realised the mechanism of evolution – survival of the best-adapted members of a species – it was Darwin, not himself, who had already put in a decade of patient, experimental investigation to underpin the theory with the data which made it unarguable.[10] And Wallace was one of the pallbearers at Darwin's funeral.

Q: Do you think that religion and science are incompatible? A: No, I don't think they're incompatible.

Q: But it is a controversial question. A: Apparently so, but that's not what this book is about.

Q: Do you have a religious faith? A: That's not what this book is about.

Q: Why do you not want to talk about it? A: Because that's not what this book is about.

Q: But are you religious? A: That's not what this book is about.

Q: Why do you not want to —

Boring, isn't it? But it's not good manners, if you're sitting on a platform, to tell a ticket-holder or a fellow author that their question is boring, and in fiction, you're not allowed FAQs.

I didn't say all that to Catriona, obviously. I'd been in the game long enough to know that, as long as I'd thought it all through in advance, I was capable of replacing my default helpfulness and conversability with a polite, pre-constructed stonewalling, and still not be guilty of bad manners.

Nevertheless, my reluctance wasn't just about external hurts, rages

---

[10] Wallace's documented dislike of publicity and public attention, which he himself said he was grateful to Charles for absorbing, and his later promotion of psychics and spiritualism, were other reasons that his crucial contribution to the theory has more recently appeared to have been obscured.

or boring questions: it came from a much deeper place, right in the middle of my creative core, and from recent experience. For the first time, now, I confessed to Catriona how difficult I'd found writing *A Secret Alchemy*.

It should have been hard but straightforward work. Elizabeth and Anthony Woodville were remote in time, I had the Wars of the Roses and the disappearance of Elizabeth's princely sons in the Tower to work with, and spaces in the record wide enough to ride a posse of men-at-arms through, let alone write fiction on. Instead, I'd found writing the novel a painful struggle. It had been the first time I'd ever suffered badly from that bane of many writers' lives, procrastination, as I faced the need to write my way out of historical impasse after impasse, and I was frightened of that happening again.

'I find real historical figures *so* difficult,' I said. 'And the better-documented they are, the worse it is. There's no room for me ... ' I was floundering, trying to put into words, without sounding hopelessly self-indulgent and unprofessional, how in building a novel on the historical record the demands of my creative imagination got trapped in an endless fight with the demand to be 'accurate', to 'not get it wrong', which is the first thing – often the only thing – that everyone seems to talk about when it comes to historical fiction. Writing *A Secret Alchemy* was, at times, like trench warfare in outer space: an arid, oxygen-less war of attrition.

I could only come up with a cliché. I said, 'With real historical figures I can't play to my strengths. It always gets my worst writing out of me.'

'Well, have a think about it,' said Catriona. 'Coffee?'

3

The Lunar Light

I sat on the top of the bus going home, and asked myself: since I couldn't, wouldn't, shouldn't write Emma, what *was* I going to write?

Silence. Traffic lights. Vauxhall Bridge.

When you don't know what to do, there's a life coaching trick which helps: you think, 'If I were a friend, what would I ask myself?'

I would, I thought, ask, 'How do you – how does one – how do I – find a new novel?'

The notion that readers enjoy is the one about how the novel chooses you. The idea hits you like thunderbolt, or a character won't go away; either that, or that the novel is 'really' about something that happened to you in real life. All of these are sometimes true, and sometimes none of them are, at least not for me. Vague ideas float in like thistledown from every part of life, all the time: the important thing is not to close the notebook as soon as something has landed safely in it, but to keep watching and listening and absorbing.

Of course, this is crucial not just to writing, but to all creative work. As one of Charles Darwin's grandchildren, the artist Gwen Raverat, said,

> The whole of a long life is spent learning to *see*, to know what one is looking at with one's inner mind: not in gaining experience, but in losing it.

As I read this, by 'experience' Gwen means preconceptions that will prevent the artist from being open to seeing what is *really* there.[11] Indeed, when my cousin, the poet Ruth Padel, took her mother – Charles's great-granddaughter, the geneticist Hilda Barlow – to a poetry reading for the first time, Hilda apparently said afterwards, 'I see the point of poets now. They notice things.'

Poets and writers observe the world as scientists do: with great attention but also – if they want to do their best work – with an open mind. When I quoted Ruth's story to the microbiologist Mark Pallen, author of *The Rough Guide to Evolution*, he pointed me towards something Charles Darwin himself said in his autobiography:

> I have steadily endeavoured to keep my mind free, so as to give up any hypothesis, however much beloved (and I cannot resist forming one on every subject), as soon as facts are shown to be opposed to it. Indeed I have had no choice but to act in this manner, for with the exception of the Coral Reefs, I cannot remember a single first-formed hypothesis which had not after a time to be given up or greatly modified. This has naturally led me to distrust greatly deductive

---

[11] Books such as Betty Edwards' mega-selling *Drawing On the Right Side of the Brain* are built on this idea: that it's our preconceptions – what we know the object 'really' to be like – which prevent us from experiencing and then drawing what we actually see.

reasoning in the mixed sciences. On the other hand, I am not very sceptical,—a frame of mind which I believe to be injurious to the progress of science. A good deal of scepticism in a scientific man is advisable to avoid much loss of time, but I have met with not a few men, who, I feel sure, have often thus been deterred from experiment or observations, which would have proved directly or indirectly serviceable.

This *dis*trust of reflex scepticism, of Gwen's 'experience', of the narrowing-down caused by too-early deductive reasoning and hypothesising, is really, it seems to me, a trust in what Keats called Negative Capability, and argued that Coleridge lacked. It's what Philip Gross calls the 'not-knowing': the capacity to stay with what we perceive and what we sense, without prematurely rationalising it into tidy patterns, and thereby excluding ideas and things which at first don't seem relevant to that pattern, but which might turn out to be significant or enriching.

But, being the very archetype of a creative scientific thinker, Darwin also recognises – as Keats, another medically trained writer,[12] certainly did – that negative capability, not-knowing, isn't enough. Darwin's last sentence seems to me to express exactly the tension that is built into creative work. If we're to get anywhere near to a finished story, theory, equation, painting, engine or dance piece, we *must* sort, order, refine and eliminate, but without completely throwing aside those things which too briskly logical a sorting process would discard. So, when I sense – it really is more 'sense' than 'think' – that a piece of thistledown has a story curled up inside it, some DNA in the nucleus, it gets pressed into the back section of my notebook, and later, when I have a story commissioned or just want to write something, I'll look for one which might repay being fertilised, inspected, planted out and allowed to grow.

And the DNA analogy works a little further because a story-idea is

---

[12] The list of doctors who are distinguished poets is very long, including Friedrich von Schiller, William Carlos Williams and Dannie Abse.

a gamete: only one strand of the necessary double helix. It's the writer who must provide the other strand from his or her hoard of observation, experience and ideas: people's voices and actions, tensions and connections, loves and hates, reasons and un-reasons, objects, places and events, smells and sounds, textures and colours, dreams and nightmares ... in short, everything that a human, writer or not, ever encounters. It's the writer's imagination which creates the 'bases' – the right pairs – to join the two strands into that famous twisty ladder, and create a new living thing. So, I decided, there was no harm in looking among the family's gametes for a strand that might fit with the strands in me.

I did know some of the family stories; in fact, I was already interested, in a non-fiction way. I grew up wanting to be a historian, and I grew up reading *Period Piece*, Gwen Raverat's memoir of childhood in an 1890s Cambridge which could be mapped by the houses of Charles Darwin's widow[13] and several of his seven adult children – which meant all his grandchildren. Gwen was a well-known artist in her field of wood engraving, and she illustrated the book as well as writing it. Indeed, one day, when she needed a model for a young man sitting with his back to the viewer and flirting with an Edwardian young lady in a hammock, chaperoned by a very grumpy six-year-old Gwen, adult Gwen left her studio to grab the first nephew who came to hand, and got my twenty-year-old father. The book was published in 1952; it's clear-eyed but warm and witty, and has become a minor and much-loved classic. So I was intrigued, many years later, to read Frances Spalding's biography *Gwen Raverat: friends, family & affections*; Spalding makes illuminating comparisons between how Gwen chose to present herself and the family, and the reality of the intellectual and creative wealth but also the unhappiness of a good deal of Gwen's actual life.

Then, in 2008, I was asked to contribute to the Darwin Day[14]

---

[13] Emma lived at Down House in the summer, but the chalk downs of rural Kent were cold, bleak and lonely for an old lady, when the roads were impassable with the winter mud.
[14] Darwin Day is an annual, round-the-world, loosely coordinated collection of events to celebrate science and reason, in and around Charles Darwin's birthday on 12th February.

programme at the University of Birmingham, on the grounds that a) I am an alumna, and b) I, as a novelist, would fit in nicely with their star speaker, Dame Gillian Beer, whose seminal book *Darwin's Plots* explores the part that Darwin's prose plays in his thinking, and the effect both his writing and his ideas had on the literary culture of his contemporaries.

I nearly said, 'No,' because what did I have to say that everyone there wouldn't have heard already? I only said, 'Yes,' because there would be a good, big bookstall which would sell *The Mathematics of Love*, and the university would pay my expenses. I'm fairly sure there wasn't a fee on offer – universities have a way of assuming that *someone*'s paying you a salary, however modest – but I'm entirely sure I didn't ask. I wasn't (I'm still not) an expert on the family history, and fifteen minutes of famous names and family stories seemed about fourteen and a half minutes too many: I felt too squeamish to ask to be paid for something which would essentially be a sloppy, ignorant piece of showing-off. And what on earth was I going to talk about?

Aunt Gwen, bless her, had the answer to that one. The chapter of *Period Piece* called 'The Five Uncles' includes her father, because 'A father is only a specialized sort of uncle anyhow', an explanation which I find delightful; here is a visual artist showing the scientific reflex to make sense of things in terms of difference, similarity, and what that means for understanding relationships. And of those five sons of Charles Darwin she said this:

> Overtly, explicitly, they would have admitted that they knew nothing at all about music, very little about art, and not a great deal about Literature, though they all loved reading. They were apt to regard the arts as the inessential ornaments of Life; unimportant matters. But this is a superficial view of them: in their scientific work they showed many of the characteristics of the creative artist: the sense of style, of proportion; the passionate love of their subject; and, above all, the complete integrity and the willingness to take infinite trouble to perfect any piece of work.

In their scientific work they showed many of the characteristics of the creative artist. Coming from a trained, dedicated, professional, passionate artist, that is a very revealing observation. And Gwen was by no means the only artist in the family, especially if you look at the whole, vast Darwin-Wedgwood oak, and look for writing as well as the visual arts and music. One of the oak's twigs is me, and though I'm a small twig, creative art is work I decided I did know something about: in 2008 I was in the middle of my Doctorate in Creative Writing. If I built my talk on how creative thinking works between and among the artists and scientists in the family then I wouldn't be standing on that platform purely thanks to 3% of my genome, I would also be standing on that platform because I have the authority of the creative practitioner to talk about how creativity works.

My brother-in-law put me onto a fascinating book, *Sparks of Genius*, by Robert and Michèle Root-Bernstein, which dissects how the same range of creative thought-processes show up across the whole range of human work from nuclear physics to dance, and I used that as a frame and spine for talking about the family. My piece went down well, although I'm glad that I didn't know till afterwards that there were no less than five Fellows of the Royal Society[15] in the audience. Then I was asked to give two longer and much more high-profile lectures along similar lines, in Mexico. I had to do a lot more digging, a lot more thinking, a lot more reading, not so much about the family but about creative thinking, and why 'Science versus Arts' is both a recent and a fallacious opposition: binary thinking at its reductive worst. Mind you, I still didn't have the nerve to ask a fee, wimp that I was, but only travel expenses. However, some months later I was asked to give the same lecture in Spain – hence dinner in Valencia – and to unveil a plaque to The Ancestor, by which time I'd got over my squeamishness.

So might the nexus of artists and scientists be the strand in the family which I could match to the strand which is my writerly self, and grow a novel?

---

[15] I had by then discovered that my father's generation of Darwins was the first *not* to have at least one FRS since Erasmus was elected a Fellow in 1761.

To say that the root of the family tree is Erasmus Darwin[16] makes sense in storytelling terms, although it's not entirely true. Erasmus' father Robert Darwin was a physician and naturalist, who in 1716 discovered the first-ever Jurassic reptile fossil: a partly-fossilised plesiosaur which is now in the Natural History Museum in London. But Erasmus is really where it starts, especially if you're interested in creative thinking. In the intellectual-cultural equivalent of the pre-Cambrian period, before the Victorian explosion of population, learning, education and printing began to drive everything towards professionalisation and specialisation, it was perfectly possible to write a serious scientific work for the general reader entirely in rhyming iambic pentameters, and Erasmus Darwin did exactly that. He also designed a speaking machine, a steering mechanism for his carriage which developed into the one used in modern cars, and a horizontal windmill for the pottery of his great friend Josiah Wedgwood, as well as supporting other technological projects financially as well as practically.

Of all my ancestors, Erasmus perhaps is the one I'd most like to spend time with. He had a huge and affectionate circle of fascinating friends of both sexes, as well as a wide medical practice. What comes over in letters and memoirs is his great zest for life, his liberal opinions on all subjects from slavery to the education of girls, his very considerable sex drive, and his capacity to be interested in absolutely everything. It's this last, it seems to me, which is so crucial to creative thinking, because by definition creative thinking brings together things which haven't been combined before, to make something new. The more things you see, know and understand, the more willing you are to try fitting what you see and understand together in new and unique ways, and the more likely it is that a new thing is created.[17]

Erasmus might be surprised by my and my sisters' PhDs, but I don't think he would be shocked; he wrote that girls should go to school, and

---

[16] There will be other Erasmus Darwins later, but this is the one who doesn't know that he will be Charles Darwin's grandfather.

[17] You will also make a lot of mistakes and create a lot of failures. Creative work is inherently very 'wasteful', which is something that politicians, bean-counters and funders of research don't, or won't, always get their heads round: it is simply not possible to reverse-engineer from a creative success in a way which will ensure that the next project is guaranteed to succeed.

study sciences, languages, arts, philosophy, manufacturing and the handling of money. He spoke from experience, too, for he fathered six girls himself, and eight boys, by two wives and a mistress, and possibly at least one other daughter by the wife of another man. His poem *The Loves of the Plants* is frankly and explicitly erotic as he explains Linnaean botany for interested gentlewomen and gentlemen; they were interested and the book was a bestseller on its own and again when combined in *The Botanic Garden* with another long poem, *The Economy of Vegetation*, which explores scientific progress as an aspect of human evolution. Erasmus managed all this despite being amazingly plain and afflicted with a bad stammer, which just goes to show that in a species whose survival depends on the size of its brain, and on its capacity for social and sexual cooperation, the mind will always be a very big and responsive erogenous zone.

But Erasmus, may his bulky shadow never grow less, was not alone, and his genius[18] could flower so widely and wildly partly because of the company he kept in person round the dinner tables of the West Midlands, and by correspondence round the world. I knew about the Lunar Society because of Jenny Uglow's group biography, *The Lunar Men*; it's subtitled *The Men who Made The Industrial Revolution*, and I'd devoured it.

Oh! I thought, sitting on the bus on my way home from lunch with Catriona: the stuffs of a Lunar Society novel would be *so* rich! There's Eramus, writing poetry about evolution, with sexual selection one of the big, evolutionary steps forward. There's the first Josiah Wedgwood, potter of genius, already a millionaire but still worried, when he had to have his leg amputated, that he wouldn't be able to work the traditional 'kick wheel' of his trade. Josiah's endlessly curious and carefully empirical search was for the combination of beauty and profit which would ensure capitalist survival, just as his grandson/great-nephew Charles set out how desirability and function operate in sexual selection for evolutionary survival.

There's Joseph Priestley, the Nonconformist minister of religion

---

[18] Can we use that word? Just because a family has one genius doesn't mean it can't have another.

showing Lavoisier how to isolate oxygen (though he called it 'dephlogisticated air'), writing about education, and being burnt in effigy by the mob which sacked his house and smashed his laboratory because he celebrated the French Revolution.

There's Matthew Boulton, the archetypal engineer-entrepreneur (and a rare Tory in the group) steadily enlarging his metal-working empire at Soho in Birmingham; there's his partner, the archetypal engineer-genius James Watt. The steam-engines they made and installed all over the world really did make the Industrial Revolution, as well as vast profits.

There's the paradox of manufacturer Samuel Galton. Most of the Lunar men were Whigs, and most came from Nonconformist backgrounds, but Galton was actually a Quaker – and yet also a gun-maker.

Mind you, a good many of the Lunar men were, at heart, atheists: Erasmus rather unkindly described Josiah's sincerely-held Unitarianism as 'a feather-bed to catch a falling Christian', and the great typographer John Baskerville described exactly how an entirely secular mausoleum should be built for him, 'as I have a Hearty Contempt for all Superstition[,] the Farce of a Consecrated Ground[,] the Irish Barbarism of Sure and Certain Hopes.' Erasmus's own unusual first name is explicitly Dissenting, in that it derives from his ancestor Erasmus Earle, who was Common Serjeant to Oliver Cromwell, and so, ultimately, from Erasmus of Rotterdam himelf. It was only later generations, gentrifying themselves away from trade and into the growing scientific and professional establishment, who tended to slide towards the Church of England, not least because only those willing to conform to Anglican norms could be students or members of Oxford or Cambridge University.

There's Thomas Day and his bestselling books for children, and also his strange, obsessive, and to our eyes deeply worrying scheme for proving that Nature could be subordinated to Nurture: he adopted a pair of orphan girls, and had them educated in the best eighteenth-century terms, with the intention of choosing which would make the perfect wife for himself.

There's Anna Seward, 'the Swan of Litchfield': rare, as a woman, in being part of the circle in her own right. The Lunar wives were frequently intelligent, well-read and genuinely interested in their husbands' work, but Anna was herself an admired and much-published writer, the first biographer of Erasmus and a much better poet.

Their loose association and vast network of connections flourished so fruitfully[19] precisely because it was loose. When I add that corresponding members of the Lunar Society included the Benjamin Franklin whose day job was as US Ambassador in Paris, naturalist Joseph Banks, astronomer William Herschel, chemist the seventh Duc de Chaulmes, and the painter Joseph Wright of Derby … I hope you get the idea, the temptation, and the potential for disaster. It's glorious, and it's overwhelming: in writing this, I could have doubled the list of Lunar men – and women and associates – that you've just read. What I enjoyed so much about Erasmus and the Lunar men, in other words, was beyond the scope of a novel. But Uglow's masterly and delightful book should have warned me (though I didn't hear the warning) that anyone less accomplished than she was going to struggle to build *any* story[20] on the connections between a busy and various group of thinkers and doers.

I would have to focus on one Lunar man or woman, I concluded, feeling the four-in-the-afternoon post-lunch gloom settling on me as I let myself into the house. But even if I did, what then? Scholars have spent years matching up pairs of letters, deducing facts from parish records as well as newspapers, court reports and recorded gossip; Joseph Priestley's Wikipedia entry alone is enough to make the experienced novelist feel weak, there are so many books, jobs, houses, sermons, scientific papers, travels towards and escapes from, so much celebration and persecution, so many letters to him, from him, about him.

At least when I built *A Secret Alchemy* on Elizabeth and Anthony

---

[19] We don't seem to be able to get away from the loves of the plants, do we? And their children kept marrying each other.

[20] For all history-writing is a storytelling of some kind: the setting out of a narrative of 'a causally related chain of events' to quote my Penguin *Dictionary of Literary Terms and Literary Theories*.

Woodville there was a complete blank – and therefore space for me – where their emotional and personal lives would have been. I could exploit fiction's inbuilt scope for interiority to find real creative, imaginative excitement in turning these slightest of ghosts into flesh and blood, and all in a violent, harsh, glamorous world full of potential thrills, spills, tragedy and happy endings.

Things are different with these children of Rousseau: they think about their own story, investigate their own experience, and write it down. There is violence, but not mostly for them, and a good few of them no longer even believe that souls continue after bodies have died. Even when letters are missing or their writers are naturally reserved or in a hurry, in terms of my imaginative work it's only a matter of reconstructing what went on in that space, not recreating it. It's a job of sticking close to what we know, researching as a biographer would, and then writing the dialogue and physical action the biographer's not allowed to play with. It might be an exciting job for a bold life writer – Richard Holmes, perhaps, in *Footsteps* mode.[21] But I was not a bold life writer.

Worst of all, there's nothing so deadly to the creative drive as having to refer everything you imagine back for checking; every decision for or against the invented thing becomes one more micro-push in the war of attrition. My heart sank then, and it sinks now, at that sort of project. How dull it is! How little space it gives the freewheeling storyteller who wants to be Emperor of her kingdom!

Where in my family tree was someone both exciting enough, and un-documented enough, for a novelist?

I moved down a generation. And there, among the Lunar offspring, including Josiah's children and Erasmus's even more formidable and rather less charming son Robert, was an old friend of mine.

---

[21] With his book of essays *Footsteps*, Holmes changed life writing, as a genre, for good. His later *Age of Wonder* explores the science-arts-culture-exploration nexus of the same world half a generation later than Uglow's Lunar Men; it starts with a very young Joseph Banks sailing to Tahiti with Captain Cook, and finishes with a very young Charles Darwin hopping off the *Beagle* in Cape Town to call on a very old John Herschel. And in *Sidetracks*, Holmes later collected together a series of essays which also explored biographical subjects that he did not, in the end, write books about.

4

Tom Wedgwood

I discovered Thomas Wedgwood on the shelves of the London College of Printing. I was doing an A Level in Photography in a year, one day a week. I'd been useless at Art at school and never done any kind of exam in it, I'd only recently learnt to work in monochrome and print it, and had never shot a single colour transparency. But this course also had a written exam on the history and theory of photography, and I knew I could do the old three-hour, four-question, sudden-death, sit-down written exams because my school despised them but also ruthlessly trained us to pass them.

Tom Wedgwood: the first photographer: as I remember, a smallish book in a 1960s reprint of the original 1903 edition, and it didn't show signs of having been borrowed very often. The author was R. B. Litchfield, who turns up in *Period Piece* as Aunt Etty's husband Uncle Richard. He was a lawyer by training but one of his great friends was the physicist James Clerk Maxwell, and they were both involved for many years in founding and supporting the progressive and philanthropic Working Men's College in North London;[22] one can imagine how this one of his wife's relatives would have intrigued him. And in the strict sense Tom *was* the first photographer we know about: the first to use light-sensitive substances to record images on a surface, first directly and then through a lens.

Tom was the fifth child and third son of Josiah Wedgwood. In the Stubbs family portrait at the beginning of Chapter Two, he's the youngst of the boys on ponies, while the young woman on a horse is Susannah, Josiah's eldest child, who married Robert Darwin.

Years later I put Tom's 'sun-pictures' in *The Mathematics of Love*; indeed, the whole of that novel is about photography (I even included a plaid ribbon, as a tribute to Clerk Maxwell's crucial experiment in colour theory) but it starts on the 16th August 1819, at the Peterloo Massacre: almost too early for photography,[23] and definitely too late for Tom (1771-1805), although I could, and did, quote his 'Essay on Vision' for the epigraph:

> Perception becomes a language ... The far greater part of what is supposed to be perception is only the body of ideas which a perception has awakened.

But to use Tom in that novel's story I had to create a link.

* * *

---

[22] Other patrons and teachers at WMC included Rosetti, Ruskin, Charles Kingsley and John Stuart Mill.

[23] If you're remembering that it wasn't till the 1830s that Daguerre and Fox Talbot started fighting in the Royal Society over priority (with added Anglo-French enmity to sharpen the fight, and glittering riches hovering over possible industrial applications), then I'll just say: google the Nièpce brothers.

from *The Mathematics of Love*

The doctor himself was being helped out of his carriage, while under the shifting of his considerable weight I saw that a few books tumbled out from where they were stacked by its open door.

Miss Durward greeted him as his footman assisted him up the steps, and led him upstairs as quickly as her good manners and his bulk would allow.

...

The doctor settled deeper into his chair and accepted a large piece of Nurse's plum cake ... 'My brother-in-law Thomas Wedgwood was much taken up with the question. I think he knew more about it than any man.' He stopped, but went on again after a moment ... 'He died many years ago. But his paper – or, rather, my good friend Davy's paper on his work – was published by the Royal Institution, I recall – I think it was in the year Two – and I could let you have a copy. And now I must go. I am putting up at the Crown, if you should need me again, but I don't at all anticipate it. If I'm absent – I've several more of those wretches to see – my man will know where I am.'

'They were not wretches,' I said.

'I speak of the magistrates and their minions. A damn— a dashed ill-managed business they made of it, it seems. But one of their number knew I was in town, rather than safely in Shrewsbury, and so I'm called to several bedsides. Besides, even those who oppose reform may bleed, and I'm bound to help all I can.'

* * *

What I'd been too squeamish to make explicit was the doctor's name. He is, of course, Dr Robert Darwin of Shrewsbury, father of Charles, widower of Tom's sister Susannah and so uncle-by-marriage of Emma. My squeamishness was partly because I had no idea whether Robert was in Manchester on that day, and decided not to try to find out. Even if there was, somewhere, clear or even circumstantial evidence either way, it was probably buried in letters or local records. And if I did all that work and found he wasn't in Manchester, would that give the mechanical-historian-monkey on my back the authority to stop me putting Robert where I wanted him? Not naming him was a bit of thin padding against the kind of reader who, instead of thinking about what a novel is exploring, knee-jerks off about minor inaccuracies. Read my lips, my friend: *this story never happened …*

I got all the information I needed – such as the stacks of books in his carriage – from Edna Healey's biography of Emma, and when I told my editor at Headline Review she said, 'Aha! I thought he was unusually 3D for a minor character.' Ever since then I have tried to hold that kind of small, particular detail as a gold-standard for bringing minor characters alive.[24]

But my main squeamishness was because to name Dr Darwin – and to do so in the early pages of the novel – would be the opposite of the small, friendly smile, the quiet, 'Well, yes, actually,' of my upbringing. To trumpet him would be that shameful social crime from which no Briton easily recovers: Showing Off. So I didn't name him, and only later did I realise that it made good interview to let listeners and readers in on the secret.

Perhaps, it occurred to me now, it would be easier to bring myself to name names in a project where the name wasn't Darwin but (by good fortune) something as memorably unusual, and as well known: not monkeys, but pots. And not just pots, but that un-shiny, blue china with white, raised figures which *everyone* recognises, though not everyone likes or knows much about. Certainly many fewer know that the blue-and-white (and a much stronger, clearer blue, at least in the early days, than is commonly thought of now as 'wedgwood blue') is only a tiny part of the whole, huge output. Wedgwood & Sons made everything

---

[24] Not that it's necessarily a bad thing to stick with the usual and the 2D. Sometimes in real life we notice the uniqueness and oddness of strangers, but sometimes we don't; so the writer of fiction must decide which kind of Sometimes is right for this character, at this point of the narrative.

from a fifty-place dinner service for Catherine the Great, Empress of Russia, to cabbage-shaped teapots for the tea-table of the middle-class Victorian housewife.[25] Their coronation mugs were just one product in the firm's long tradition of using well-known artists: the 1953 mug for Queen Elizabeth II is by Eric Ravilious. Royalty was both a market and a motif for Wedgwood & Sons even though many of the Lunar men bordered on the Republican – Erasmus Darwin certainly did. Capitalists must work with the buyers that existing society offers them.

I rolled up my mental sleeves, hunkered down in the glorious Victorian back-stacks of the London Library, and set about seeing if I could build a novel on Tom. In 1909, Uncle Richard's Preface to *Tom Wedgwood* set out his problem, and my opportunity, at the beginning:

> This Memoir appears, it must be confessed, rather late. It was in the year 1806 that the little world of Tom Wedgwood's friends and relations – a little world, but it included some of the most notable Englishmen of the time – were expecting the appearance of a book which was to give an account of his life and character, with an essay expounding his philosophical theories. This essay was to be written by Sir James Mackintosh,[26] and the Memoir by Coleridge. But neither of these eminent persons did what he promised. It is not certain that either even began to do it. Of Mackintosh, Coleridge once wrote: 'He is one of those men with whom the meaning to do a thing means nothing.' Of Coleridge himself this was absolutely true, and it was not quite untrue of Mackintosh; for he was noted for his infinite capacity for procrastination, as if his rule of life was never to do a thing to-day which could possibly be put off till to-morrow. The plan of a joint Memoir by two such

---

[25] And so to the present day: in a family in many ways very free of opinions about what one must do, it was still rather assumed that the china on my wedding list would be Wedgwood.

[26] James Mackintosh's involvement in that little world is of course professional – he was a qualified doctor but became a famous jurist and historian – but also personal: his wife's sister was married to Tom's brother Josiah II, and his daughter married that Josiah's son Hensleigh, of whom more anon.

collaborators, two men, as it happened, not the least in sympathy one with the other, was thus virtually hopeless from the first. Mackintosh, moreover, had gone to be a Judge in India, and Coleridge was nearing that saddest time in his life when his best friends could only describe his condition (produced by opium) as one of 'paralysis of the will.'

In the following century some letters had been lost, but enough remained for Uncle Richard to write a slim – well, these days we'd call it biography, not memoir.

So was this the right project? I knew there was space for me in Tom's experiments with sun pictures – a delectable, visual, metaphorical, physical and Physics-based potency – but I also knew that ideas and metaphors can't carry a novel. A story *has* to have people as the carrier signal – characters-in-action and characters-in-interaction – because the basic connection that a reader makes with fiction is human-to-(fictional)-human.[27] The book industry's shorthand may too often shrivel that deep truth to an over-simple requirement for characters we can 'care about', but it is still true. Image, theme, metaphor and non-fiction hooks may be desirable or even necessary, but they are not sufficent, and woe betide the writer who forgets it. The interest of Tom for the reader was obvious: everyone's interested in love, friendship, and the human need to make sense of one's life, and everyone reading historical fiction is interested in history. But where was the interest for me? Was there enough in the events and stuffs of Tom's life to keep me getting up each writerly morning to go on marrying the DNA in his story with mine, and creating something new? Were those events and stuffs things which would allow me to play to my writerly strengths?

The London Library has two first editions of *Tom Wedgwood*. I borrowed one then, to work on the novel, and to write this I've borrowed it again. The bookplate says 'Presented to the London Library by Dowager Lady Farrer, Jan 1917', and in one corner of it a

---

[27] Or, obviously, stand-ins for humans such as rabbits, hobbits or small, charming robots who find themselves alone in outer space.

librarianly hand has pencilled in '?Farrar'. Then, I didn't hunt down the Farrar reference because it wasn't relevant to the possible novel, but to write this I have, and as I click to and fro in the *Oxford Dictionary of National Biography* I can't help laughing, though this footnote[28] explaining why is strictly for the genealogy nerds.

It was already clear that Tom's story might allow me to play to some of my strengths. I like writing men, and I'd loved writing in the flavour of 1819 for *The Mathematics of Love*; Tom's voice would be very little earlier. Even if I decided to work with an external narrator – 'in third person', to use the writerly shorthand for a decision with enormously important consequences – it would be Tom's voice and sensibility which would dominate.

Tom, aged eleven, writes to his father, who is in London: during the Potteries bread riots of 1783, a canal barge of grain was stopped and plundered, and Tom's oldest brother John was at a meeting of the Master Potters who 'harrangued to the Mob on the bad way they had begun in to lessen the price of corn'.

I'd first explored Stoke-on-Trent many years before as a little bit of ancestor-worship (and ancestor-in-law worship for my personal anti-Darwin). The Wedgwood Visitor Centre made a pleasing temple, since it collects and exhibits the unique Wedgwood archive[29] as well as showing some of the crafts and processes. I went back to the Potteries a few years later, when I had the idea of setting a novel in a family-owned pottery. The novel never quite worked and wasn't published[30] but I'd been simultaneously impressed and horrified by what's left of one of the earliest Industrial Revolution landscapes.

In the late 18th century, when Tom was a boy, it was little more than

---

[28] If that long-dead librarian is right, this Lady Farrar must be Katherine, the second wife of the distinguished civil servant Thomas, Lord Farrar: she was a daughter of Emma's brother Hensleigh Wedgwood, and so a granddaughter of both Josiah II and of the deplorable Sir James Mackintosh: I'd love to think of her donation as some kind of atonement for her Grandpapa Mack's failure to do what he promised for her Great-uncle Tom. What's more – you did want more, didn't you? – her step-daughter Ida Farrar married Horace Darwin, Charles's youngest son.

[29] The archive came very, very close, recently, to being sold abroad as a consequence of a change in the rules of pension funds which hit the Wedgwood company hard. Fortunately, the campaign by local and national historians and art historians to save it had the support of the historian Tristram Hunt, who also just happened to be Labour MP for Stoke-on-Trent Central.

[30] But the idea of the family firm built on an ancient craft eventually became *A Secret Alchemy*.

a cluster of over-grown villages, their industrial practices unregulated, as Manchester's were unregulated, by any ancient tradition of guilds or early-modern royal charters. The form-follows-function of the bottle-ovens is deeply satisfying, and yet the pollution that their kiln fires and the different chemical processes spilled out was as toxic as anything else in the eighteenth century. It was Josiah Wedgwood who campaigned, with Erasmus's help, to build the Trent & Mersey Canal so that china clay could come directly from Cornwall, and the finished ceramics could glide safely away to the showrooms in London's West End and the ports of Liverpool and Bristol. It was Josiah who, despite being in many ways a comparatively conscientious and benevolent employer, pioneered the ruthless division of labour and separation of processes, a century and more before Henry Ford. In other ways the Six Towns of the Potteries are apparently unremarkable, but there's a powerful sense that only just under the pavements is the clay on which and out of which all this work and wealth was built. That building was done by brutal working lives made of specialist but casual labour. Putting out the shout for workers to empty a kiln before the heat and fumes had dissipated to safe levels might be illegal or at least disapproved of, but it made all the difference to the pottery's profit. One display in the Gladstone Pottery Museum explained how it all worked, and quoted a witness: 'But I never knew an oven-man live over forty.'

Tom, aged fifteen, joins his next oldest brother Jos at Edinburgh University; 'the Divinity students are the dirtiest set I ever saw; a company of old potters look like gentlemen compared to them,' writes Jos, the closet atheist. The letters are full of chemistry, literature, news of Priestley and Lavoisier, the student who is imprisoned in the Tolbooth for trying to pass a forged bill at a shop and 'stands no chance for his life,' and all the other things that would now flit about on Twitter. Tom sets out on organised scientific work which leads to two significant papers before he is twenty-one, including one which provides very early experimental evidence of the basic fact of physics that when almost all substances are heated, whatever their melting point, they fluoresce at the same temperature.

And what was there in this story which would play to … not necessarily to my weaknesses – that's dangerous – but certainly to my unexplored capacities? The problems which I'd be excited by? The things I didn't know if I could manage? That isn't from a sadistic desire to make my agent and my publisher nervous – though I don't blame them if it does – but because it's the only way I can go on being interested.[31] Writing a novel is in part a business of working out the practical answer to a practical problem, and that business takes too long, and the outcome is too uncertain, to set yourself a problem you won't enjoy solving. So where in the story were the things which would be new, perhaps difficult, but potent for me: things that I would *want* to crack?

'No ideas but in things', said William Carlos Williams but, as Philip Gross points out, that doesn't mean 'no ideas', and it's enfleshing the ideas in the things which shapes the working process of a novelist. That's why I've never been interested in writing about the normal business of normal, contemporary family life – it's important to me as a person, I enjoy reading that kind of fiction, but I find the working process of embodying those ideas in those things very dull.

Mind you, I used to say that I couldn't imagine writing all-male sex in detail, since by definition I wouldn't be in the room. Then I decided to write Antony Wydvil.

* * *

from *A Secret Alchemy*

From the best scrivener in Bruges I bought an exquisite miniature copy of the *Summa Theologica*, and had it on the tavern table beside me when a dark young man, seeing me unable to resist opening its casket and stroking the sweet, new leather of the binding, asked me what book it was that I read.

He was Louis de Bretaylles, come to Bruges to offer his services

[31] I used to tell my Open University students that I'd rather see a heroic failure than a cowardly success, because no one ever got better by only doing things they already know they can do. And I said that as far as I could, within the grade descriptors, I would award marks accordingly.

to Edward, for he was a man accustomed to work in secret between old allegiances and new.

...

But soon our talk turned to poetry and philosophy: he knew Christina of Pisa, and Chaucer, Aquinas and Livy. His eyes were black and his hands long-fingered, and his voice had the tang of one born speaking the *langue d'oc*, though he spoke the *langue d'oeil* well enough, English and Spanish too. And when he laughed at me that my face was still so pale-skinned, for all my years' campaigning, and began to quote Chrétien de Troyes from the The *Story of the Grail* – 'Ainc mai chevalier ne conui ... ' – I wanted to reach across the tavern board and seize him by his thin, hard shoulders, the better to kiss him long into the night. And I did kiss him so, and many nights thereafter.

My love for Louis was almost more than my spirit and mind and body could bear. Sometimes I would rise in the moonlight and watch his sleeping face, his copper-coloured skin and whipcord arms, and wonder that I did not die, there, in that breath, for the love of him.

* * *

I see Tom carefully setting up a sun-microscope, and his hand touching a friend's, so that they both realise what is happening – but now what can they do about it? And is that Act One, where my story starts? Or what if it's the midpoint, the heart of Act Three,[32] the crux after which nothing can ever be the same? And if that tiny, burning moment is the crisis of Act Five, what does that say about where the story should start?

I seemed to be planning to make Tom Wedgwood fall in love. Would he let me exercise my craft? My art, dammit? His real story is beyond recall, buried in a Dorset churchyard, and I would be working with a mercifully thin and broken skeleton of recorded facts; with luck, I

---

[32] For more on all that, I refer you to John Yorke's *Into The Woods*, which is by far the best of the legion of books about story-structure that I've yet read.

wouldn't be creating a narrative that merely represented a historical figure, I could claim the fiction-writer's birthright in enfleshing this skeleton into full life and consciousness.

Tom, aged nineteen, wants to set up a house near the Wedgwood factory and estate at Etruria with a rather older acquaintance, John Leslie, as both friend and scientific tutor. Tom describes his purpose: 'My aim is to strengthen the power of reason by the habit of reflection, and by cultivating the virtues of the heart in a temporal retirement from the world at large'. Litchfield puts it in the context of the Romantic period, as well as the excesses of a teenager's idealism only nine months after the fall of the Bastille: 'one feels the ring of the new ideas which the great upheaval of 1789 was stirring in the young and ardent souls of the time'. Leslie stayed at Etruria for about two years, from June 1790, Litchfield explains.

> His stay there was doubtless a great help to Tom Wedgwood in his scientific work. One may doubt whether his influence was good in other ways. He pours out his admiration for his pupil in language which is too exuberant to sound sincere, and whether sincere or not, it was hardly wholesome reading for a lad of nineteen.

Later, Litchfield edges closer to the problem, being as explicit as was feasible in 1903:

> What degree of personal attachment existed between Tom Wedgwood and Leslie is not easy to say. It was apparently a warm feeling, on Wedgwood's side at any rate, in the early days of their acquaintance...

Towards the end of the time with Leslie, Tom seems to have had a severe nervous and physical breakdown. My ears pricked up again when in 1792 – perhaps to help get over the depression – Tom and Jos travelled to Paris as good Whigs joining in the celebrations of the third anniversary of the fall of the Bastille.

> ...I lodge here in the same house with young Watt – he is a furious democrat, detests the King and Fayette.... Watt says

that a new revolution must inevitably take place, and that it will in all probability be fatal to the King, Fayette, and some hundred others. The 14th of this month will probably be eventful. He means to join the French Army in case of any civil rupture…The English here are all Aristocrats, and I do not intend to dine again at the Table d' Hote [*sic*], as politics are discussed with such freedom that it is difficult to avoid disagreeable disputes…

Was there space for me in the disastrous trip to Jamaica in 1800? The successful second trip to Paris, then Geneva, in 1803, even though the Peace of Amiens between Britain and France was beginning to fray? Tom got out of France the day war was declared but his travelling companion, the painter Underwood, had decided to stay on in Paris to study; he was arrested and imprisoned, and for two years Tom sent him money and comforts, and worked hard to get him released. As the war got going and in Britain the invasion scare mounted, Tom paid for the raising, equipping and paying of a company of volunteer militia, while letters flew to and fro in the family about the dangers of living, as Jos now did, in gentlemanly rurality in Dorset, and therefore uncomfortably close to the south coast and Napoleon.

It's hard to know what caused what, but Tom had been a delicate, sickly child, and from that first breakdown his bodily health was never good; he fell repeatedly into deep depressions. There's a heart-breaking letter to his father, when he's only in his early twenties, setting out his reasons for finally giving up all hope of a scientific career. It's impossible not to wonder how the history of science might have been delayed or changed if Charles Darwin had suffered the same kind of ill-health from a young age as his Uncle Tom had.[33] My private theory is Tom had something like coeliac disease, or maybe Crohn's, which led, as chronic disease so easily does, to clinical depression.

Doctors, including Erasmus Darwin, sometimes helped; cures which

---

[33] Although the jury is out on the causes of Charles's genuinely grim physical symptoms later in life, all the evidence is that he had been as robust as any other young man of the time, until he returned from the *Beagle* voyage.

sound strange to us, but were logical given what was known, sometimes helped. Tom might have been desperate, but he wasn't foolish to try, for example, the cure which involved living above a butcher's shop to inhale the airs. One of the things it's difficult for historical fiction to conjure up convincingly is how, in the history of science, different explanations and models could genuinely make equal sense to intelligent, scientifically-minded adults at the time. With our hindsight-spectacles we ignore, or laugh at, the paradigms which so clearly turned out to be dead ends; but our characters not only mustn't laugh, they mustn't seem stupid for not laughing. Tom supported the weird new Pneumatic Institute, where its founder Beddoes had a new young second-in-command called Humphrey Davy, joining in the fashionable experiments with laughing gas, but also taking Beddoes' medical advice seriously and hoping for a cure.

However, he had plenty of money, and when his health allowed he could afford to travel, tinker with science, read, write, observe, and enjoy music (he played the flute and the piano, both apparently very well) and the company of friends and family. Was there space for me in the warm, clever life of his brothers, sisters and cousins, including the Darwins not so very far away in Litchfield and Shrewsbury? Tom loved his sisters, although he never shows a flicker of interest in women as possible wives, while Jos's devotion to his brother was possibly the most important relationship of Jos's reserved, businesslike and successful life. Later, Tom spent long hours in the nursery with Jos's children, observing, listening and making notes about how humans develop. This was a family habit that had its origins in a thoroughly Rousseauian belief that much of human nature could be explained by studying children, and it developed into a philosophy of child-rearing which seems remarkably modern. Jos II when quite young had written extensive notes on bringing up children, against 'interference and direction' except when otherwise the child would be harmed, and he also hid behind the nursery door to record what the children said when the grown-ups were absent. Charles's more careful, daily observation of the first three years in the lives of his babies Anne and William are to this day valuable data for developmental pyschologists. These detailed observations and explorations make the small, grey shapshots of my parents as children, and the one VHS tape I have of my own children when young, seem very lazy and unrevealing.

Tom and Jos were fond of, but not so close to, their older brother John. He, as first-born son, was the natural heir to Josiah I and the great Wedgwood firm, but although he was very intelligent as well as kind, he was gentle, easily swayed by others' opinions and desires, and constitutionally hopeless with money. As a banker – i.e. a partner in a private bank – he kept nearly going bankrupt, and as he still had shares in the family firm, his disasters endangered the wellbeing of the business as well as that of his wife and their several children. It says something for the affectionate and reasonable spirit in the family relationships that even when Jos and Tom sorted him out for the umpteenth time, and arranged things so his dependents were safe and he couldn't touch his own capital, everyone stayed friends. However, affectionate, reasonable spirits don't tend to make very good novels either, unless they come up hard against something much less affectionate and less reasonable, and on the whole the Wedgwoods didn't.

Could I make something of Tom's life in London, where he was supposed to be keeping an eye on the Wedgwood showroom as well as keeping his spirits up with intellectual company? The search for suitable travelling companions focused on musical young men – the artist Underwood, the poet Thomas Campbell – which *is* a nice space for me. A young flute-player crops up once, and, beady-eyed, I began to wonder …

Would I be justified? Tom's support of poor Underwood, locked in a French prison, isn't in itself evidence of more than what I already knew: that Tom wanted to do right, to behave well, to use his money and connections on behalf of less fortunate friends, as well as charities and the defence of the realm. He gave loans and gifts of money, and even annuities, to those, like Leslie some years later, who would do good work if only they could put bread on the table. In the era before the professionalisation of science, it wasn't only artists and writers who needed £500 a year and a room of their own; what's more, the scientists needed a room which could withstand the occasional explosion.

He supported writers too: William Godwin, James Mackintosh, Thomas Campbell. When Coleridge was offered a preaching position that he didn't want and would have been terrible at, but needed in order to eat, and support his wife and children, Jos and Tom combined to give him a pension, on condition that he gave up the post and concentrated on writing. Coleridge – Col, to his friends and patrons – repaid the favour, I can't help suspecting, by introducing Tom to the recreational, as opposed to medicinal, use of opium.

Coleridge. Even if Keats was right, and he was a bit short of negative capability, he is the perfect embodiment of the open-ended, open-minded habit of enquiry across art, science, philosophy and experience, but in a far more glamorous form than the sensible, pragmatic, well-grounded, well-funded Darwins or Wedgwoods could ever hope to be: a man so charismatic, so fascinating, so frustratingly brilliant and so disaster-ridden that it's almost impossible to read a book about that world without him dominating it.

A hundred years later he was almost equal to Tom in importance for Uncle Richard Lichfield and his publisher: *TOM WEDGWOOD, the first photographer* is subtitled *An account of his life, his discovery and his friendship with Samuel Taylor Coleridge including the letters of Coleridge to the Wedgwoods*, before an academic sting in the tail: *and an examination of accounts of alleged earlier photographic discoveries.* Coleridge's name is set bigger than the rest of the subtitle, and a hundred years later I still had a couple of poet friends in thrall to him, but this was one of the times when my lack of an English degree has been a minor drawback:[34] I didn't know his work well. A nice little Oxford University Press *Poems*, printed in 1940 with the thin, crisp paper of proper letter press, and a note from one of those poet friends

---

[34] Not that I regret my Drama degree in the least: I learnt vast amounts about both storytelling as character-in-action, and practice-led research in the arts, which I never would have learnt otherwise. What's more, I was spared the experience of many writer friends, who read English but then struggled for years or even decades to get out of the shadow of all those great authors, and claim their own entitlement to write.

pointing me towards the best of them, put that right. And his prose?

Oh! Coleridge is daunting. Differently daunting from Erasmus, but daunting for some of the same reasons: too many words, too many ideas, too many books by him, about him, and grown outwards from him. How on earth would I – who till a couple of months before hadn't got much further than 'Kubla Khan' – be able to bring him alive, and yet hold the dam against his personality, and stop him swamping the novel?

* * *

from *The Mathematics of Love*

'... My father and I were fascinated, although it was not easy to make out the images, for they must be kept in the dark lest they darken further, and may only be looked at by candlelight. Mr Wedgwood explained how his late brother brushed paper or white leather with nitrate of silver – in solution, you understand – and then the object to be copied was placed on top of it, and the whole put in the sun. It took only a few minutes, he said, if the sunlight was strong enough.' Miss Durward pulled her chair close in, propped her elbows on the table, and continued, 'You see, the nitrate of silver tarnishes by the agency of light, where the object does not protect it, even to the degree of translucency of each part of the object.

...

'Mr Wedgwood showed us one of a vine leaf. Every vein and stem was as clear as if I had drawn it, only white, of course, on a darkened ground, like a white-line wood engraving. My father was mainly interested in the precision of it, for he has an idea of copying prints automatically by such a process, but it was so beautiful, too! There were some pictures of insect wings, made through a sun-microscope so that they appeared larger than in life. I almost feared that they would float off if I breathed too close ... The strangest thing was, to be able to make a picture of something real with no intervention – no agency – except the natural properties of the sun. The object creates its own image. Mr Wedgwood referred to the image as a simulacrum – a replicant. And then suddenly it has an independent life.'

'It is like a ghost,' I said. 'The object is – may be – long lost, in another time. Its image lives on, in a different place—' I could not continue …

'Yes,' said Miss Durward. She tucked her hand into my arm, and I felt the thin firmness of her through my sleeve. 'But only when it is kept in the dark.'

* * *

So where was the spine of my putative novel about Tom? What would the story be?

The obvious one was the spine that anyone's story has: the beginning-middle-end of a life, which makes a biography interesting in the way that an accurate photograph of an absent person is interesting: the closest delineation we'll get to the real thing. But a cradle-to-grave biographical *novel* would be like taking a photograph and repeating it carefully in embroidery or paint: ploddingly literal for the reader, utterly boring for the writer.

What if I took a narrower section of the life? Was there a good beginning-middle-end which would have drama and meaning within itself?

I had been to the Potteries twice, and had some sense of them. Now I went looking for the older Tom in north Dorset, where the River Tarrant runs through ancient hills like a silk thread strung with little villages for pearls. Their names could make a skipping rhyme, or perhaps a vocal piece by Philip Glass, if he'd submitted to immersion in Thomas Hardy: Tarrant Crawford, Tarrant Gunville, Tarrant Hinton, Tarrant Keyneston, Tarrant Launceston, Tarrant Monkton, Tarrant Rawston and Tarrant Rushton.

In 1795, only a few months after old Josiah Wedgwood, mortally sick, in pain, and as clear-headed and practical as ever, locked himself in his bedroom one night and took a fatal overdose of laudanam, Jos II handed the day-to-day running of the firm over to his managers and moved to Surrey, the better to follow the scientific and country pursuits of a cultured gentleman. Surrey didn't turn out as nice as the family had hoped, however, and in 1799 he and the sickly, peripatetic Tom agreed to look for adjoining estates somewhere else. They found them in tiny Tarrant Gunville, a mile or so north up the river from the main Salisbury-Blandford Forum road. Jos bought the recently-built Gunville House, all clean stone and plain lines, while Tom bought Eastbury Park, just across the lane. Eastbury was originally a much bigger, grander house, designed by Sir John Vanbrugh almost a century before. As well as his famously cynical Restoration comedies, Vanbrugh designed the impossibly, magnificently grand Blenheim Palace; it seems fitting, in a painful way, that by the time Tom bought Eastbury Park, most of the house had fallen into disrepair and been demolished, so that the only wing still standing was a size fit for a sad, well-off, single, dying man.

It's late summer. I drive gently through the lanes, seeing the wheat waving as if the breeze has brushed a hand across it. The cottages, says the parish website, were partly built with brick, flint and stone liberated from the demolished wings of Eastbury, the gardens are fit for opening to the National Gardens Scheme, and the farm shop is full of ancient breeds of pork loin, legs of new-season's lamb, punnets of local strawberries, and cold-pressed olive oil from Kalamata. The village hall's bunting flicks and flutters, and the purr of lawnmowers is damped by the deep lanes and the thick, dark green of late-summer trees. The church, when I gently open the door, is full of flowers for a wedding that afternoon, and the altar has its posh frock on.

My natural writerly territory is history and its presence in our present, but somewhere at the heart of most of my stories is an exploration of how two people in a certain section of historical time and place work out whether they can be together, while still being themselves: call that some kind of love story if you want to. Sex and love are always also the carrier signal for all sorts of other ideas and themes, but could I build a novel on Tom's search for that kind of love?

There was plenty for me to work with, in a world where his search for love would have been a societal crime, and his finding it a legal one. But to write a novel with that imagined story as the spine, when there's so little evidence for it of any kind ... What story was it, really? I'd have to do some stretched-to-the-point-of-dishonesty readings of what letters there are, or some far-too-lurid imaginings.

Not every reader liked my 'take' on Anthony Woodville in *A Secret Alchemy*, although quite often in the context of such an anachronistic or ill-informed understanding of fifteenth century lives that their comments didn't sting, even if they did exasperate. More than one blogger said, rather more perceptively, 'How can she say that? Who knows?' The answer of course is that with the historical Anthony nobody knows, and that's why we write fiction about him. It's hardly possible, in any case, to map our concept of homosexuality onto those times. With Tom though, maybe someone knew.

Nonetheless, I'm typing this, and wondering all over again whether the Underwood story would work – or the Invasion scare – or – or – or. The fuel of a fiction-writer's mind is 'what if?', and Tom's own life is one long chain of 'what if?'s. But the more I stared at the space after each 'what if?', the more it turned out to be a dead end. Everything that Tom tried seems to have ended in failure – and not heroic failure but the dull, grey misery of the chronic depressive. He never loses his mind or his love for his family but as, one-by-one, he gives up the work and the activities that he loves, as his letters are taken up ever more with his physical and mental suffering, the story peters out in the most depressing way possible, until at last he dies just before his forty-third birthday.

The more I played with changing Tom's personality and his actions in order to find a plot – the more I embroidered my way away from the incomplete but faithful photograph, towards the complete but ever more fictional story – the less connection my Tom and my Tom's story would have with the real Tom and his real story.

That shouldn't matter, of course. 'How many times,' I scolded myself, 'have you reminded students and friends and readers of the blog that they're "allowed" to do whatever they like, as long as it works? That it's their novel so it's their rules? That you can't libel the dead? That this is a novel, y'know: fiction? Oh, physician, stop whingeing and go and bloody heal thyself.'

But it did matter, and it's actually in thinking about the different houses in this story that I've finally found the right image for the wrangle at the heart of this project.

Historical fiction gets written about real historical characters because so many writers and readers are passionately interested in historical minds and lived experience, and that's what fiction does best.[35] However, although we're explicitly claiming the creative freedom and greater psychological penetration of a novel, if the story loses *all* its anchors in the historical facts, then why are we bothering to write and to read it?

Imagine writing a novel explictly about Blenheim Palace. Failing a record of what the morning room, say, actually looked like, most writers would decorate it with carefully-researched and therefore plausible colours and patterns; if the original was known but their plot required something else, many would cheerfully paste that different plausible decor up instead, and quite a few would tuck in an ante-chamber or an extra side-door, if it meant the story could work better. Having done what their book needed, the more nervous, or naturally scholarly, would put a note at the end to explain what they'd invented.

But adding a storey to Bleheim Palace? Moving the stairs? Demolishing the ballroom? Reversing the entire orientation of the house, so the setting sun can shine into different rooms? Each of us would set the threshold we can't cross at a different point, but all of us know that beyond our personal threshold we're only using the façade and bolting it onto a completely different internal architecture. If nothing about the house in your Blenheim Palace novel is remotely like the real Blenheim Palace – if you really can't say that the novel is *about* Blenheim Palace in any real and substantial sense – then as a creative

---

[35] It also gets written, of course, because those real historical characters are a built-in 'non-fiction hook' for the industry we need to sell it.

act it's either artistically pointless, or nakedly cynical. Very possibly both.

Real historical people are no different. I was shackled, even if loosely, to the facts of the real Tom because the further I took this story away from the essential truth of him, the more transparently I was being driven simply by the need to use his real name – and by extension my surname – in order to sell a book.

* * *

Thursday, July 16th, 1805: Early on the morning of the funeral, Jos walks out of the house and across the lawns towards the church. The dew is as thick as foam on a sea-wave, and from among the slate-green mid-summer trees the tower of the church scarcely rises. The sun is warming, but his shoes are soaking and his feet cold. It doesn't matter.

Jos opens the little gate in the wall and walks down the three steps into the churchyard. The church itself is cramped close to the path and the wall, with graves tucked alongside its flanks. And now there is a new one: the Dorset earth pale and summer-dry, even in the depths of this damp, green spot: paler than the Staffordshire clay they grew up on; made mud pies of; threw at each other and turned to hurl at their common enemies; mortared tree branches with to make castles; learnt to roll between their fingers, reading it as a blind man reads an inscription: grain, grade, density, porosity, moisture, pliability, shade, hue, firing point, cracking point. *Feel it, boys,* Papa would say to John and Jos and Tom, *Feel it – sample after sample – careful to keep them in order – feel it, and look at the figures in the record. You must know how the figures will feel, and you must know how the feel will measure.*

He is standing outside the porch. He has no desire to enter the church, although of course he does as often as seems polite; that it's politeness, his neighbours know well. It's one reason they don't care to admit him to their confidence. The other is that Staffordshire clay, still there, invisible, on his hands and his shoes.

The porch is square and plain – medieval – and on the right-hand pillar is carved what's left of a sundial. The gnomon is long-gone, not even a stump of iron left in the central hole. But the markings are still there: concentric rings and radial lines carefully measured and worked although a little worn, now, to the windward side. *Sixteenth century, it seems,* the Rector said once; *pity about the gnomon.* His visits to Gunville House on parish business are cordial and his condolences sincere.

Jos puts a hand up to the sundial. He doesn't think to himself what is true: that although Tom was ill for so many years, it's with his death that Jos has lost half of himself and, he would say, the better half. He's not a fanciful man, not emotional or Romantick, rather a man of business and an extremely successful one at that. He feels the truth through his fingers, in the lines carved in the granite ready to register the motion of the sun, which is really the motion of the earth and of all the creatures on it.

That the gnomon has gone makes no difference, and not just because Jos has in his pocket the most accurate and beautifully made watch that money can buy. It makes no difference because 11 o'clock will come, and the carriages and black coats with it, while Bessy gathers the younger children in the nursery and reads the funeral service for Uncle Tom to them.

Jos wonders for a moment how Col is getting on in Malta – perhaps it will be the making of him, finally – and hopes that the news of Tom will not distress him too greatly, whenever it finally arrives.

His hand is still on the sundial marks, but there is much to be done. After a moment he lets go and walks back to the house.

Later, Col will write an essay about Tom, which Jos will read before it's published:

He is gone, my friend; my munificent co-patron, and not less the benefactor of my intellect! — He who, beyond all other men known to me, added a fine and ever-wakeful sense of beauty to the most patient accuracy in experimental philosophy and the profounder reaches of metaphysical science; he who united all the play and spring of fancy with the subtlest discrimination and an inexorable judgment; and who controlled an almost painful exquisiteness of taste by a warmth of heart, which in the practical relations of life made allowances for faults as quickly as the moral taste detected them ...

TOM WEDGWOOD
THE FIRST PHOTOGRAPHER

AN ACCOUNT OF HIS LIFE, HIS DIS-
COVERY AND HIS FRIENDSHIP WITH
SAMUEL TAYLOR COLERIDGE
INCLUDING THE LETTERS OF
COLERIDGE TO THE WEDGWOODS

AND AN EXAMINATION OF ACCOUNTS
OF ALLEGED EARLIER PHOTOGRAPHIC
DISCOVERIES

By R. B. LITCHFIELD

" *A mind perhaps the finest I ever met with.*"—T. CAMPBELL

LONDON
DUCKWORTH AND CO.
3 HENRIETTA STREET, COVENT GARDEN
1903

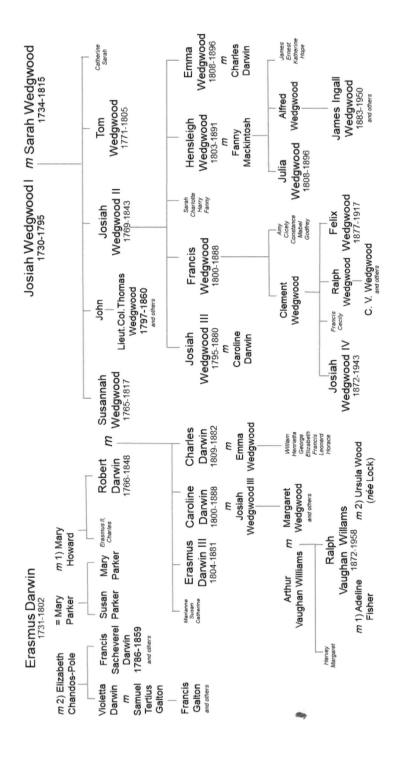

5

Scrambling Around in the Family Tree

So if not Tom, then who?

Those same Whiggish, Nonconformist genes, mutating as they are transmitted down the generations towards me, have become a general unease about talking or thinking in terms of the casual, common rhetoric of social class, and a much more solid anger at the reductiveness and lazy thinking which bases any action, policy, understanding or analysis on such crude labels. So it was only *very* reluctantly that I tracked down an article which crops up often in bibliographies and almost as often when I've mentioned the topic of my family tree: Noel Annan's 1955 essay about the networks of friendship, collaboration and family which dominated eighteenth and nineteenth century scholarship. Of course it is by no means solely made up of Darwin-Wedgwood-Galtons, but there's no denying that the clan figures very largely in what you could call an early example of life-writing or even psychogeography. Annan takes the reader on a 'gallop' across the Midlands, roughly from Shrewsbury to Cambridge, exploring the web of kinship, geography, discipline and intellect which resulted in – or resulted from? – the formation of what he calls, and then titles his essay, 'An Intellectual Aristocracy'.

It's a project irredeemably of its time and place: by the 1950s it was no longer all right to argue that it was natural for the aristocracy of birth to run the county and the country, but it was still possible to approve of an established intellectual élite of (almost entirely) men, with their marriages, wives and children, who dominated the institutions of scholarship and philanthropy.[36] A twenty-first century more aware of the indirect, systemic and lethally covert forms that discrimination also takes, and Tweeting demands to each other to 'check your privilege', is less indulgent. The best I can do, then, to soothe my embarrassment and spike the guns of your class-warrior rage, is to point out that, at the end of his essay, Annan admits that he could write just as substantial an essay about the same time and space, based on bakers.

The thing is, it seems to me, that the human race has evolved to operate best in villages. Humans work together, live together, marry together, and then their children do the same. It's not only Darwins who can say things like, 'Who was our cousin before she was our aunt', as Gwen says of the moment when Uncle Leonard married his second wife, Mildred Massingberd, who was descended from one of Robert Darwin's sisters; later, Uncle Frank's third wife was also a quasi-cousin. But, in a species with the faculty of abstracting and generalising from particularities, as well as projecting from experience towards possibility (the species which has invented the novel, in other words), the sense of living in a geographical village, in a physical dwelling-place, can overlap with a mental one: villages of professions, of crafts, or of minds. In Saxon England Johan the Baker may have genes and upbringing in common with his brother the farmer and his sister the midwife, but he has just as much in common with Jean le Boulanger, who arrives with Guillaume le Conquerant to keep those invading Normans well fed, and it might be *their* children who marry. Cousinly cooperations and courtships are just as likely to happen in a mental and intellectual village, such as the late-Victorian world of the natural sciences.

So even some Darwin enthusiasts are surprised, given Thomas Huxley's central place in the mid-Victorian sciences,[37] and his well-

---

[36] A nice example of the kind of network I mean is that Eglantyne Jebb, founder of Save the Children and prime mover in creating the UN Declaration of the Rights of the Child, was the niece of Gwen's great-uncle-by-marriage Richard Jebb, while another node in the web is that Eglantyne's great and cosummated love was Margaret Keynes, the sister of Maynard and Geoffrey Keynes, and later the wife of the Nobel laureate physiologist Archibald Hill; meanwhile Geoffrey married Gwen's sister Margaret Darwin.

[37] He was largely self-taught, but became a brilliant anatomist. As well as establishing the now accepted theory that birds evolved from dinosaurs, Huxley coined the term *agnostic*, to describe a fundamental principle of modern science and matters of the intellect: 'follow your reason as far as

known role as 'Darwin's Bulldog', that the two families were only linked by marriage in 1947. Andrew Huxley was Thomas's grandson and much younger half-brother to Aldous and Julian, while Richenda Pease's maternal grandfather was 'Colonel Jos', Josiah Wedgwood IV, of whom more in a minute. Andrew was a brilliant and imaginative experimental physiologist who, among many other honours (including an Order of Merit and a knighthood) became a Nobel laureate for his work on the electroconductivity of the nervous system. Then, in 1964, my uncle George Darwin was married to Andrew's American niece Angela Huxley, and *Punch* magazine was moved to riff on the famous rhyme about the Brahmin families of Boston, where 'the Lowells talk only to Cabots, / and the Cabots talk only to God':

> A DARWIN is marrying a HUXLEY
> A fate which no Darwin escapes;
> For the Huxleys speak only to Darwins
> And the Darwins speak only to apes.

Andrew Huxley died in 2012, and the next year the *Notices* of the American Mathematical Society collected many pages of learned tributes to him and his work; the last described the memorial party gathered in the grounds of the house in Granchester, just outside Cambridge, where the Huxleys had lived for decades. Of course, as intellectual activity became increasingly professionalised, intellectual villages in turn become physical ones, whether in early-twentieth-century Bloomsbury or Enlightenment Edinburgh, and Cambridge was typical. It might have been Annan, not molecular biologist David R. Trentham, who wrote:

> It was a beautiful summer's day and memorable for the gathering of Huxley, Darwin, Pease, and Wedgwood family members. One could imagine a similar reunion of such

---

it will take you, without regard to any other consideration... do not pretend that conclusions are certain which are not demonstrated or demonstrable'. Only recently has this term tended to be applied only to conclusions – or lack of them – concerning religious belief.

names in the same idyllic surroundings a century earlier.

Not that reading Annan's essay, amusing though it is in its pre-Sixty-eight, pre *les evennements*, Oxford-in-the-Fifties way, told me all that much I didn't know. What interested me had never been so much the individuals, in their reasonably successful, moderately interesting personalities, but the connections *between* the individuals: the habits of thought, the art and the science, the interests and the tastes. I so regret never knowing Andrew, for example, more than very slightly, so that I might have asked him about the creative, imaginative side of his work, and tried to map across from that to what I know of creative and imaginative work in the arts and humanities.

So reading 'The Intellectual Aristocracy' to find the story for a novel turned out to be about as much use as using a Tube map to find out what there is to see in a weekend in London. Tower Hill is a safeish bet, but the unhappy tourist will find Wimbledon very dull for fifty weeks of the year, and there's a distinct absence of Earls in Earl's Court.

I needed not a map but a guidebook. Luckily, I am by no means the first monkey in the family tree to write about our habitat.

I drop by my parents' house and borrow a book which is the nearest thing there is to a history of the Darwin family. Inside the cover I recognise my grandmother's pencilled writing: 'To Henry, on his birthday 1980, from Mama'. Henry was my father; it would have been his fifty-first birthday, the age I am now, and the book is *The Wedgwood Circle 1790-1897*, by Barbara and Hensleigh Wedgwood.

So why was an anti-Darwin giving a Darwin such a book? One of Aunt Gwen's uncles used to mourn, 'You've none of you ever seen a Darwin who wasn't half Wedgwood', and I had a personal demonstration of the truth of this fact during the Bicentenary of my great-great-great-great-grandfather, the first Josiah Wedgwood, in 1995. It was celebrated with a lunch in his own Etruria Hall, since it had, most conveniently, been converted into a hotel, and something like two hundred of the six hundred or so living descendants were present. In a pleasing example of the family habit of organising knowledge in a systematic way, we all had labels carrying not just our name, but a number – by definition unique – showing how our descent traces from Josiah I. So I was numbered 1.5.5.2.3 (i.e. Josiah's oldest child Susannah, then her fifth child who was *the* Charles, then George, Charles and my father Henry).[38] The organisers had even dealt with the problem that, because of cousin marriages, some of the guests could trace descent by more than one route: people like me had a second number, in my case 4.8.5.2.3 (i.e. Josiah's fourth child Jos II, then his youngest, Emma, then George, Charles, Henry). A very small baby had *nine* digits on the label stuck to the pram, and it was very clear, not least from the spectacular genealogy that went round two sides of an anteroom, that the un-prolific, late-marrying Darwins are only a slimmish, single branch of a very large tree.

Unfortunately, as Catriona would say, the rest of them aren't Darwins. But while the Darwins, so far, had not proved to be the stuff of which novels are made, quite a few of the Wedgwoods looked distinctly interesting.

There's James (Ingall) Wedgwood, who in 1904, when he was 21, went to a Theosophist meeting in order to denounce Annie Besant, definitively, as a crackpot, but joined her Theosophical Society four days later. His vocation and spirituality were life-long and genuine, there's no doubt, and deeply inflected by music: he became being particularly expert on organ-music and organ building. His involvement with Theosophy and the Co-Masons lead him to join the schismatic Original (later re-constituted as Liberal) Catholic Church, and after various scandals and renunciations he became its Bishop. But all that ran in parallel with what we would now call a homosexually-oriented sex addiction: at one point, he boasted, he had made eighteen visits to public lavatories in two hours, for sex. Then, in 1919, he and other senior members of his Church came under investigation for sexual abuse of the young boys in their school and he resigned, going off to study Music at the Sorbonne. In Paris he eventually gained a Doctorate but also an addiction to cocaine, which in later life he smuggled into

---

[38] My husband, being a spouse, had the same number in brackets; the speeches started 'Ladies, Gentlemen and Brackets.'

England concealed in the head of his bishop's crozier; he died in his sixties of an accident caused by syphilitic dementia. There's a photograph on Wikipedia: the long, strong Wedgwood chin is much in evidence, but otherwise ... well, I do, of course, believe that one should never be prejudiced by people's appearance, and that there is no art to find the mind's construction in the face, etc. etc. ... but his eyes are *so* mad. Personally I wouldn't have trusted him with a penny stamp, let alone a soul or a child.

Then there's ...

However, if I were faithful in reproducing here the way in which I scrambled – or more often fumbled – my way from branch to trunk to branch of the family tree, missing my grip and barking my knees, you would get as tired and frustrated as I did. To bring some order back to the proceedings, what follows is the family's chronology, not mine, and it leaves out dozens of dull, well-intentioned direct and collateral ancestors who lead reasonably virtuous or only slightly careless lives, and offer nothing of the least interest to a novelist.

Once I'd set aside Tom, these were the people in my family tree who I thought just might make a novel:

Erasmus Darwin. I reconsidered him. If the Lunar Society was overwhelming, what about him as a father? His adored oldest son, Charles, died while at medical school of septicaemia caught during a dissection; he was only 20. With Erasmus II dreamy, depressive and frail, all their forceful father's hopes centred on turning the youngest, Robert, into a replacement for Charles: he would become a doctor, and no argument was allowed. From that time Robert, too, became prone to depressions, while at the age of forty Erasmus II died in a drowning 'accident' that was clearly suicidal. There does seem to have been a streak of both physical and mental ill-health in that side of the family; when Robert, 'my' Charles's father, is accused of being cold and brusque to his thin-skinned sons and nephews (spendthrift John Wedgwood got more than one dressing-down from Uncle Robert), one should perhaps remember that by then both Robert's own brothers had died tragically, and that he'd hated being a doctor from the first to the last of his professional days.

Erasmus' illegitimate daughters. Miss Mary Parker was governess to the widowed Erasmus's children by his first wife, and she bore him two daughters: Susan (or Susannah) and Mary Parker. They were brought up alongside his legitimate children, as equals, and Erasmus, never being one to accept the world's conventional attitudes unquestioningly, observed that whereas his legitimate daughters' hopes of happiness could only rest on becoming a gentleman's wife and a mother, Susan and Mary had a much better chance of a satisfying and self-determined life, because they would have the necessity of supporting themselves by finding a profession. Their equivocal social position was actually an advantage, in other words, although it helped that their father's status had some value. Indeed, Erasmus's own second wife, Elizabeth Chandos-Pole, whom he courted for years before she was widowed and they could finally marry and have a slew of more children, was herself the illegitimate daughter of the Earl of Portland. Erasmus gave his Parker daughters the wherewithal to set up a boarding school for girls and they ran it very successfully for a good many years. But even though Erasmus knew that women, too, might be happier if they were given the chance to think, experiment and work their ideas and interests out to the full, he was too much of his time – or perhaps too much of a realist – to encourage either sort of daughter to tread a more radical path than schoolmistressing.

This was promising stuff for fiction. But deciding what novel to write is a strange business, whether you're eating chips with your agent, or crouched among the ghosts that flit to and fro over the iron grids which are the floors of the London Library's back stacks. It's part objective, part subjective, and part downright physical. Would this work?

The objective sense was in favour. Here was a classic job for historical fiction: recovering the voices that history has silenced, not just women's but those of servants, subject races, children. And though Mary and Susan's surname isn't Darwin, their paternity's no secret;

they are Lunar children, albeit by the left hand, and their world is the same world. Subjectively … there was surely *something* there. As I read what I could find about them, which wasn't much, I began to sense that inside it might be the DNA of a five-act story. There was a sense of roundness, of a curling back so that the story's resolution can be made to echo its beginning, so that those echoes reveal that everything which matters has changed. Yes, the subjective measure was in favour.

And physical? My skin and solar plexus both voted Nay.

Yes, I get angry when it's assumed that only 'big' lives make 'big' novels – for both of which, too often, one has to read male lives and male novels. Yes, I love and admire fiction which finds treasure and bigness in apparently small or unsatisfactory lives, whether it's by Graham Greene or Elizabeth Bowen or Jenn Ashworth. Yes, if you forced me to an either-or (but please don't), I'd personally take Jane Austen over any Brontë, and even, perhaps, Henry James over Dickens. However, whether it's a sign of a feeble imagination, lack of spiritual growth, or an inadequate commitment to feminism, I can't find all the energy a novel needs in an everyday story of female folk sewing and washing up and bearing children, nor in their doing the equivalent for a bunch of girl pupils in a school of its time. Doing any of those things in the context of some wider, weirder world brings scale and interest to such a life, and doing those things in the context of big history such as political turmoil, war, or famine, makes such lives bigger still: the domestic becomes heroic.

Did the Misses Parker look outwards? Was big history lapping at their doorstep? The secondary sources were pretty thin, so I couldn't be sure, but it didn't look like it. True, it's good professional and artistic practice to learn ways to find interest in something that you, personally, find at first dull. But some stages of writing a novel are quite boring enough already; it seemed to me (and seems to me now) asking for trouble actively to choose a project that feels dull from the outset.

What's more, as John Gardner puts it in *The Art of Fiction*, the writer's side of the contract is always that we'll deal 'honestly and responsibly' with the reader; the reader's side of the contract is that, in return for that honest and responsible dealing, the reader will 'agree to forget' that the events in the novel never actually happened.[39] But with real historical characters the bar of 'honest and responsible' is set significantly higher; what you invent and imagine doesn't only have to fit cleanly and convincingly into the generality of that historical world, it has to fit cleanly and convincingly into the recorded specifics of that particular life. The more I was forced to ramp up the fictional drama for want of the real thing – bolt on a haunted dormitory, a flirtatious arithmetic mistress or a terrifying suit in Chancery – the more likely it was that any reader would sense the dishonesty, feel unfairly dealt with, and consciously or unconsciously drop their commitment to their side of the contract.

Jessie Sismondi, née Allen: 'my' Emma's favourite aunt on her mother's side. Those Allen girls might have come straight from Jane Austen: nine Misses Allen (and a couple of brothers), almost all beautiful, clever, lively, charming, not richly dowered but much fallen in love with, and living with a tyrant of a father at Cresselly, near Tenby in Pembrokeshire.

Bessy married Jos Wedgwood II and Louisa Jane married his older brother, the feckless John Wedgwood, while Catherine married Sir James Mackintosh.[40] Most interestingly of all, when she was no longer in the first blush of youth, Jessie married the irresistible Jean Charles Léonard de Sismondi, a famous economist, historian, writer, and diplomat. It was a surprising marriage, you could say, but it absolutely wasn't a case of Jessie merely trying to avoid spinsterhood, and the marriage appears to have been very happy. Sismondi was born Swiss, of mixed French and Pisan blood; he was highly educated, then had to work on the farm his parents bought when they lost their money. But he made his way nonetheless, becoming a friend of Madame de Staël

---

[39] Gardner's is one of the founding texts of Creative Writing as an art and a discipline. 'Supension of disbelief' is the usual phrase, but I think Gardner's 'agrees to forget' much more accurately evokes how the reader experiences that intuitive 'buying into' the story.

[40] Of the rest, Caroline married Edward Drewe, Octavia died young, and Harriet, Emma and Frances never married. The brothers were John, and Baugh.

and a passionate and prominent supporter of Napoleon. He wrote novels, books on politics and economics, and huge and (for the time) definitive political histories of Italy and France. He and Jessie lived in Geneva – where Emma visited them – and moved in the literary and diplomatic salons of Europe. His portrait seems to me the male equivalent of a *jolie-laide* – ugly-sexy, if you like, rather as Erasmus is – while the entry in Wikipedia (which sounds very translated-from-the-French in its elegant formality), is just sexy, at least to your average leftie-liberal:

> as an economist, Sismondi represented a humanitarian protest against the dominant orthodoxy of his time. ... in *Nouveaux principes d'économie politique* (1819), he insisted on the fact that economic science studied the means of increasing wealth too much, and the use of wealth for producing happiness, too little.[41] For the science of economics, his most important contribution was probably his discovery of economic cycles.

Was there a story there? Again, who knew what I might find with enough research? But the thought of my main sources being in French was daunting, and the family connection was increasingly tenuous. It might make a carrier signal for some other story, and they would unquestionably be wonderful secondary characters, but I couldn't see how they could make a novel themselves.

Francis (Sacheverell) Darwin was a son of old Erasmus by his second marriage.[42] Like so many of the family, he was a doctor by training and a naturalist by inclination, and in 1808, at the height of the Napoleonic Wars, he spent two years travelling – mainly by sea – from England, via Corunna, to Belgrade and back. His diary was published by his grandson in 1927; I found it when I was researching *Black Shadow and*

---

[41] Shades of John Maynard Keynes, it seems to me. Of whom more in a moment or three.
[42] He was therefore also a Lunar child, being uncle (and godfather) of the biologist Francis Galton, whose mother was Erasmus' daughter Violetta and father the son of Samuel Galton.

Bone, and was very fed up that I hadn't known of it when I was researching the Peninsular War for *The Mathematics of Love*. But although it would have been useful as a source of local colour, it doesn't exactly teem with riches for the twenty-first century novelist in search of a compelling character on which to build a twenty-first century historical novel.

> Chap.I: Corunna, St Jago, Vigo, Oporto
>
> …
>
> 16th January. – The wind being fair we sailed for Cadiz in the 'General Wolfe' Merchant ship … Here, in a noisome ship of fish from Newfoundland, did we toss about the Atlantic until Sunday the 22nd. Having doubled Cape St Vincent, the first thing to attract our notice was a fine turtle asleep on the waves; but he escaped being taken. The next day a large whale entertained us by his mode of throwing up the water, at no great distance from the ship. It was midnight when, in the direction that our captain expected to make Cadiz, a light appeared which he mistook for the lighthouse near the town. The ship was then going eight knots an hour and we did not seem to gain upon the light, which shortly afterwards disappeared – and we heard the breakers up on the shore, which greatly alarmed the crew…

He went ashore frequently, to explore sites of natural history and classical interest:

> Chap. VIII: Abydos, Troy, Tenedos, Smyrna
> …15th September … the wood appeared on fire, and the flames spread over the valley and cut off our retreat. It was necessary now to hasten on with all expedition, the fire before us raging through the thicket and increasing rapidly; and we had just time to accomplish our end, when the whole road which we had just left was in one vast conflagration. Over the smoking embers we observed numbers of roasted serpents, tortoises, and a few of the larger animals.

This was no gap-year backpacking jaunt: of the five friends who set out – one of whom was his brother-in-law Theodore Galton – only Francis lived to return home. But though his observation of natural phenomena is a delight, this isn't a memoir, nor even travel writing in the sense of setting out to tell a tale. It's certainly not a Romantic journey through the Other in order to discover the Self: it's an endearingly calm set of notes about what he did, where he went, how much it cost and what he saw, from a mixture of ships, packet-boats, horses, carriages, mules and his own feet. I found myself thinking how much better a job C. S. Forester would have made of a scene like this, where Francis has quite legitimately hitched a ride with a Royal Navy ship which has captured an enemy brig. Francis writes that

> On the 20th and 21st we were becalmed off Sardinia; and two French privateers came out of Cagliari in the night, and carried off three of our convoy …

but no more about that little excitement. The story ends thus:

> July 9th. We sailed for England, but put back next day on account of bad wind, and anchored close to the Packet – which had followed us from Malta. Mr Wilkinson, of Smyrna, was on board and persuaded me to take my passage in the Packet – as I should have to perform Quarantine if I proceeded home on the prize brig. I paid Captain Bullock £47.15s.0d, and joined the 'Express' Packet. We sailed on the 16th and witnessed the operations of the siege of Cadiz, but did not anchor here … Major Howard, one of our fellow passengers, was very ill with a remittent fever – the effects of Walcheren fever: on the 27th this unfortunate and gallant officer expired.

For the writer of historical fiction, there are little scraps of period-detail gold in there: would you have thought that the verb that goes with quarantine would be 'perform', and use it in your novel instead of 'go into' or 'submit to'? I don't think I would have known that. And

'Mr Wilkinson of Smyrna' is somehow a name to conjure with – I'm imagining Charlotte Brontë as a Graham Greene *avant la lettre*. But oh, poor Major Howard! Now we'd call his ailment malaria; it was common in the army, not least among those who'd served in India, but it was named after the fever that so many caught during the disastrous military expedition against France on the Dutch island of Walcheren at the mouth of the Scheldt. That was in 1809, after Francis had left home. Did he, as a medical man, keep up with professional developments? Did the unfortunate Major Howard speak of it as he was dying in 1810? Or, in writing things up back home, did Sir Francis apply a name for the ailment which he'd learnt later? If so, what else did he change, or mis-remember? I love novels which carry with them a sense of this being only one version of what could be written, and so implicitly invite the reader to imagine another: Golding's *Rites of Passage*, say, or Allan Massie's *Caesar*. If only Francis Wedgwood had a teaspoonful of those characters' unreliability and charm!

Even though I'd missed Sir Francis in researching *The Mathematics of Love*, I had known about Colonel Thomas Wedgwood, who was present at Waterloo as a very new Ensign in the 2nd Battalion of the 3rd Regiment of Foot Guards. I'd first thought to use him for the link between Stephen and 'my' Tom's photographic experiments, but I couldn't work out how to link him in the Foot Guards with Major Fairhurst of the 95th Rifles in the middle of a huge, world-rearranging battle which took place before the novel began and was only recalled in shell-shocked flashbacks. It was far more elegant to bring Robert Darwin in as a real, if minor, character at the beginning.

Now I tried harder: this Thomas was a son of 'my' Tom's improvident older brother John.[43] The day after the battle, he wrote to his mother, Louisa Jane, describing the battle, literally, from the inside: his regiment was commanded to defend the farmhouse of Hougoument which was at the centre, both physically and strategically, of the entire battle.

---

[43] And so both Emma's and Charles's first cousin.

They sent balls of fire upon the house and set a barn and all the other houses on fire. After being exposed to a heavy fire of shot grape and shells for two and half hours in which we had three officers wounded, besides a number of men, the right wing of our regiment and my company went down to the assistance of the Coldstreams in the wood in which there was a very heavy fire of musquetry.

The French were directing nearly the whole of their fire at the house into which my company and another entered, nearly 100 men having been consumed in the flames. The French forced the gates three times and three times were driven back with immense loss, for we were firing at each other at about a distance of five yards. There was a large garden to the house which was surrounded by a wall on two sides, on the third and remaining side by a hedge. We had another company brought in and a few Dutch who lined the garden wall in which they made port holes and annoyed the French very much.

At five o'clock the French gained ground very much and made the English retire from their position on the heights but were again driven back by a strong column consisting of cavalry and the 2nd Battalion of the 1st Guards and the remaining part of ours. After a hard struggle [they] were obliged to give ground and retire through the wood when they attacked the house again with renewed force and vigour. They knocked a great deal of the walls down with their cannon but could not gain admittance. My company was sent out to skirmish [at] about eight o'Clock. The 1st Guards and a part of ours charged the French with the bayonette and drove them entirely from the house.

About that time a body of about 30,000 of the Prussians came up at a great pace and the French immediately retreated at a great pace and all our cavalry following them with our regiments and drove them back double quick and dispersed them entirely.

> My regiment has lost 16 officers killed and wounded, including Lt Colonel Sir A Gordon and Canning of my company who were among the number of killed. Capt Ashton of my company is also killed. The Duke of Wellington told us he never saw troops behave so well as the Guards.

A few weeks later he wrote to his uncle, describing the cannon fire in the battle as 'carnage':

> ... We had two officers wounded and one killed that way. The latter was Ensign Simpson, he had the whole of his backbone taken away by a shot which also killed a sergeant and men near him.

Would Ensign Tom make a novel, even if it did mean writing another Waterloo? After all, I wasn't the first to write Waterloo and I'm sure there will never be a last: my personal favourites are John Keegan's and Georgette Heyer's,[44] and that's before you've counted *Vanity Fair*, *Les Miserables*, and any number of others from Stendhal to Sharpe. But I couldn't find out any more about Colonel Thomas in the books on my shelves, and he doesn't have an entry in the *Dictionary of National Biography*, or even Wikipedia. After Waterloo, even *The Wedgwood Circle*, comprehensive as it is, gives him only passing mentions, so it seemed reasonable to assume that Colonel Thomas is a very ordinary twig on the tree and his only historical interest is in being typical. At which point, 'Yes, but he's not a Darwin', begins to ring again: if there's nothing inherently exciting or intriguing about him, then why would any reader be interested? And if I manufactured the quantity of wholly fictional events that it would take to make a novel worth reading, how could I describe it – how could it honestly be promoted - as a novel 'about' my family?

So, back to what is, for the purposes of writing a Darwin novel, the central trunk of the tree.

---

[44] In *The Face of Battle* and *An Infamous Army*, respectively.

Emma and Charles: I'm putting them in for the sake of completeness, but see Chapter One.

Emma and Charles's children. Ten were born, and the mortality rate was about what you'd expect of their class and period: their second child, Mary, and tenth, Charles (Waring), died when very small, and Annie died aged ten. The other seven grew up and made lives of some academic and professional achievement:

William was a partner in a Southampton bank: he married an American, Sara Sedgwick, but they had no children. When he was widowed he moved to London, next door to his brother Leonard, and 'flowered into a second youth and became a really first-class uncle', as Gwen puts it.

Henrietta ('Etty') married R. B. Litchfield, the biographer of Tom Wedgwood. She helped edit her father's *The Descent of Man*, and went on to edit his contribution to Krauss's biography of Erasmus Darwin, as well as producing the definitive edition of her mother's letters and private papers. They lived in London and had no children: after Richard died Etty moved to Gomshall Park in Surrey.

George was a physicist, and Plumian Professor of Astronomy at Cambridge: he worked on geophysical topics such as the tides and the moon. After he married he lived all his life at the house he called Newham Grange, which his son Charles inherited, and which ultimately became the University's postgraduate-only Darwin College. He had five children (one of whom died in infancy) with his American wife Maud du Puy, and they are my great-grandparents.

Elizabeth ('Bessy') never married, and possibly not from the Victorian habit of leaving one daughter a spinster, so as to look after the parents: she seems to have had some kind of mild, specific learning difficulty. As a beloved aunt she divided her time between Cambridge and Down, and after Emma died she proved quite capable of an independent life with 'only a little help', as *Period Piece* puts it.

Francis ('Frank') was a biologist and his father's assistant at Down, as well as his biographer. His Welsh first wife Amy (née Ruck) died at the birth of their son; his second wife Ellen (née Crofts) was an English lecturer at Newnham College, and they lived in Cambridge, but she died when their daughter was a teenager. He later married the widowed Florence Maitland (née Fisher), and acquired two step-daughters.

Leonard was Major Darwin of the Royal Engineering Corps, living in London and doing almost no ordinary soldiering. Instead, he worked on ballistics and other scientific projects, such as photographing the 1874 transit of Venus in New Zealand, and the 1886 total eclipse of the sun in Jamaica: his portraits of his father are some of the classic images of Charles in old age. Later he was elected MP for Lichfield. His first wife Elizabeth Fraser died quite young; he later married his cousin Mildred Massingberd[45] and they built a house in Ashdown Forest, but had no children.

Horace was an engineer who founded what the family called 'the shop', which became the Cambridge Scientific Instrument Company; he later twice crossed the then considerable barrier between Gown and Town, to become mayor of Cambridge. He married Ida Farrar, and they had three children.

George, Frank and Leonard were all knighted and, like anyone else, they're of their time in some ways, and not in others. They went to church rarely, and then purely to save trouble and argument: they were liberal with a small and quite often a large L and supported charities and good cause. Although very comfortably off financially they would

---

[45] Definitely one for the genealogy nerds: Mildred's grandmother Charlotte was one of Emma's sisters, so she and Leonard (Emma's son), were first cousins once removed. But since Charles was also Charlotte's cousin, Leonard and Mildred were also second cousins once removed.

never have dreamed of giving up work, abandoning professional ambition, or splashing money about in ostentatious ways. Like so much of the Victorian population in general and the scientifically-minded in particular, they accepted eugenic ideas very much more willingly than we now find comfortable; Leonard took over the presidency of the Eugenics Society of Great Britain from his cousin Francis Galton, and later my grandfather, Charles Galton Darwin, took it on. Other well-known members of the Society included birth control campaigner Marie Stopes, novelist Naomi Mitchison, economists William Beveridge and John Maynard Keynes, Nobel laureate biologist Peter Medawar, biologist Professor Steve Jones and Prime Ministers Arthur Balfour and Neville Chamberlain.

Still, these sons of Charles Darwin were also kind, clever, conscientious, hard-working and personally benevolent, and if they were no more imaginative in their understanding of other people and the wider world than any other members of the upper-middle class intelligentsia, then their only failure was, you could argue, in not being exceptional for their time and place.

And that's the problem. Of *course* there were griefs and tensions: the story of Annie has already been written and filmed; the death of the very young and beautiful Amy Ruck is heartbreaking; while her son Bernard's relationship with his stepmother was difficult. But if ever there was a group of people who wouldn't make a novel worth reading, without re-writing history, it's this lot.

So baffled was I by how to write about these nice, dull people, that I took the problem to the heartland my creative friendships of the time.

* * *

June 2011 www.writewords.org.uk

How Do I Write About My Family?

Emma: Encouragement needed, if WriteWorders wouldn't mind.
I'm finding this novel about my family incredibly difficult. Not because of my hangups (well, not mostly), but just because

everyone's terribly nice and kind and well-intentioned, and comfortable. It's all very domestic and rather dull, and making it anything else feels forced and vulgar. And yet everyone I mention it to (which isn't many because, y'know, not talking the story out and all) says "Oh, that's a fantastic idea!" Am I missing something? Is there a way I could write it which wouldn't be domestic and dull?

Ruth: How about you write a Margaret Atwood style spec fic where Darwin is executed by the religious right a la Galileo, and Emma is filled with a burning widow's zeal to carry his standard?

Caroline: Yes, how about dystopian steampunk...and could you squeeze in a vampire?

Emma: Caroline - clearly it needs vampires. Thank you for pointing that out - my agent will be either thrilled or relieved. Or maybe it needs Frankenstein and Monster.

Actually, it's not so mad to get involved with Romantic dystopias and potential steampunk. There's Punk: as one of the many ways they supported good causes from anti-slavery to the arts, some of my Wedgwood ancestors gave Coleridge an annuity so he could keep writing. Coleridge repaid the favour by introducing one of them to opium, and the addiction killed him. There's Steam: earlier still Erasmus D and Josiah Wedgwood were deeply involved in the Boulton & Watt factory which exported something like 80% of the world's steam engines...

The world clearly needs a detective series with Emma fighting her way through a Steampunk world run by Creationists, who are holding Charles hostage in a dungeon until she discovers the real murderer of God. Her search takes her from the British Museum reading room where Marx is collating Engels' industrial data, to Freud's Vienna and the trenches of the First World War, which was started by a mad Creationist dictator to make such a mess of Northern France that they'd never realise it was chock-full of dinosaur bones about to prove the truth of the theory of Evolution.

Ruth: Emma PLEASE write that book! I can see the Hollywood film already. Starring Natalie Portman as Emma and Harrison Ford as the captive Charles. John Malkovich to play the mad creationist prime minister of Great Britain. I think there should be a role for a kick-ass feminist Queen Victoria. Maybe she could join Emma as a punchy side-kick?

Emma: Emma can sail around the world in an amphibious steam-punk Zeppelin/submarine called "Beagle 2". It would need a catchy/edgy title for the film. Something like "R:Evolution: The Bones of God". Argh! Now I really want to do it - have just had a vision of the wicked Creationists building a tunnel under the Channel and turning up near Down, and their feisty daughter Etty defeating them by getting the fruit flies to evolve into killers...

Sally: Emma could have great fun putting up a quiet, country-house persona for the visiting greats - hiding her musket under her tapestry and her dynamite under the coffee-table. And can someone please re-animate the dinosaurs to fight for the forces of science?

Emma: Entry from Charles's Diary:
"Spent morning dissecting a fine specimen which was sent to me by Benjamin Franklin Jr as a female Barnaclouses Hydropiensis, but the hermaphroditism had confused his normally fine powers of discrimination, and I determined - after 6 hours at the microscope with only a few minutes spared several times for vomiting - that it is actually a male Barnaclous WriteWordsii with a poorly toe. Several

explosions from the cellars put paid to the day's work when the lens of my big microscope was shattered by a tremor which I measured at 3.2, although later I compared it with the instrument in the billiard room, which read 3.5 - I cannot altogether account for the anomaly. At the time, my dearest Emma, being occupied with helping Etty with the fruit flies, sent Leonard running up from the cellars to apologise, and Lenny and I agreed that any price (even one of Dollond's best 3" lenses) is worth paying to repel those Creationalists…"

Sally: It could be a Victorian 'Jonathan Strange and Mr Norell'-type alternative-history novel - lots of historical detail, lots of cameos by famous Victorians, told very seriously and only slightly bonkers round the edges.

Ruth: I'm starting to feel this may be YA…? The younger Darwins do seem to be having a lot of the fun.

Emma: They do, don't they. I think Beagle 2 is the one which they sent to photograph Mars, so this one would have to be Beagle 1½ or Beagle V-1 or some such. There's even a Darwin to build it: the youngest son Horace was an engineer who started his own company to build scientific instruments… If it was a series they wouldn't have to get older or anything, just as Bertie Wooster doesn't. It would be such fun… If I got things "wrong" – places, voice, science – y'know what? IT WOULDN'T MATTER.

* * *

Hensleigh Wedgwood: He was Emma's brother and therefore Charles's cousin as well as one of his great friends – 'Hensleigh' is the maiden name of the Allen grandmother they all shared – while his wife Fanny, née Mackintosh, was also a first cousin. Indeed, Charles and Emma's first married home was in Gower St., a few doors down from Hensleigh and Fanny, round the corner from the British Museum, and at the heart of academic and intellectual London. But what caught my interest most is that while Charles was writing *On The Origin of Species*, Hensleigh was writing *A Dictionary of English Etymology*, setting out the first real evolutionary tree of the origins of language in general, and the English language in particular.

I've been trying to avoid the modern cliché of 'I can connect', but here I can. Not just because words are the stuff I think with, and about, but because my own father's hobby was languages and most particularly etymology. How languages connect and evolve was always somewhere in family conversations about history, science or literature. The parallels of languages and species are delicious, the ideas endlessly fascinating, the opportunities for playing with and enriching the prose delicious to contemplate.

But where was the *story*?

I needed William Carlos Williams's Things – for which read people and their actions – to put those Ideas in.

I started to dig. Fanny had a love affair for many years – and probably a consummated one – with Charles's older brother Erasmus III; at one point the scandal threatened to get into the papers, and Emma had actually been considered as a bride for Ras, by way of damping it down. This Erasmus never married (and here that phrase presumably isn't the euphemism that it often was) but lived the life of the sociable intellectual dilettante that Charles so easily might have lived, if Charles's temperament, his twenties, and his wife had all been different. Adultery is one of the oldest story-engines of all, and as powerful as ever, but Erasmus III didn't feel like a personality to build a novel on, and I couldn't find much out about Fanny Mackintosh. What was more, their whole milieu – the Royal Society, hill-walking in Scotland, dinner-party, Cambridge-oriented, London-living – would probably have been good to live in, but certainly wasn't appealing to write about.

And Hensleigh? Whatevever the reasons – the family depression showing up again? the unhappy marriage? my lack of interest in mid-Victorians? – he didn't attract me in either the writerly or the personal sense. He doesn't even have the spectacular awfulness of James Wedgwood, which some writer other than me (J. S. Lefanu? Denis Wheatley?) could unquestionably have a lot of fun with. Hensleigh is reserved, grumpy, negative in the original sense: a glass-half-empty person. Imagine spending a couple of years in Mr Casaubon's head – albeit a Mr Casaubon who did actually produce a magnum opus worth writing – and you'll know why I decided he wouldn't make a novel.

I tried to take stock of this thick, mid-Victorian wodge of Darwin-Wedgwoods. By this time I had encountered three Charles Darwins, five Erasmus Darwins and four Josiah Wedgwoods, and that's without chasing down almost any of the descendants of Erasmus Darwin's second marriage. There are six Thomas Wedgwoods listed in the index of *The Wedgwood Circle*, for example, several native Frances Wedgwoods – always called Fanny – and several more Fannies who became Wedgwoods by marriage: 'Fanny Frank', née Frances Mosley, was married to a Francis ('Frank') Wedgwood,[46] would you believe, and with clear logic Hensleigh Wedgwood's wife was always called 'Fanny Hensleigh'. What's worse – at least for the long-suffering biographer – is that with amazing frequency they would give a child two names, as many of us still do, but in reverse: as with aunt Etty, who is really Emma Henrietta, the name in memory of a parent or ancestor is put first, and it's the less confusing, perhaps more individual second name that's for everyday use.

So it's perhaps not surprising that it took me a while to realise that one of many Julia Wedgwoods, who was actually Frances Julia, was the same as the one called Snow, and that she wrote novels. It took me even longer to realise that here was someone else whom, in a disguised and coded form, I had met before.

* * *

from 'Reading, Writing and Desire in A.S.Byatt's *Possession*: a critical paper' in *Shadows in the Glass*, unpublished MPhil Thesis, University of Glamorgan

By contrast, we are not, for the most part, told in these terms – in the narrative form that novel-readers are so used to – what Ash and Christabel feel or think. Instead we are shown it, partly through Roland and Maud's reading and partly through our own, but always

---

[46] Shades of Frances and Francis Cornford, of whom much more in a minute.

in Ash and LaMotte's own voices. Their desire was first set alight when they met at Crabb Robinson's breakfast: Ash recognises 'after all one clear-eyed and amused reader and judge'. (p.6)

> Now would you not rather have a poem, however imperfect, than a plate of cucumber sandwiches ...? (p.87)

replies Christabel. Desire is kindled in each by finding a reader for their public writing, and this desire powers in return their desire to write and to read these private letters, so that the reading of each letter is the springboard for the writing of the next. Their letters together make, or rather the novel-reader makes from them, the emotional truth of the story of the courtship, with its rushes, hesitations, evasions, deletions and unfinished sentences. Letters 'do not know, from line to line, where they are going,' (p.131) realises Roland, and in that they reflect the nature of any courtship as well as forming this one. Ash acknowledges the connection between reading, writing and love:

> My true thoughts have spent more time in your company than in anyone else's, these last two or three months (p.181)

and right at the end of their lives, LaMotte writes,

> I regret most of all not those few sharp sweet days of passion – which might have been almost anyone's passion, it seems, for all passions run the same course to the same end ... I regret ... our old letters, of poetry and other things, our trusting minds which recognised each other. (p.501)

If the advantage to the novelist of using the reading of private writing to form a narrative is the kind of subjective immediacy that is one of modern fiction's defining characteristics, it has the disadvantage that the demands of plot mean that at certain points letters in particular simply may not, convincingly, be made to exist. The subsequent, central event of Ash and Christabel's relationship – the crime that the detective story first sets out to examine – leaves no written evidence. It is as if the core event – the culmination of desire and of all this writing and reading – does not actually exist either. The narrative that the reader constructs is the embodiment (or rather, lack of embodiment) of the postmodern sense that there *is* no central truth to be discovered, through reading or any other investigation, about anything: that 'reality' is only the ever-shifting construction of a series of perceptions. But then the privileged reader is given a reality that Roland and Maud are not: Ash and Christabel in Yorkshire, focalised through Ash. There is – or was – a reality, which formed the letters.

6

Julia

I had gone to Victorian London, as embodied in the London Library, to look for members of the family (many of whom were members of the library) on whom I might build a novel. I was deep in the back stacks when I found Julia, and then, when I held the book up towards the striplight and turned the thick, clean pages, I realised I had found her once before or, rather, a life which was wholly fictional but partly hers.

Possession actually begins in the London Library, and Byatt's poet Randolph Ash is so clearly based on Browning that I thought she must have come across the book I had found: *Robert Browning and Julia Wedgwood: a broken friendship as revealed in their letters*. It's a smallish volume, edited by Joseph Conrad's champion, the critic Richard Curle, and published in 1937. And if Byatt coded some of Browning's DNA into Ash, then surely some of Julia Wedgwood's DNA is LaMotte. Byatt literally pairs her with Ash, and figuratively sets her against him, to explore the struggle of the creative artist who happens to be female.

Frances Julia Wedgwood was called 'Snow' because she was born during a violent snowstorm. That she hated the nickname, but was always called by it, seems emblematic, so I try to think of her as Julia, and my interest first latched onto the fact that she published two novels. She was Hensleigh and Fanny's oldest child, she was very deaf (it ran in the family), very tiny (less than 5ft), and very, very clever. In the sober language of the *Oxford Dictionary of National Biography*:

> At the height of her reputation, in the 1870s and 1880s, Julia Wedgwood was seen as one of the great female intellects of Victorian England, second only to George Eliot in her ability to handle difficult, 'masculine' subjects and 'modern' themes.

She wrote a major biography of John Wesley, and assisted Mrs Gaskell with her *Life of Charlotte Brontë*, and her uncle Charles Darwin with his translation of those works of Linnaeus which grandfather Erasmus had never got round to. Earlier she had published a substantial examination of the theological implications of the *The Origin of Species* which prompted Charles – always kind but incapable of intellectual dishonesty – to write that 'I must tell you how much I admire your Article ... I think that you understand my book perfectly, and that I find a very rare event with my critics.'

Sometimes I think Julia's life is the archetype of the fate of the clever, creative woman in the civilised intellectual family of the time. She was never sent to school, which was probably just as well, given how feeble virtually all Victorian girls' schools were before Miss Beale and Miss Buss took a hand,[47] but such families usually cared enough to engage

---

[47] The notable exception was Queen's College in London's Harley St., which was founded in 1848 to help governesses between jobs, but also to educate them and so improve the education of women in general. It was the first institution in the world to award qualifications to girls.

adequate governesses, and she would have had free run of the conversation and the library, while her parents' salon was at the heart of the London intelligentsia. As with Fanny Mendelssohn, Alice James, Alma Mahler (née Schindler), Margaret Wittgenstein and so many others, what is transmitted explicitly or implicitly is not, *Thou shalt not think/write/paint/sing*, but only *Thou mayst* – or even *Thou shalt* – *go thus far, but no further*.

The novels were written in her twenties, but she suffered painfully from lack of confidence in them, as in many things. She published the first, *Framleigh Hall*, anonymously: only her sister Effie and her great friend Meta Gaskell, and later her Uncle Charles and Aunt Emma, knew her to be the author, as if she could only face putting it out into the limelight if she stayed safely in the dark of the wings. For the second, *An Old Debt*, she did step onto the stage, but masked as 'Florence Dawson'. The novels went down well with readers – Harriet Martineau and Meta's mother Elizabeth Gaskell both praised them – and she started to write a third, with Gaskell's encouragement.

This was not a case of the stereotyped Victorian woman whose idleness is a badge of respectability or social status and who therefore has nothing better to do: Julia wrote 'between five and seven in the morning', because the rest of the day was taken up with whichever part of the clan needed nursing, or childcare, or company.

I'd love to think that with her third novel she would have taken the mask off, but if – to paraphrase Joanna Russ's immortal *How To Suppress Women's Writing* – the wretched woman *will still write*, the next tactic is to tell her that what she's writing isn't worth it. Her father, who had form for consistently underrating not just his daughters' but also his sons' capacities and achievements, read *An Old Debt*. Her male characters gave him 'a pain in the stomach', he said, rewriting both story and moral for her, and would she please write 'something more chearful [*sic*] next time.' She decided that she lacked any capacity for imaginative or original thought, and never wrote fiction again. You might say that Mr Casaubon got his revenge after all: a century later *The Wedgwood Circle* is still being dismissive of both Julia's personality and her achievements.

Then, in 1863, when Julia was thirty, one of the guests at her mother's dinner table was the well-known poet Robert Browning; he was fifty years old, and his even more celebrated wife Elizabeth (neé Barrett) had died a few years before. He got a severe migraine: Julia, the dutiful and knowledgeable carer, was the one deputed to do the caring. Something happened, though we can't know what, some kind of revelation of a new and natural intimacy, which they both acknowledged. Upstairs, Julia's brother James was dying of cancer, and a few days later Browning, who knew very well how dreadful a deathbed could be, called to express his sympathy but found Julia not at home (for which read 'in the house but not free to see him'). He wrote. She wrote back, telling him when she would be at home, and that he might call. He seems to have arrived at the right moment, and afterwards sent her a note:

> My dear Miss Wedgwood
>
> I shall only repeat, though unnecessarily, that if I can ever be found capable of the least use to you, it will make me glad and grateful indeed. I daresay that I have managed to give you a notion that the distance between your house and mine is formidable: the time of the journey from door to door cannot exceed twenty minutes, by railway.
>
> Faithfully yours ever
> Robert Browning

James died, and Julia wrote to tell Browning, continuing

> ... At this solemn moment it seems easy to go on, rather it seems impossible to stop, till I have said all I want to say ... A woman who has taken the initiative in a friendship with a man, as I have done with you, has either lost all right feeling or has come to a very definite decision on the issue of all such friendships. I have told you what your intercourse has been to me ... it would be bitter, oh very bitter, to feel that you had drawn back from mistaken kindness to me, that you had feared to inflict a pain against which I am shielded by the

deliberate decision of my mature life … I shall very soon wish
to see you again, and perhaps you will let me summon you…
When I can see any one, it will be you.

Browning replied on the same day, offering a heartfelt and honest expression of some kind of hope, though his belief was 'a very composite and unconventional one', that each would meet their dead loved one again. He went on,

What you say … respecting our intercourse – your feeling
and mine – on that, too, I must write a little – the impulse
being to write much, because very many earnest thoughts are
excited by your letter – and while each of them is, in some
sort, proper for you to hear, all of the multitude would
confuse us in speaking and hearing … I shall tell you then,
that I do understand you, and know that you understand me.
Be assured that your friendship has been always precious to
me, and that while I live it will be most precious: it would
have been so any time in the past … in the meeting of our
hands, mine has seemed somewhat to lift, rather than be
lifted by, yours. But that has been only a chance – and any
day you would help me as much. Simply, I value your
friendship for me, as you shall know, if you will but wait.

So what happened? Julia wouldn't be the first person to scent danger to her own heart and try to ward it off by expressing 'a very definite decision' that there is to be no sexual element in the friendship. At the beginning Browning is the more openly ardent, although always – as was proper – insisting that she must be the judge of what their intercourse (the word comes naturally in this idiom) might and might not be. But that may reflect not any lack of ardour in Julia, but simply the burqa of indirectness and abstraction in which a well-brought-up Victorian woman had to dress her words. Perhaps she should have remembered that although *An Old Debt* starts with a witty evocation of an idle and decorative brother set against a determined and forceful sister, in *Framleigh Hall* she evokes her heroine's pain in these terms:

The thought that the most intense, spontaneous feeling of her soul was one with which she must struggle as a deadly sin, overwhelmed her with a sense of injustice. At what point was it in her power – when could she have stopped and said, 'Here esteem ends, here passion begins – I will go no farther.' She could remember no such point. She knew her love was hopeless ... and yet so much dearer was it to her than any other joy that she wished to sink into nothing rather than survive it.

For over a year they met in company and alone, wrote long letters, and talked about everything under the sun, although it's not easy to reconstruct the details because, in a city with several posts a day, a note from one might appear to have gone unanswered, when in fact the answerer came in person. They date their letters sketchily, greet each other casually – 'dear friend' – and sign off with initials. The letters are sometimes short sections of a rolling conversation which just happens to shift onto paper when they can't meet, or scraps and passing mentions of the minutiae of everyday life. Sometimes they're long, detailed, philosophical: two writers using their craft to the full, as naturally as breathing, to explore what they're both thinking about. And writers, too, are well-equipped to say things indirectly, and know their real meaning will be read.

It's a true meeting of minds, although their editor Richard Curle has no doubts about their relative status: Browning is, as it were, the one in big print, as Coleridge, not Tom Wedgwood, is for Litchfield. Leaving famous-in-their-time women out of posterity's canon is another of the strategies Joanna Russ points out. To be fair, as the generations pass scholarly interpretations by either gender tend to wear less well than original art does, but a feminist can't but wince at this, from Curle's Foreword:

> She was rather a prosy and long-winded letter writer, not unintelligent, by any means, but with a constant tendency to moralize; but for the sake of unity all her letters which

> answered letters from him have been given … In fact, only a
> handful that are of no particular significance and do not
> carry on the story are omitted. Needless to say, all of
> Browning's letters [to Julia] have been printed, and as they
> have been checked twice with the originals the text may be
> taken as accurate.

Needless to say, my blood did a little boil at how only Browning,
evidently, merits being reproduced in full, and with the full scholarly
effort and apparatus.

And then, rather more than a year after their first encounter and
after a books-worth of letters and who knows how many meetings,
Julia writes this:

> I have been intending to write to you for several days, dear
> friend, to say – what I do not say willingly – that it would be
> better that we did not meet again just now, at least that you
> did not come here … I feel a great desire for something more
> than the friendly acquiescence which I know I should have
> from you at any rate. I want your sympathy, the support of
> your longer experience and more mature judgment, and so I
> tell you the simple truth … that I have reason to know that
> my pleasure in your company has had an interpretation put
> upon it that I ought not to allow. I have no doubt the fault
> has been mine, in incautiously allowing it to be known that
> I made an object of your visits. You will feel at once that it
> is a mistake which must be set right by deeds, not words… I
> have drawn it upon myself … but I cannot explain this to
> those others who impute to me anticipations irreconcilable
> with that fact … Dear friend, I spin out my letter in
> reluctance to say goodbye, but it must be said – you know
> all that it means from me, all that you have been to me and
> how my thoughts will twine round you and yours – and yet
> you know, too, that I am not giving up more than I can
> afford; you must believe both facts … And so you will strip

away almost all the pain of this last goodbye for your ever
grateful

F.J.W.

His reply is undated.

> My dear friend, this comes to me as no surprise – I thought
> from the beginning it was too good to last, and felt as one
> does in a garden one has entered by an open door, – people
> fancy you mean to steal flowers ...

And having established this extremely revealing metaphor he accepts
her assertion, and promises to withdraw to exactly the distance she
prescribes:

> I left you always to decide (as only you yourself could) on
> what length into the garden I might go: and I still leave it to
> you.

Now, though, he backtracks:

> But I would remark – as common sense must, I think – that
> to snap our outward intercourse off short and sharp will
> hardly cure the evil, whatever it be: two persons who
> suddenly unclasp arms and start off in opposite directions
> look terribly intimate ... Therefore, no goodbye! But, out of
> sight or in it, there will never come a change to my
> impression of you... Of course I will send you the poem,
> when it is done ...

She, too, is not very good at letting go. A month later she writes to
thank him for returning some books of hers:

> I have your photograph now ... I have felt much tempted to
> give myself one more sight of the original before we leave
> town for the summer in 10 days time, but I thought perhaps
> my asking you to give it me would frustrate the object with
> which I asked you not to come ... Farewell, I must stop

writing – it seems difficult – but you know everything I am saying, I think, before you read it.

And that really *was* the end, for a good two years, largely because of her strength of mind. He did send her 'the poem' – *The Ring and the Book* – when it was published, and they began to write to one another again: the intellectual understanding is there, but there's no glow about what they write, and she dislikes the poem and says so. Their 'trusting minds' no longer 'recognise each other', as Christabel LaMotte puts it in *Possession*, and Richard Curle captures the difference rather well:

> It is as if, having lost the key, they were now resolved to express their own personalities, to come out into the open, as it were, where formerly they had wanted to enter sympathetically into each other's minds. It is all rather sad and strange, and the last letters they exchange have a real poignancy as of a grey twilight falling upon everything.

However, unlike LaMotte, Julia didn't sink into nothing: Browning's friendship had given her the confidence she needed. Within a year she had published her *Life* of John Wesley, and not long afterwards she left her parents' house and set up a home of her own. Her novels were reissued and she wrote substantial articles on science, religion, philosophy and politics. She wrote more books, including a major survey, *The Moral Idea*, of the evolution of ethics since the first human societies: years later she admitted that the dedicatee, given only as 'a friend', was Browning. But she was also kept busy with the guardianship of her nephews Bertram and James (Ingall) Wedgwood, after their parents' marriage hit the rocks, and when her following book did less well, her family persuaded her that her work was old-fashioned and out of date, and she wrote less. She did, reluctantly, give in to the family plea that she should write a biography of Josiah I, to correct the 'twaddle' of an earlier one, and when her mother died she succumbed to tradition again, and moved back to look after her father – was that a victory for Mr Casaubon?

So should I write the story of Miss Wedgwood and Mr Browning?

And did they ever call each other 'Robert' and 'Julia' – or even 'Snow'
– in private? It certainly has a classic shape: a bluestocking, poetic tale
not of boy-meets-girl but man-meets-woman, an autumn-tinged story
of second chances and love come late. And we wouldn't dream of seeing
Elizabeth Barrett as Rebecca, would we?

Nor was it easy to resist the letters, although in a strange way the
fact that they're not histories and poems, but the informal, casual
conversation of friends, makes one more aware of the gap between their
voices and our equivalent. To my mind, Byatt's 'ventriloquism' – her
term – of Ash and LaMotte and their writing, in fact edges their voices
rather more away from strict fidelity to the period, and towards an
authentic-*seeming* fusion of the different voices of 'then' and 'now',
than it might at first appear.

Long before I studied *Possession* I'd explored the uses of letters in
fiction, at first as a way of teaching myself how to get a reader to
understand things that a narrator – the letter-writer – can't or won't
talk about, or is scarcely conscious of. Later, in *The Mathematics of
Love*, I'd enjoyed the business – the struggle, on occasions – of working
with the physical letter-y-ness of letters, because they made plotting
easier as often as they made it harder: the time they took to travel; the
assymetrical way they could therefore shape the plot; the characters'
own consciousness of their act of writing; the physical presence of the
ink on the paper and the crossings-out; the gradual closing of the gap
between writing and reading, until a character is interrupted in writing
by the recipient, and hands it to her for her to read it in his presence.
When I'd sought a novel to study for the critical paper element of my
MPhil, I'd chosen *Possession* because it, too, was a parallel narrative –
two stories in two completely different eras – shaped and connected by
letters. *Possession* had sent me to Browning and I'd fallen for his
dramatic monologues. On the other hand, although years before I'd
read and enjoyed Margaret Forster's *Lady's Maid*, about Elizabeth
Barrett, my consciousness of Forster having been there before me was,
now, daunting as much as encouraging.

But the best way to overcome dauntedness is to condense the huge, cloudy, problematic project in one's head into something more distinct and so more analysable. Back to the London Library. Some catalogue searching found *Robert Browning: A Life after Death*, by Pamela Neville-Sington. It's a really interesting product of our own era, when both biography and literary criticism have to find new lights by which to look at old lives. She explores Browning's relationships with women after Elizabeth's death as a way of illuminating his work and his marriage, and she has interesting things to say about the dynamics of his love affair – you really can't call it less – with Julia. Unlike the pre-feminist Richard Curle and the rather catty *The Wedgwood Circle*, Neville-Sington gives Julia her due, but also avoids the excesses of the sort of feminist recovery that writes as if every thwarted creative woman is an embryo Aphra Behn, Hildegarde of Bingen or Artemisia Gentilleschi, tragically un-born. In some ways I felt better for poor Julia after I read it Neville-Sington's book, because her analysis is convincing: Browning's feeling for Julia was very real but not unique to her, and there were other women with whom he had, simultaneously, the same sort of intellectual and personal *amitié amoureuse* that, in those coded, euphemistic days, could so easily hover, tantalisingly and for years, between *eros* and *agape*. Ultimately, Julia didn't have the talent or sheer scale and force of character that Elizabeth Barrett had: she wasn't emotionally stable or mature enough – as EBB was – to have made a successful marriage to a man such as Browning. And yet, although Browning was so fearful of what would be written about him after his death that in old age he burnt many of his papers, he kept all Julia's letters, and his sister returned them to her after his death. Did Julia know just how important she must have been to him?

So their heartbreak at the time is clear, and real, on both sides, and as a writer I do love a bit of heartbreak. What's more, sexual tension is one of my favourite story-drivers because as well as the tension between the two (or more) parties to it, there are tensions inside each: there's feeling the fear and doing it anyway, versus the safety of staying inside your own defences; there's the desire for autonomy versus the need for connection; there's the urge towards selflessness, versus the urge towards self-preservation.

But where was the story? Novels, like televisions series, but unlike films and short stories, are multi-sitting narratives: we must not only hold the reader, but make them want to come back next time. Was there enough sheer drama in this story to make readers come back?

Having had the good sense to implant Robert's and Julia's DNA in purely fictional characters, Byatt could send Ash and LaMotte to bed. But I was being baulked not only by the higher bar of 'honest and responsible' that real-people fiction sets, but also by my own interests and capacities. At heart Julia and Robert would be talking, walking, writing, and nothing else. What was more, many of the spaces that any record of a human life leaves empty were already filled with their own excellent writing: there were no blank pages left for mine. What other action there was – the travelling and living, the tensions and dramas of family and friendship, the enmities and the interfering aunts, the growing-up of Browning's son, the death of Julia's brother, even the childhood of James Ingall ... all of it would only really be the backdrop to an almost entirely mental story going on inside their individual consciousnesses. The things I had done in earlier fiction to embody consciousness in character-in-action were not available to me now: I couldn't make Julia risk social leprosy by boarding a boat to Spain, I couldn't send Browning to live in a brothel for his sexual re-education.

Could I not? Or might I be so wildly un-true to Julia's story and everyone's reading of her character – not to mention the entire manners and mores of her world and era – and send them to bed?

But 'alternate' historical fiction is a control experiment, a thought experiment: it's about exploring what's perennial and what's contingent in a given moment of history, and so it only works if the reader has a really strong sense of the real history from which you're deviating. So alternative fiction about Germany winning the Second World War is plentiful, and I could – well, I couldn't, but maybe you could – write a 'What If?' novel about Charles Darwin having drowned off Tahiti and never writing *The Origin* or anything else. But there's not much point in writing a 'What If?' about this Miss Wedgwood marrying that Mr Browning and finishing her third novel after all.

Might I, I wondered, do as I had also done once before, and frame Julia's story with Miss Wedgwood herself building a novel, her fourth, on the story of her great and only love and the loss of it? Should I perhaps simply re-write Julia's history, and fulfill the love that, unfulfilled, shaped the rest of her life? Or even – this, to me, is where thinking in terms of parallel narrative gets really exciting – might I interweave the story of what really happened, with her version of what she wished had happened? Could I make Julia, post-heartbreak, realise that you can create a reality by writing fiction that you can't by writing history?

But, try as I would, I just couldn't make myself want to. Was it weak-kneed of me to find writing Browning differently daunting, but just as daunting, as writing Erasmus Darwin or Coleridge? Was it snobbish of me to turn down Julia as a central character, simply because she wasn't, in the long term and to twentieth- and twenty-first century eyes, a very exciting literary figure? Was it vulgarly commercial of me to turn Julia and Browning down because, to be true to her real story, I'd have to acknowledge that they would have been a disaster?

Call me a snobbish vulgarian, I thought miserably (probably half-way down the bottle) but I just couldn't see – couldn't *feel*, is more what it's like ... I just didn't know how to write a novel which was both Julia's, and mine.

And besides, she isn't a Darwin.

Yet, as with Tom, in writing this I'm feeling again the longing to fulfill all the promising parts of Julia's story. Was I wrong, those years ago? Should I put an end to this parallel project, and return to fiction? I know I shouldn't – and yet, again, the longing, just now as I type, is extraordinarily strong.

Where does it come from, the longing of the creative artist, not just the writer, to re-express and re-create what we discover or experience? We tell ourselves and others that it's because we need to earn a living, or want something to do in the evenings, or want to ignore the washing up. But at times that drive to write, and to send our writing out to find readers, is desperate, and its thwarting unbearable; and no emotion so visceral is only about mere living-earning, or skiving-off.

It isn't just writers, of course. Tourists have always sketched and taken snapshots to keep a little of what they have seen for after they've gone home; wedding photographers are booked partly for fear that, without such processing of the experience – the framing, the recording, the making recoverable – the experience in some way doesn't or didn't exist. If creators of art, too, simply want to make sure that these things are recoverable, then we could save a whole lot of trouble and keep what we create safely on the shelf or under the bed. But we don't.

The thing is, when a singer or an actor doesn't have an audience she calls it practising or rehearsing, not performing, and many singers stop singing if they can no longer get chances to perform. Writers, too, want an audience, and that's where Julia's pull-push over putting her name on her novels is a clue. The great psychologist D.W.Winnicott said that artists are people driven by the tension between wanting to communicate and wanting to hide, and he said elsewhere that, for a child, hiding is a joy but not being found is a disaster.

If I suggest that creative art, too, fulfils an infant need, it's not to imply that artists are childish, only that a human being's oldest drives – which is to say our youngest drives – are also our strongest ones, and cause the most trouble when they can't be fulfilled. Besides, Winnicott observed that children's play is their work, and working at art is like working at play: the doing of something for its own sake, the seriousness, the imaginative recreation, the deliberate evoking and replaying of emotions and actions, and – perhaps most overtly in fiction – the acceptance of the doubleness of 'real' and 'not real'.

So hiding is a joy but not being found is a disaster, and yet many actors are personally very shy. Many writers of fiction, too, respond like performers as their imaginations run and words rise up and get put on the page, but nonetheless shrink from the glare of light on their own, un-masked face and body. Fiction is the armour, the helmet and visor, which make it possible to put ourselves in emotionally dangerous places, and those places include both the imagined action of our stories, and the imagined stage – the reader's mind – which our stories must stand on. Projecting not our actual selves, but a creation of that self, outwards to an audience resolves the tension between communicating and hiding, and when the audience responds we feel both hidden and found.

'Stop it!' I have just said to myself. 'When it came down to it, you *didn't* want to write Julia. You know that.'

Yes, I did know it. I do know it. Perhaps it's because she's not a photographer; perhaps it's because the smells, sights, minds and loves of the mid-Victorians don't draw me in at all, compared to other parts of the past; perhaps (oh, the feminist shame!) it's because she's a woman and I like the built-in distance of writing men … My decision not to write a novel of Julia Wedgwood was carefully made, but not, in the end, difficult. I mostly minded that I still couldn't find a way into *Black Shadow and Bone*.

So, back to the family tree, and down (up?) to the next generation: the generation of Charles Darwin's grandchildren.

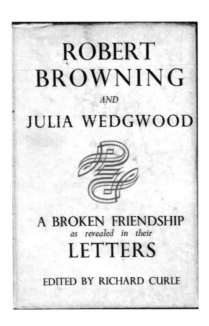

ROBERT
BROWNING
AND
JULIA WEDGWOOD

A BROKEN FRIENDSHIP
as revealed in their
LETTERS

EDITED BY RICHARD CURLE

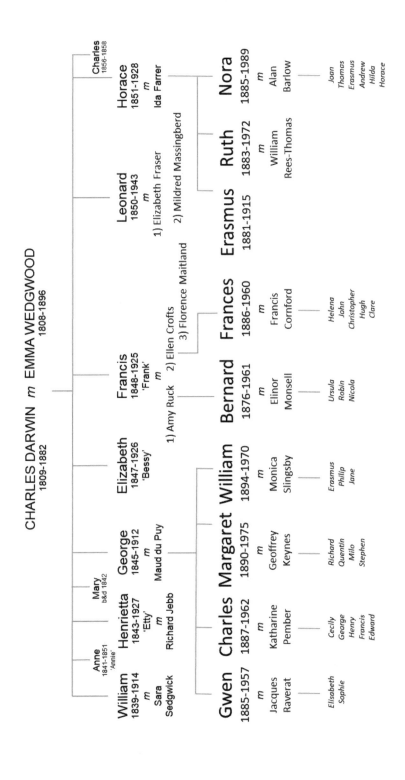

CHARLES DARWIN *m* EMMA WEDGWOOD
1809-1882   1808-1896

William 1839-1914 *m* Sara Sedgwick	**Anne** 1841-1851 'Annie'	**Henrietta** 1843-1927 'Etty' *m* Richard Jebb	**Mary** b&d 1842	**George** 1845-1912 *m* Maud du Puy	**Elizabeth** 1847-1926 'Bessy'

Francis 1848-1925 'Frank' *m* 1) Amy Ruck 2) Ellen Crofts 3) Florence Maitland	**Leonard** 1850-1943 *m* 1) Elizabeth Fraser 2) Mildred Massingberd	**Horace** 1851-1928 *m* Ida Farrer	**Charles** 1856-1858

Gwen 1885-1957 *m* Jacques Raverat	**Charles** 1887-1962 *m* Katharine Pember	**Margaret** 1890-1975 *m* Geoffrey Keynes	**William** 1894-1970 *m* Monica Slingsby	**Bernard** 1876-1961 *m* Elinor Monsell	**Frances** 1886-1960 *m* Francis Cornford	**Erasmus** 1881-1915	**Ruth** 1883-1972 *m* William Rees-Thomas	**Nora** 1885-1989 *m* Alan Barlow
Elisabeth *Sophie*	*Cecily* *George* *Henry* *Francis* *Edward*	*Richard* *Quentin* *Milo* *Stephen*	*Erasmus* *Philip* *Jane*	*Ursula* *Robin* *Nicola*	*Helena* *John* *Christopher* *Hugh* *Clare*			*Joan* *Thomas* *Erasmus* *Andrew* *Hilda* *Horace*

7

The Grandchildren's Generation

Once or twice I've had an email via my website which says something along the lines of 'My mother's surname was Darwin, and so we've always wondered if we are descended from Charles Darwin; can you tell us?' And the answer has to be a delicately-phrased version of No, such as, 'I can see why you might wonder, but I'm afraid there aren't many Darwin-surnamed descendants of Charles, and they're all documented.'

There are more if you back-track to Erasmus – that second marriage of his produced many descendants, not just the startlingly debauched James Wedgwood – but, compared to the Wedgwoods, the Darwins were not prolific. If you wanted to speculate about my family as an example how the inbreeding of populations leads to infertility, you wouldn't be the first, although apparently you'd also be wrong.[48] Still, if *Black Shadow and Bone* needed to be built on a Charles Darwin descendant, my options were narrow.

But although I've never yet found someone in the tree to beat James Wedgwood for sheer story-pizzazz, there are some not-quite-Darwins, parallel to Charles's direct descendants, who I felt were too delicious, in the writerly sense, not to spend a library-hour or three dissecting, in case somewhere in their life there was an episode with story-DNA curled up inside it.

Ralph Vaughan Williams isn't a Charles descendant, but if you want to

---

[48] See, for example, Adam Rutherford's *A Brief History of Everyone Who Ever Lived: the story of our genes.*

explore creative thinking in my family, then one of Britain's great 20th century composers isn't a bad place to look. And he is closer than you'd think: remember Charles's sister Caroline Darwin marrying Emma's brother Josiah Wedgwood III? Ralph is a grandchild of that marriage. That makes him a double-second-cousin to my grandfather (though in fact fifteen years older), and if I want to make a geneticist look *very* green about the gills, I speculate about just how much genetic damage would show up if a child of RVW's had married a child of my grandfather's.

With RVW, as with the other more famous monkeys in the family tree, it's easy to find possible story-stuffs, beginning with the family letters about dear Ralph: 'it will simply break his heart if he is told that he is too bad to hope to make anything of it.'[49]

There's the story of him sitting on a cliff watching the troops embarking for France in 1914, and being arrested thanks to the boy scout who saw a stranger making notes and reported him to the police: the notes were the song of a lark, which much later found life in 'The Lark Ascending' – a piece which to me breathes of the fields of Flanders.

There's his uneasy marriage to Adeline Fisher:[50] she was incapable of putting herself and him before the demands of her siblings and parents, and then, early in the marriage, she began to be slowly but inexorably disabled by rheumatoid arthritis of the most awful sort.

There's his volunteering in 1914 as an ambulance driver, though he was a pacifist and over military age; he served in France and Salonika and then, when things were really dark in 1917 and defeat was looming, he switched into the Royal Artillery, and was partially deafened as a result.

Possibly the first piece of classical music I ever really loved was RVW's *Fantasia on Greensleeves*; I can remember dancing to the

---

[49] I quoted this letter of Emma's to the music critic Humphrey Burton, who said, 'And he never did get much better'.
[50] Strictly for genealogy nerds is this entanglement: Adeline Vaughan Williams' sister was Florence Fisher, who as Florence Maitland became the third wife of Frank Darwin. Adeline and Florence's aunt Julia Fisher was the mother of Vanessa Bell and Virginia Woolf; their brother Herbert was the great historian H.A.L. Fisher.

gramophone record as a small child,[51] and I soon grew to love the rest: *The Lark Ascending*, the *English Folksong Suite*, and one of my top ten of all music, *Fantasia on a Theme of Thomas Tallis*. But if that kind of music – the much-maligned English Pastoral school – is what you think of when someone says 'Vaughan Williams', then it's worth listening again, to something like the *Sinfonia Antarctica*. Inside those tweedy photographs, that Establishment genealogy with its small, not specially valuable but probably silver spoon-in-the-mouth, is the modernist who studied with Ravel, and who Ravel said was the only student he ever had who didn't end up sounding like Ravel (make of that what you will). He's the tall, dark, staggeringly handsome man who looked 'like a hawk in repose' and carried on a long affair (consummated? It seems likely.) with the great pianist Harriet Cohen; the cosmopolitan city-lover who for his invalid wife's sake moved to live in the suburbs of the small Surrey town of Dorking; the professed atheist who produced not one but two of the great Anglican hymnals;[52] the composer of a deeply un-pastoral *Pastoral Symphony*, and a Sixth Symphony which is some of the most troubling music to come out of war that I know.[53]

And RVW is the devoted husband and carer who, in his sixties, fell passionately in love with Ursula Wood, who fell just as passionately in love with him although she was forty years his junior and also married. Here is the good man, the old-fashioned radical and philanthropist, who established a ménage à trois which lasted thirteen years and led to his second, very late marriage to Ursula. *Surely* there was something there which would mean I could build a novel on him? I hunkered down

---

[51] We had no access to pop music: there was a gramophone, and one small radio which lived on the Third Programme (as my parents still tended to call it) unless you were ill in bed and were given the radio to stave off boredom. I didn't know what Radios 1 and 2 were for: after all, the *Radio Times* only listed something like 'Tony Blackburn'? What did that mean? What was the programme *about*? So I was baffled by what was sung in the playground: The Beatles' 'Yellow Submarine' when we lived in New York, and Abba's 'Waterloo' in my London primary school. It was only when my mother's sister, executing their childless aunt's will, distributed some keepsakes that I got a transistor radio and discovered Capital Radio and such joys as the first ever episode of *The Hitchhiker's Guide to the Galaxy*. And I only lived with a TV when I left home in my early twenties.
[52] First the *English Hymnal*, which he felt was compromised by its High Anglican brief, and later *Songs of Praise*.
[53] And I'm including his great friend Gustav Holst's 'Mars' from *The Planets*, as well as so much Shostakovich.

with more books and more websites, and started looking for places which would give me atmosphere and emotional substance as well as facts.

The only accessible house, of the places he lived, is where he grew up. His father, the Reverend Arthur Vaughan Williams, died when RVW was only two, and his Wedgwood mother moved herself and their three children back to live with her own parents at Leith Hill Place in Surrey, south-west of Dorking. The house is classical and plainish, built in the mid-eighteenth century of silvery stone. It passed down to RVW's older brother Hervey, and when RVW inherited it from Hervey after the Second World War, he gave it to the National Trust.[54] These days it's open to the public, but it's not a case of a treasure-house left or restored to be just-as-it-was. The rooms are often used for musical events and are sparely furnished, but they have RVW's piano, and the most astonishingly beautiful views, out over the Surrey Hills, which are so thickly wooded and contoured that it's scarcely possible to see evidence of the twentieth century, let alone the twenty-first.

The first difficulty about writing a novel of RVW was that I'd be living not in my first love and happy zone of photography and visual arts, but in music. True, it was possibly a plus that I'm not a professional musician or musicologist; fiction isn't musicology, and at the very least I wouldn't suffer from the 'curse of knowledge', as Stanley Fish puts it in *How To Write A Sentence*. Nevertheless, I would be making fiction from the *experience* of making or listening to music, and whoever described writing about music as equivalent to trying to dance about architecture was understating the problem. Vikram Seth manages it in *An Equal Music*, but it's a hard trick to pull off, and perhaps harder still if your central character is a composer, not a performer. Compared to Julia Wedgwood and Robert Browning, there would be more scope for an exciting plot, what with two world wars to play with, but most of the story – if the story was music – would still be going on inside people's heads.

---

[54] Who did not at that time open it to the public, but instead leased it back to RVW's cousin, the railway engineer Sir Ralph Wedgwood.

If the story-driver couldn't be music, then clearly it was sex, love and marriage. Ursula's *Life* of her husband is still the biography of record, and it's exemplary, neither hagiography nor hatchet-job. Here were the same old problems: how *much* material there was in the archives, how well-documented everything is, how many good and sober historians have been there already, how the bones of that story have been sorted out and told, how little space there would be for me. What was more, while Ursula doesn't conceal, she has what you might call an old-fashioned reticence: the biographer as collater and (lively, engaging, honest) explainer, not the biographer as psychoanalyst or gleeful opener of closets full of skeletons. In principle, that's exactly the reticence which leaves a role for a novelist. But, still, my job would merely be to put the flesh of feelings and ideas onto the recorded growth and death of love, to add small gifts and betrayals, to chart the accommodations and irritations that were known, and imagine a few more.

As it happened, in my teaching life I'd just ground my way through a particularly trying batch of marking for the Open University. Had I really spent four years on a PhD in Creative Writing in order to spend weeks doing little more than explaining comma splices for the third time to the same student? And – I asked myself grouchily as I coaxed the system into zipping the files and uploading them back up to Milton Keynes so such students could download their grades and ignore all my comments – had I really spent even more years learning to write novels, only to find myself as the scriptwriter and wardrobe mistress of a docudrama?

As well as these familiar problems, there was a new one. These are people I sort-of know. My parents knew Ralph and Ursula well, and I think I met Ursula[55] once or twice: certainly she only died in 2007. RVW is only an arm's-length away, in other words; was I really proposing to go into his head and presume to write about what went on in there?

---

[55] Though I can't be sure, because there's another Ursula in the family tree: Ursula Mommens, the potter, who was Bernard Darwin's daughter, and married first the artist Julian Trevelyan, and then Norman Mommens. Bernard's son Robin was a painter, and Rector of the Royal College of Art for many years, with his cousin Christopher Cornford as Dean.

Which was the point at which I realised that maybe I am wired for that same old-fashioned family reticence as Ursula's. In my fiction I've broken hearts, heads and horse's legs, made the horse's loving owner have to fetch a shotgun and *then*, shamelessly, made the gun jam so the beloved old mare realised what was happening. I've written childbirth, murder, euthanasia by pillow and abortion by screwdriver, judicial hangings and extra-judicial beheadings, instant death by cannon ball and weeks of death by septicaemic battle-wound. I've written good, bad and (in)different sex, both gay and straight; I've written masturbation, deflowering and rape. My real life is much duller, but I thought I might be able to write that bedroom outside Dorking, when the Blitz had driven Ursula from the London flat and she lay on the floor between Adeline's bed and Ralph's, while they all held hands and listened to German bombs raining down outside.

But if they found their private, quiet, sensible way to a *modus vivendi*, who was I to become the gutter-press reporter, splashing them all over the front page? And I knew I'd never, ever be able to write even a blissfully consensual sex scene between my double-second cousin twice removed and his wife, let alone that cousin and his mistress who I may once (or twice) have actually met.

So, was there someone else with as good a story and less call for reticence? Some of the Wedgwoods looked promising.

Josiah (Clement) Wedgwood, Josiah IV if you like, was a great-great-grandson of the first Josiah, and the Whiggish nonconformity showed up extra-specially strongly in him, which explains why when his niece, the great mid-century historian C. V. Wedgwood, wrote a memoir of him, she titled it *The Last of the Radicals*. Colonel Jos (he was later ennobled as Baron Wedgwood of Stoke-on-Trent) was incapable of ignoring a cause he believed to be right, and it's hard not to think that 'right' for him was anything which ran counter to the received opinions of most of the ruling class and a fair slice of the working one.[56] He was MP for his local seat in the Potteries, Newcastle-under-Lyme, for thirty-six years, holding it first for the Liberals, then for Labour. After being wounded in 1915 during the Dardanelles campaign, manning the machine gun in the bows of his ship and thereby winning the DSO, he – like John Maynard Keynes, and on similar grounds – opposed the punitive reparations imposed on Germany at Versailles. He was also a lifelong and leading supporter of Zionism[57] and Indian independence.

However, it wasn't only foreign affairs that drove his political convictions and actions. He married his cousin Ethel Bowen, the daughter of a lawyer and writer, and they had six children, but the marriage was tempestuous; during the war Ethel left him for someone else, and then asked him for a divorce. At the time that meant one party providing evidence of adultery so the 'innocent party' could apply to a court to divorce the adulterous spouse; of course the only honourable arrangement was for the husband to provide the evidence and take the blame, since his reputation would suffer far less than his wife's at being branded an adulterer. But the job of the court, in the person of a splendidly medieval-sounding official called the King's Proctor, included investigating the 'crime' on which the petition was based. If the King's Proctor suspected a put-up job – that the couple had colluded to create or fake the necessary evidence, or the 'innocent party' was herself not innocent of adultery – then the divorce wouldn't be granted. Even if it were granted, the decree *nisi* was a matter of public record, and such a scandal that to much of the population it was equivalent to being convicted of an actual crime.

The Wedgwoods' divorce was granted, on the grounds of Josiah's adultery, and Josiah's constituents were predictably horrified that their MP could have behaved so wickedly; some demanded that he resign his seat. So, as soon as the divorce was absolute, he told the truth: that he

---

[56] Ralph Vaughan Williams had a similar cast of mind: he once said of an impending election that although it would be in his own interests to cast a mid-to-right-wing vote, he would never be able to do so, partly from genuine conviction and partly from sheer cussedness: he hated fulfilling people's expectations of how a man of his background would act.
[57] There have been several streets in Israel named after him, as well as two Israeli warships and a *moshav* community.

was not an adulterer, and the whole thing was staged. From then on he became a passionate advocate of divorce law reform.

That story felt more like my territory, but again I came up against the problem of the well-documented life: there are three other studies of him, including a full biography by Paul Mulvey, as well as his own autobiography, characteristically titled *Memoirs of a Fighting Life*. What would there be for me?

Reluctantly – Colonel Jos is another twig of the tree I'd love to have met – I crossed him off my list, and went looking for more people. I also – not least thanks to having read Richard Holmes's *Footsteps* and other creative non-fiction such as Janet Malcolm's *Reading Chekhov* – went looking for more places.

The Darwin-Wedgwoods might have become gentlemen by the late eighteenth century, but even in the nineteenth century they weren't landed gentry of the sort that Adam Nicholson explores in his book *Gentry*. It was Wedgwood & Co., and other industrial money, sensibly invested, which bought or built a house and land wherever work or family suggested was most desirable. Robert Darwin was one of the biggest investors and lenders of money in Shropshire, and became a very rich man; he only kept on with the hated doctoring because it maintained his social status as a gentleman, which also secured the family's social life and matrimonial prospects. In such families the land is not the work, and the children marry and move on to work elsewhere: their houses are rarely kept for more than a generation or two. It's true that Gwen Raverat suggests that for all Charles's children and grandchildren Down was such a paradise that nowhere else could ever rival it, and of course, more recently, the family was delighted when Down House was restored by English Heritage and awarded World Heritage Site status. But even when such a place is much loved, and stays in the family, the identies of those who live there are not formed by it, as are the families that Nicholson studies, where the intertwined history of a place and a family creates a deep sense of the house and land as a quasi-sacred trust.

So there are dozens of ordinary old houses in the family's story. For the earlier stages of research, Google Street View is a wonderful thing until you are sure enough that you need a place to start bothering the owners. In real life I'd looked at the outside of Gunville House and Eastbury Park and I was ready, once I'd found the subject of the novel, to investigate further.

It's only some of the other biggish houses in the family's history – Down of course, but also Leith Hill Place and Erasmus Darwin House in Lichfield – which are both lucky enough to still exist, and interesting enough in either history or architecture to be carefully preserved, and then opened to the public. Mind you, such houses are still bigger than most of us could ever hope to live in or, frankly, would want to, in terms of maintenance, upkeep and fire insurance premiums. But it is possible to *imagine* living in them, as you can't imagine living in the great political-territorial powerhouses such as Blenheim, Knole or Chatsworth.

I'd been intrigued to find that when one of Charles's son's, Leonard Darwin, married for the second time he and his wife, Mildred Massingberd, went to live at her family house, Gunby Hall, on the Lincolnshire coast. If Chatsworth is Pemberley, then Gunby Hall would make a very convincing Longbourn, and when the area was going to be turned into an airport, after the Second World War, the Massingberds saved it by persuading the National Trust to take it on. It's Aunt Mildred that Gwen, in *Period Piece*, explains as having been 'our cousin before she was our aunt', and there are other connections, including a Vaughan Williams one.[58] Digging among the Massingberds, I found the now familiar combination of establishment science, unostentatious money, and a thick, reforming streak of social and political action: Mildred's mother Emily Massingberd, in particular, was a notable feminist (as a widow, she gave up her married name of Langton) and anti-vivisectionist. So in late October I took the chance of a literary festival gig in Harrogate to come back by way of Gunby.

The autumn rain and the steep, green fells of West Yorkshire give way to the quieter landscapes round the Humber and, once I'm over the

---

[58] Mildred's grandmother and RVW's grandfather were siblings, both being children of Josiah II.

A1, the clouds roll away and show the Lincolnshire Wolds rumpled under the autumn sunshine. Almost in the North Sea, and hard by the gates of Skegness Butlins – built on land bought from the Gunby estate – I turn left in accordance with the signs and trundle up the drive.

It's a lovely, flat-fronted eighteenth-century manor, built of pinky-red brick and creamy stone, and slightly asymmetrical: very much the product of an ordinary builder and an ordinary gentry family. There's a walled garden and a stream, and a path through the grounds that joins Gunby village to its parish church. There's a small stable-block too, and I'm struck again by what a lot of hardware and housing horse-transport required. No wonder 'keeping a carriage' was, like so many markers of social status, not only about genuine convenience but, too, about conspicuous consumption of not just money but also time and fuss.

Gunby is much the same age as Leith Hill Place, and inside looks much as Leith Hill once did: thoughtfully decorated and arranged but slightly shabby, book-lined, photograph-packed, old-piano-ed, with chintz chair-covers, well-polished but well-worn furniture, stair-treads which protest faintly under your feet, and wide, uneven stone flags in the kitchen.

I've planned to pour over the photographs, perhaps get chatting to the volunteers, or even reveal my particular interest in the house and the family. I might be very, very brave and ask to talk to the house manager, by way of making a connection ready for later. I always find that difficult: my wanting-to-hide wiring always seems to be on high alert, and it's worse when it's family stuff because then it's also painfully like showing off. Perhaps, I think, I can make the connection now, in the hope that the Trust manager would be interested (I toss a sop to the gremlins by adding, '*If* the novel gets published') in hosting an event. At the very least I can find out his or her email, and ask questions later, or arrange a visit when someone's free to show me the archive.

But all · my plans are scuppered, because it's half-term, it's Hallowe'en, and Gunby Hall is in half-light. Doors creak mysteriously, light-fittings are festooned with archival-quality, National Trust-approved, acid-free, fire-proofed cobwebs; curtained windows and dust-sheeted chairs heave and howl with phantom presences (I imagine a work time sheet: '3 hrs as ghost') and both over-excited children and volunteer room-wardens are given to emitting sudden shrieks. My idea of some gentle, modest, grown-up research and networking will have to wait.

I stroll through the rooms before going outside to stroll round the gardens in the last, warm, autumn sun. The ever-reliable National Trust supplies me with tea, and over a heroic wedge of Victoria Sandwich I reflect that though Leonard was obviously a lovely man, he never did look like very promising novel material. Besides, it's still a very long drive back to South East London, and I can always come back to Gunby if I need to.

Felix Wedgwood was a mountineer and adventurer – Wedgwood Peak in the Canadian Rockies is named after him – as well as an engineer who specialised in marine salvage and shipwrecks. That last bit, particularly, might have been promising, but I'm phobic about water and all my nightmares are about ships. Surprisingly (or perhaps not suprisingly at all, given any writer's need to work with things which are potent to them) terrifying maritime moments tend to crop up in my fiction, but I really, *really* didn't want to build a whole book on them.

However, Felix also published a novel and I found it in the London Library, not for the first time blessing them for their policy that they never throw away a book, although also giving a little feminist snarl at the fact that they evidently acquired his, but not Julia's. *Shadow of a Titan* draws vividly on Felix's travels in South America and doesn't merit throwing away. There's humour here, a vivid imagination and some striking writing: imagine that Isabel Allende had a great-grandfather who wanted to emulate Rider Haggard at Dickensian scale. *The Times* apparently described it as 'a masterpiece on a South American dictatorship that [George] Meredith might have fathered', but 'masterpiece' is pushing it, and it's a fat book. I can't honestly say I'm surprised to see by the label in the front that it was last borrowed in 1968, although it's doubtless good for me to be reminded that even books which get brilliant reviews in their generation fade so quickly from sight. I do wonder what Felix might have written next – it was published in 1912 – but by then he had married and had two daughters. He was killed on the Western Front in 1917, six months after his son was born.[59] There was something very poignant in discovering, as I did, that his wife, Canadian fellow-climber Katherine Longstaff, lived until 1976, when I was twelve. I wondered for a short time whether Felix – away from the shipwrecks – would support a novel, not least because the Centenary of 1914 was ticking ever closer. But without doing full-scale work on primary sources I had no way of finding out what, if anything, there was which was more than the individual kind of ordinary. So, again (again, *again*, *again*), I would have had two possibilities: embroider a largely fictional story and lose the 'non-fiction' hook, or stick to non-fiction, and do a lot of biographer's work that I've never done, would need to learn from the ground up, and had no appetite for.

Oh, and of course he's not a Darwin.

It was time to get methodical with Charles Darwin's grandchildren so here they are, in order of age.

Bernard Darwin: the oldest. He grew up at Down House where his father Frank was Charles's assistant. Bernard's memoir is called *The World that Fred Made*, because to infant Bernard it was Fred, and the other gardeners who collaborated with his grandfather at Down, who created the world of his childhood. He married the artist and illustrator Elinor Monsell ('Eily') and they had three children. Bernard became a noted golfer and a journalist specialising in sports; he was the only grandson too old to serve in the First World War. As well as publishing several books he was was the golf correspondent for *The Times* for fifty years.

Erasmus Darwin: fourth of that name. He was an engineer like his father Horace, but Ras worked in 'big' engineering for various steel

---

[59] His uncle Cecil Wedgwood had died on the Somme the previous year.

companies. By 1914 he had been involved with the Territorials for some years and was commissioned immediately; he was killed in France in April 1915.

Ruth Darwin: older daughter of Horace Darwin: she worked in mental health and married William Rees Thomas late in life.

(Emma) Nora Darwin: youngest of Horace's children. She worked as a geneticist under William Bateson and then at the John Innes Institute, publishing two important papers. Later she produced new, definitive editions of Charles Darwin's *The Voyage of the Beagle* and *Autobiography*, restoring various cuts that Frank Darwin and Etty Darwin had made at Emma's request; she also edited several other collections of important scientific letters. She was married to Alan Barlow, who was a civil servant and, among other senior posts, principal private secretary to Prime Minister Ramsay Macdonald, and they had six children.

Gwen Darwin: the oldest of George Darwin's children. She studied at The Slade and became an artist and wood engraver, marrying a French artist, Jacques Raverat; they had two daughters but Jacques died of multiple sclerosis in 1925. Gwen also designed for the stage and worked as an art critic: during the Second World War she engraved topographical maps for the military. Towards the end of her life she was too crippled with arthritis to engrave, and it was then that she wrote and illustrated *Period Piece*.

Frances Darwin: Bernard's half-sister, from Francis Darwin's second marriage; Frances and Gwen were particularly close friends. She suffered for much of her life from deep and recurring depressions, but as Frances Cornford she became a well-regarded poet, one of her closest friends being Rupert Brooke. Frances married the Classical anthropologist Francis (F.M.) Cornford; they lived in Cambridge and they had five children.

Charles (Galton) Darwin: third of that name and second of George Darwin's children. A physicist like his father, he worked with Rutherford and later Niels Bohr. He was in the Engineering Corps in the First World War, winning a Military Cross for his work on the Western Front in sound-ranging and flash-detection. Later he was Master of Christ's College, Cambridge, before moving to be head of the National Physical Laboratory: in the Second World War he travelled to the US to work on radar and then the Manhattan Project. He married Katharine Pember, a mathematician, and they are my grandparents.

Margaret Darwin: George Darwin's younger daughter, read History at Oxford but left before graduating to help nurse her father, who was terminally ill. In 1917 she married Geoffrey Keynes,[60] a surgeon and expert on William Blake. Much later she wrote *A House by the River*, a history of the house which became Newnham Grange and then Darwin College.

William Darwin: ('Billy'); George's younger son. Served in the Royal Artillery 1914-18, became a stockbroker and married Monica ('Mona') Slingsby.

The grandchildren grew up more-or-less together, as all three of the child-producing brothers, George, Frank and Horace, lived in the physical and mental village that was academic Cambridge. Bernard was a good deal older, but the rest were close in age, and though the boys went to boarding school the girls were educated at home. Indeed Ruth, Nora, Gwen and Frances were all born within three years of each other, and the cousinage formed something of a pack outside schoolroom hours; there were often Wedgwood cousins about too. Frank's house Wychfield was next door to Horace's house The Orchard and both adjoined Emma's house The Grove, where Grandmamma Emma and Aunt Bessy spend the winters. The area has since become Murray Edwards College, but then the grandchildren had free range of a vast

---

[60] Geoffrey's older brother was the economist John Maynard Keynes.

patch of gardens, meadows and waterways, while in the summers much of the family shifted to Down.

I dug around in *Period Piece* and *The House on the River*; in *The World Fred Made*; in Geoffrey Keynes's memoir *The Gates of Memory*; in biographies such as Frances Spalding's *Gwen Raverat: Friends, Family & Affections*, plus Robert Skidelsky on Maynard Keynes and Judith Mackrell on Lydia Lopokova, and, among a small forest's-worth of other Brooke-iana, Paul Delaney's *The Neo-Pagans: Rupert Brooke and the Ordeal of Youth*. I spent ages to-ing and fro-ing in the indexes of dozens of other books – histories, biographies and academic studies – and at last came upon something which seemed to embody all the things that I really, actually might want to build a novel on.

* * *

Where were they going when they stopped in Manchester to see Charles, wondered Gwen; it was long before the War. They'd met in the lab: Rutherford down the other end talking to students, and Charles tidying up before they went out to lunch, and the physics lab smell of ozone and rubber and machines, and always a whiff of gas from the bunsen burners. She and Jacques and Imogen had all being going to walk in the Lakes. It must have been – what? 1911? Something like that. But Gwen and Jacques weren't married, said the parents, and Imogen was no good for a chaperon for Gwen and Jacques anyway: neither old enough, nor young enough. They would have to stay with Charles until Frances, who *was* married, could join them, and they could all set off for Keswick.

All those rules, instead of just letting people decide for themselves! Of course at home, for those river-picnics – tours of the Colleges – visits to the play – evenings in the garden – it was enough insurance against disaster for parents simply to tie a bored, grumpy little Gwen, or Margaret, to a couple's heels. Although Gwen had always wondered what on earth she was supposed to do, if they had started to do … whatever the disaster was.

She'd asked Nana several times: If Miss Thing and Cousin Mr That started to kiss, what should she do?

'Och, just clear your throat, Miss Gwennie,' Nana said, checking to see if she'd washed behind her ears. 'Give a nice little cough, and the young lady will remember what's what. And the young gentleman will understand. Now, you do the back of your neck again and no skimping, and get that green paint out of your fingernails, while I get on with washing Miss Margaret.'

A nice little cough didn't seem like much of a weapon to stop them doing whatever it was, Gwen had thought in those days, soaping her hands. Even the back of a hairbrush was more frightening than a nice little cough. 'What if they ...' she began, but foundered: what was it that they might do? Not that she cared, specially, any more than she cared what the grown-up's wine tasted like, or why they fussed so about Home Rule. It was just that she did need to know what her job was.

It wasn't long after that, she had a feeling, that Billy was born. God had sent her and Charles and Margaret a new little brother, said Nana. It was years and years before she connected her mother's delighted fretting over the young ladies and gentlemen with the entirely different business which started when you got married, and ended with a baby. And it *was* an entirely different business, of course. No one really thought that the young lady would succumb, or the young gentleman try to make her: it was all about What People Would Think.

Strange, Gwen thought now, how those cousins and brothers and uncles, including her father, could be as unorthodox in their science as a poet might be in his morals – they could have as good an eye for beauty and balance in their theoretical work and their experiments as a great artist has – and yet when it came to love and sex they accepted the rules without a snarl or even a sigh.

8

Masques

In 1908, Cambridge University's Marlowe Society was only a year old. It had been founded by undergraduate Justin Brooke – friend but no relation to Rupert, as I expect they were sick to death of explaining – with an explictly anti-Victorian agenda and ethos: to produce neglected plays from the past, using the original, unexpurgated and uncut texts, with men playing women,[61] and clean productions to let the texts speak.

---

[61] This was, of course, authentic for pre-1660 texts, but must also have been convenient, as the University authorities were suspicious of mixed productions. The men's colleges worried about the distraction and potential immorality of having women around, and the women's colleges, challenging gender conventions by their mere existence, were forced to be extra-careful of the proprieties, and were often particularly reluctant to allow their students to take part.

Now, the celebrations for the tercentenary of Milton's birth were centering on his college, Christ's, and it was decided that the heart of it would be a Marlowe Society production of the masque Milton wrote for the sons and daughter of his employer, the Earl of Bridgewater. Clearly authenticity in producing *Comus* demanded at least one actress, and also extras such as dancers, and there would be a vast amount of work. Frank Darwin was a Fellow of Christ's, and thought his daughter Frances might be able to help with the designs.

Rupert and Justin went to ask, found Frances with Gwen, (they were in their early twenties by then, and studying art together), and four hours later everything had been set in motion. Indeed, it was Gwen and Frances who persuaded Rupert that as well as being the stage manager (in our terms, director) he should play the important role of the Attendant Spirit; it was they, too, who then persuaded the young Classics lecturer F.M.Cornford, who had been drawn into the Society largely to supply a respectably senior element, to play the glamorous villain Comus. Frances played The Lady, Gwen designed and made the costumes, and virtually all meetings happened at Newnham Grange, culminating in an after-show party which Gwen persuaded her parents might be held in their garden on the Cam. By all acounts the night was magical, even if Rupert's costume was so tight, he said, that he was unable to sit down.

Along the way, Francis Cornford proposed to Frances and was accepted, and with Frances – who'd suffered from more than one serious clinical depression – safely embarked on a new life, Gwen felt able to embark on her own new life. Her campaign to be allowed to move to London and study art at the Slade finally succeeded, and she went to live with her beloved Uncle William in Kensington Square.

Comus sowed the seeds of the group that Gwen and Frances's step-cousin-by-marriage Virginia Woolf later christened the neo-Pagans: Rupert Brooke, the parentless Katherine ('Ka') Cox, the four very beautiful and virtually un-chaperoned Olivier sisters,[62] Geoffrey Keynes

---

[62] Unchaperoned because their father Sydney Olivier, a civil servant and noted Fabian, spent many years working in the government of Jamaica, and was then appointed India Secretary.

and his friend Jacques Raverat, Gwen and Margaret Darwin, and Francis and Frances Cornford, while the fringes of the group included Maynard Keynes, Lytton Strachey, Ermengarde and Fredegonde Maitland[63] and other Bloomsburies.

There was something else. Until *Comus*, Francis Cornford's closest female friend had been Jane Harrison, a notable and much older Classics don at Newham College. Together they had had been part of the scholarly revolution which studied the great Classical texts not simply as literature, but through the lenses of archaeology, anthropology and evolutionary theory; she had, in fact, presented George Darwin with a copy of her new study of ritual in Greek religion, *Prolegomena*, writing in it: 'You will see that most of the important points are contributed by your illustrious family.' She was twenty-four years older than Francis Cornford, and in their *amitié amoureuse* – working together, going on holiday – there had been nothing obviously sexual. Many of Jane's most intense relationships were with women and it was actually Jane who had, years before, introduced him to the fifteen-year-old Frances – the daughter of Jane's great friend and fellow-Newham lecturer Ellen Darwin – as one might introduce a beloved great-niece to a favourite nephew. But beloved great-nieces grow up, and favourite nephews may not be so much older after all. It was only when Francis announced his engagement to Frances that Jane admitted what she had known for some time: that she herself had been in love with him for years.

As well as being Milton's tercentenary, 1909 would be the centenary of Charles Darwin's birth, *and* fifty years since *The Origin* had been published. Frank Darwin was President of the British Association for the Advancement of Science, which had played a notable role in the early battles to get evolution by natural selection accepted as scientific fact, and now was at the centre of the celebrations; Frances acted as her widowed father's hostess for major events. Indeed, Francis Cornford had to set a subject for a poetry competition for the Chancellor's Medal:

---

[63] They were Frances Corrnford's step-sisters; Fredegonde married the economist Gerald Shove, and became a poet of some distinction.

did Frances think that 'Evolution' would be a possible topic? Jane started to write an essay on 'The Influence of Darwinism on the Study of Religions', but suffered a physical and mental breakdown, and left Cambridge, not returning until after the wedding.

So, could this be the start of a novel? As an ex-wannabe actress I was tempted. There are few smells more evocative than glue-size, dust, hired costumes and sweat, and few better sources than a drama production for what books about creative writing call 'conflict', which is shorthand for what happens when a character wants something, tries to get it, and encounters practical, physical, human or psychological obstacles.[64] And then I discovered that Joseph Wright of Derby, painter-in-ordinary to the Lunar Society, had actually painted a picture of The Lady: how could I not recognise such a sign?

* * *

I creep into the theatre, and no one stops me. The entrance is quite grand, but it smells of black paint and dust, and in the auditorium the odd bits of light which trail in from the lantern of windows above only make it seem dimmer and dustier. On stage Margaret's playing the piano and they're rehearsing a dance, for the Beasts, I think, although Comus – Mr Cornford – is sitting in the stalls with Rupert. Margaret keeps going, even though the score's handwritten, and even when the dancers stumble. And when they stop altogether, she picks up the music at just the right point again. I wish I could play like that.

The dancers stop again and Francis says something to Rupert, leaning sideways all in one: like a Spanish grandee, Gwen said once. I suppose I shouldn't photograph without asking, but then they'd move to answer me, and I like the way that as they talk their heads are close, as if what they're thinking about joins them.

---

[64] I learnt in my Drama days that, however smoothly a production is going, someone, somewhere, will always discover a problem that entails a great deal of rushing around and talking and coping in order to ward off the looming disaster. Eventually I realised that such crises were usually born of psychological necessity, to get everyone's adrenalin running, so that actors and stage crew alike could then use the blast of energy to enter into the state of controlled, single-focused disinhibition that performances need.

I click the shutter just as Rupert laughs, flinging his head back and into a shaft of light so it seems that a few more scraps of sun are thrown round the theatre.

Frances is standing at the end of their row. Mr Cornford turns towards her, suddenly swift and supple. 'My Lady?'

'We've finished the backcloth. Come and tell us what you think, before we sew the sovereigns on.'

'The what?' Rupert leaps to his feet and, rather than waiting for Francis to uncoil himself from the seat, steps over the row in front, and almost runs along it and through the pass door.

'Oh, Imogen, hello,' says Frances. 'How nice – have you been given a half-holiday? Come and see.'

I follow them through the pass door onto the side of the stage, where things get blacker and dustier and shabbier. We go up some clanking iron stairs to a room high up in the light, where a sea of dark-blue canvas is spread on newspapers on the floor. The air's thick with the chalky, oily smell of paint, and Gwen's kneeling by one edge, threading strips of webbing through big eyelets in the cloth. Rupert says, 'What do you mean, sovereigns?' and she looks round.

'Sewn on the cloth. Rothenstein wants there to be stars,' says Frances, going over to where the scene designs are tacked to the wall. 'Just held on with a stitch – Gwen borrowed a punch for the hole – so that whenever there's a draught, or the actors are moving, they'll twinkle.' She puts her finger on one of the pencil notes. 'Look.'

Rupert explodes. 'Sovereigns? Gold sovereigns? Gold *sovereigns*? Why not bring in a troupe of can-can dancers to liven things up, while we're at it? And real rabbits for the audience to coo over?'

'But Rupert,' says Frances, 'it says —'

'I don't care what it says, we are *not* turning Comus into a pantomime. It's a Masque – it's Milton, for God's sake! I won't have it. It's completely against everything the Society's trying to do. Francis, you're on the committee, you agree with me!'

Gwen gets off her knees and picks a small bag off the table. She plunges her hand into it, then brings out a handful of coins and tosses them towards the backdrop. They fly out, dark and bright gold, taking the light and falling with it down onto the midnight-blue of the canvas.

Someone gives a little gasp, a happy sound, and when Gwen smiles at me I realise it was me. Then she looks at Frances, but *she's* looking at Francis. I usually think he has an indoor face, old parchment, but today he looks like a book read by firelight.

'No!' says Rupert again. 'Francis, back me up.'

'Well, there is plenty of precedent,' says Mr Cornford and his hand goes to push the spectacles he isn't wearing up the bridge of his nose. 'Inigo Jones's designs for the Court masques —'

'That's not the point!' cries Rupert. 'This isn't Court, it's Ludlow – a family party! It's like Gwen and Margaret doing theatricals in the garden at Newham Grange. How are we ever to persuade a world raised on Dan Leno in Cinderella at Drury Lane that it needn't be – mustn't be —'

Frances puts out a hand. 'Rupert—' He stops. 'Would it be more bearable if we used half-crowns?'

There's a big, buzzing silence and then everyone – even Rupert – starts to laugh. In the end he says, 'All right, you can have three. And somewhere they can't be seen,' and I crouch down and start collecting all the sovereigns, to give them back to Gwen.

When we get back down to the stalls it seems that the dancing rehearsal has finished; there's another production coming in. It's only four o'clock; I'll be in time for tea.

Frances only has to go a few yards down the road to Christ's College – her father has asked her to join him in greeting some professors from Germany – so we walk together. Luckily she doesn't look painty; she's one of those people who always manages to be clean.

'Will Mr Rothenstein be cross if you don't do what he says in the design?'

Frances sighs. 'I don't suppose so. I do hate it when everyone argues. Gwen just keeps painting. Sometimes I think she'd keep painting if the sky were falling in. I do see what Rupert means – and of course it matters. It's just – so much noise...' Her voice trails off, as if it's run into the sand, the way Aunt Claudia's does when she talks about my parents, even though she never refuses to answer questions if I ask.

'I think people are allowed to argue about things which matter,' I say. 'What I hate is when people argue about things which don't matter.'

'Like what?'

'Oh, whether tapioca-pudding is bad for you if you put jam on it, or if you should leave cards on someone before they've been widowed for at least three weeks. Mrs Bailey spent half an hour discussing that with one of her friends. I know it was half an hour, because I was watching the clock.'

* * *

Even though no novelist would ever be so insane as to have three important characters named Frances, Francis and Frank, maybe – just maybe – it would work.

A story doesn't just have a beginning, middle and end, it *is* a beginning, middle and end. This time I'd found the beginning, so what did that tell me about what the end needed to be? In 1909 they were all children: adolescent spiritually if not in years, and still living, emotionally speaking, in their parent's houses while they tried to find their way out. It was a growing-up story, but what was 'grown-up' for these late-Victorian, Edwardian children?

There were only six years till August 1914, of course. But, instinctively, I recoiled from finishing them off in the mud of First World War France. Not that I could avoid it altogether, with all the male members of the clan in khaki and most of them junior officers, with the heartbreaking casualty rate that went with that rank. And I'm certainly up for working with the human consequences of war: my publisher had sold my debut as '*Birdsong* told the story of the First World War, *Atonement* described the Second, now there is *The Mathematics of Love*'.[65] Most of the reviews said similar things, plus or minus a reference to *Captain Corelli's Mandolin*: they were the natural namechecks although at that time I hadn't read any of them. But I didn't want to write a novel about the First World War, and even less did I want to write a novel which pretended to be about the First World War and wasn't. I was damned, in other words, if I was going to just sprinkle mud and poppies onto *Black Shadow and Bone*, like sprinkling monosodium glutamate onto cheap ingredients, just to get it published.

Mind you, perhaps I was right in a practical way too to eschew the First World War, since the weeks were ticking away towards 2014; it's rarely foolish to be pessimistic about how long everything takes in the book industry, from your own writing of a first draft to your publisher's decision about how to exploit the big buyers' promotional cycles. But if the end of the story wasn't at the Front, where was it?

I did know, I realised: I'd discovered it when I was first researching creativity in the family. If the beginning was *Comus*, the end was *Job*.

The story goes something like this:

A surgeon and scholar of William Blake named Geoffrey Keynes – who had married Margaret Darwin – had long been a keen ballet fan, despite the fact that classical ballet (as opposed to troupes in pantomimes and music halls) was not easy to find in Britain. But he haunted the stage doors of visiting companies such as the Ballets Russes, drawing in his older brother Maynard, who was already the rising star of British economics. Many merry and gay (in both senses) Bloomsbury evenings ensued, but then the cheerfully and openly homosexual Maynard not only became a ballet fan, but stunned everyone by falling in love with and, in 1925, marrying the extra-super-starry Russian ballet dancer Lydia Lopokova. Of all the books I read in order to write *Black Shadow and Bone*, Judith Mackrell's *Bloomsbury Ballerina* was the most fascinating, the most fun and possibly the most touching. I'd always vaguely assumed that Maynard's marriage, in his forties, to a

[65] A mathematical friend, reading that, said, 'So is yours about the Third World War, then?'

Russian ballerina had been a *marriage blanche* for some reason of passports or cover for the door of the closet. Not a bit of it: it was a real love story, and passionately and devotedly sexual. Mackrell, a dance critic, is also remarkably good at the very difficult business of conjuring up a sense of Lydia's professional and personal magic, from her origins in the Imperial Ballet School that we know from Tamara Karsavina's memoir *Theatre Street*, to her nursing the dying Keynes through the Bretton Woods conference that was shaping the post-Second-World-War world.

But the Bloomsburies were furious, struggled to adjust to the changed dynamic of Maynard's place in the sexual and intellectual politics of Bloomsbury, and took years to recognise and respect Lydia's intelligence and capacities. Meanwhile, the Ballets Russes had collapsed with the death of Diaghilev in 1929, Pavlova was also dead, and though Britain had two true and native-born ballet stars in Anton Dolin and Alicia Markova, there was no visiting or resident ballet company for them or anyone else to dance with. In 1930, the ballet critic Arnold Haskell joined up with composer Constant Lambert and, with Maynard as treasurer and the by now semi-retired Lydia as choreographer, they formed the Camargo Society. The explicit aim was to foster the establishment of a native British ballet tradition, and it succeeded: within three years the Society had produced sixteen new one-act ballets and several revivals of classics, and demonstrated that both the talent and the audience existed for home-grown ballet. One of those new one-act ballets was William Walton's *Façade*, and another was *Job, a masque of poetry and music*.

Job was based partly on the Bible story, but had roots just as much in William Blake's art. Geoffrey Keynes conceived it, writing the book with some help from his old friend and cousin-by-marriage Frances Cornford, by now a well-established poet, and asking Ralph Vaughan Williams to write the score. RVW would only join in if it was called not a ballet but a masque; he wasn't usually a cultural snob so I suspect his stipulation reflects the particularly low artistic status of ballet at the time. The Ballets Russes might be admired, but to a composer writing tough, Tallis-steeped symphonies, the nineteenth century trappings of pink tights and silly plots were presumably too much. Frederick Ashton choreographed it – bare feet and Robert Helpmann at his most spectacular as Satan – while Gwen Raverat, by now a well-known artist and experienced stage designer, designed the sets and costumes.

At the première in June 1931, *Job* was promoted and hailed as the first all-native English ballet;[66] shortly afterwards the Society cleared its debts with a spectacular production of *Coppélia*, and wound itself up, handing its more successful productions on to Ninette de Valois' Vic-Wells Ballet which, along with Marie Rambert's Ballet Club (later Ballet Rambert), was by then clearly here to stay. *Job* remained in the repertoire of the Sadler's Wells – later Royal – Ballet for many years; it was last revived in 2008.

Of course, whatever end you've decided for your story, the lives of your characters don't stop, whether they're real or imaginary. Ursula Wood saw *Job* early in its life, although it wasn't until 1935 that she got in touch with the composer and found herself instantly in love: 'I hadn't expected someone so large, and so beautiful', she wrote. I hovered over this – could I get it in after all? Big-age-gap relationships interest me.

Could I even – oh, please let me! Please could I somehow explore how Gwen's sets and costumes for *Job* were lost? As far as I could find out at the time, they'd disappeared when the Sadler's Wells ballet, having embarked on a tour of Holland in 1940, had to flee on the morning that Germany invaded the Netherlands.[67] What's more, a few hours later and not just Gwen's sets but the entire revival of British Ballet might have died shortly after it was born, because, along with de Valois, among those watching the 7th Flieger-Division floating down

---

[66] Mind you, research has shown that, like so many great innovators, Ninette de Valois deliberately drew a thick veil over a substantial preceding British tradition of dance, in order to emphasise both the need for and the newness of what she was doing. There was more of a real, original dance culture in late 19th and early 20th century Britain than until recently was recognised. But that's not to deny the central importance of de Valois and Sadler's Wells to the history of dance and ballet in the UK.

[67] I have since discovered that Gwen's sets were not lost then, but simply became shabby and outdated, and were retired some years after the war. I'm glad I didn't have to choose between the better history, and the better story, on that one.

were Margot Fonteyn, Michael Somes, Robert Helpmann, Frederick Ashton and Constant Lambert. The whole troupe then crammed themselves onto a blacked-out bus which struggled along roads clogged with terrified Netherlanders, before wedging themselves into the hold of a rusty Dutch ship at Flushing and praying not to be bombed. Even I know there's a limit to how many quarts of story you can squeeze into the pint pot of a novel, but maybe?

Or ought I to listen to the cry in my ears of 'But there weren't any Darwins on that rusty ship!'

It would depend on how I tackled it. But how on earth *was* I going to tackle it?

To get a sense of who and what I'd be starting with in the pre-War world, I re-borrowed Paul Delaney's book *The Neo-Pagans: Rupert Brooke and the Ordeal of Youth*. It's not a coincidence that before the Great War many of the central figures had been at the new, shockingly liberal, co-educational boarding school Bedales. The Neo-Pagans were all about socialist politics, mostly of a Fabian sort; faith in the mental and physical effects of fresh air, plain living and plenty of exercise; mixed, naked bathing at Granchester; plays and music; and a general air of doing things that parents and neighbours were being stuffy to disapprove of. There was, too, a strong homoerotic streak[68] which in some was merely the confusing remains of adolescence in non-Bedalian single-sex boarding schools, and in others the beginning of a life-long orientation. But underlying how they acted wasn't just a desire to shock maiden aunts and frighten parents; it was an honest rebellion against – or at least an honest exploring of – the boundaries of politics, sex, human relationships, art and what life was for. Like their cousin groups such as the Bloomsburies and the Cambridge Apostles, the neo-Pagans were genuinely trying to work out new ways of living, loving and thinking.

---

[68] Frances Spalding argues convincingly that Jacques Raverat's sometimes aggressive homophobia, which sits oddly with his passionate devotion to his friend Gide, and friendships with the likes of Duncan Grant and Maynard Keynes, has all the hallmarks of psychological projection. She also points out that a characteristic of the multiple sclerosis from which he suffered is violent mood swings, which goes a little way, though not nearly far enough, to explain his tone in writing about this and other issues such as the post- and anti-Dreyfusard anti-Semitism which was typical of him and his background.

Then I bumped into a writer friend and, as ever, the conversation turned to work. Like most writers, I'm cautious about talking about work-in-progress: perfectly well-meant reactions, catching you at the wrong stage, can really damage your confidence in your project's value and prospects, and that's the quickest route there is to ballsing up a book. But we'd had useful conversations before, so I told her. Had I read Jill Dawson's *The Great Lover*, she asked. 'It's all about Rupert Brooke.'

'No, I haven't. I didn't know she'd done him.'

'But you must,' my friend said. 'It's so good, and you need to know what how others have tackled it.'

As it happens, I actively avoid books set in the period I'm writing about, let alone those using the same characters.[69] Besides, I added, I tended not to read a lot of fiction when I'm in first draft mode, because I pick up voices terribly easily.

'But you *must* read this one,' she said. 'You really can't write this book without it.'

I didn't read it then of course – I have since – but I was disconcerted. It wasn't discovering that someone had written Rupert: that was hardly surprising, and in my novel he was only going to be a secondary character. But it did bring home to me the true nature of my project: here were huge monoliths of facts that many people know and many biographers and historians have worked on, and not only was I planning to write a novel in some very thin cracks between those monoliths, but even those cracks were not mine alone, but cracks which many novelists had already had a go at filling.

How – how – how on earth was I going to get free of this huge weight of *stuff* … when the stuff was so much part of what interested me?

Here was the trench-warfare in outer space again.

In her essay 'The First Mystery', Rose Tremain explores the process of turning researched material into creative work, and describes it so

---

[69] By which I mean historical fiction set then. Not, obviously, things written *during* the period of my novel: those are essential. I didn't read any fiction set in the late Middle Ages for about ten years, because that was how long I spent working in and around the story that became *A Secret Alchemy*.

perfectly that I have actually learnt this quotation by heart, the better to produce it for students:

> ...all the research done for a novel – all the studying and reading, all the social fieldwork, all the location visiting, all the garnering of what is or what has been – must be reimagined before it can find a place in the text ... Graham Greene, when asked by a journalist how he would make use of an important experience he'd had in South East Asia, replied: 'It's yours to remember and mine to forget.' He was talking about the novelist's task of reimagining reality. Reimagining implies some measure of forgetting. The actual or factual has to lose definition, become fluid, before the imagination can begin its task of reconstruction. Data transferred straight from the research area to the book will simply remain data. It will be imaginatively inert.

That freewheeling work of imagining something which doesn't exist is what used to be thought of, crudely, as 'right-brain'[70] stuff: disorderly and a-rational, intuitive and heedless, simultaneous and un-hierarchical, spinning together things that logic and experience would keep apart. The creative brain, in this mode, has no sense of the duty to be correct, to conform to the necessary conventions of communication, society or the book industry. It's the later stages which used to be labelled 'left-brain': the Inner Editor which is[71] orderly and logical, conscious and judicious, sequential and rule-observing, 'conventional' in the proper sense of working with what's common to both writer and reader, such as cultural context and knowledge, and language and its conventions. Of course any sustained creative imagining is actually the product of a constant to-and-fro between these two 'sides' of the brain, but it is true that a new idea – and the writer's first shot at a paragraph or a novel is essentially, a very rough new idea – is tender and must

---

[70] I know the relationship between the two sides of the brain is *much* more complicated than that really, but it's a useful shorthand for a difference that so many creative artists recognise.
[71] Mind you, many writers find that sometimes what they think is a constructive Inner Editor is in fact a disguised, and destructive, Inner Critic.

acquire its own form and substance before you're safe to let the Editor in, and start work on making it better.

In 1932, a schoolmaster of Frances Cornford's seventeen-year-old son John sent some of John's poems to W. H. Auden, who was then teaching in a prep school in Scotland. Auden treated the poems respectfully – what sort of a poet John would have made is one of the more interesting 'what if?'s of the history of the art – and went on to say:

> The real problem for you as for every other writer ... is that of the Daemon and the Prig. Real poetry originates in the guts and only flowers in the head. But one is always trying to reverse the process and work one's guts from one's head. Just when the Daemon is going to speak, the Prig claps his hand over his mouth and edits it. I can't help feeling that you are too afraid of making a fool of yourself.

Notice that both Daemon and Prig are necessary; because poetry 'only flowers in the head', simple outpourings from the gut will never make a poem any more than the fluid, undefined, 'forgotten' stuff that Tremain talks about will make a story on its own, without undergoing the process of reconstruction. The difficulty – not unconnected to Charles Darwin's distrust of scepticism – is to stop the Prig trying to control what is originated. You can't reverse-engineer creative work, Auden is saying: you can't work your guts from your head.

In a project like *Black Shadow and Bone*, the factual-historical Prig could so easily claim too much power, too soon, over the Daemon-driven imagination. My creative sense of story, of humans and their actions, might work to unfold – to evolve – who these characters were and how they experienced and acted in the story's events. But on every shelf of the library, in every Darwin expert, enthusiast or nut, and above all in my own mind, there waited a judge whose hand was poised to clap over the mouth of my imagination, and silence me.

* * *

John was never tired for long; Frances used to say she'd never had or known a child who needed less sleep. One June morning in Cambridge I'd got up at dawn, as I often did, to catch the light on Coe Fen and the Backs, and found him and his brother Christopher up to their knees in a stream, building a pontoon bridge to attack the enemy that intelligence had discovered were in ambush behind the mill on the far bank. John would have been – what, about ten? – and by the time hunger began to clamour in all our stomachs, we had quite a serviceable construction, although when I walked on it it my grown-up weight sank it a good foot below the surface. The boys did better: I took a photograph of Christopher, still featherweight enough to be walking on beer crates and scaffolding planks, and then John, seeming to walk on water, and then I took them back to Hardwick St with me to dry out and have breakfast before they ran home. But once he'd left school he was at once too close to his home, and pulling too hard away from it, for me to reach him safely.

And then, of course, we all began to realise that if you wanted to fight fascism you might have to embrace war.

What would John be becoming, if he hadn't gone to war? What's the future that he's lost? How would he have been shaped by it? How would he have shaped it? Would he have changed from his black-and-white Marxism, and begun to see colours again? It's so hard to know, of these boys and girls who were born into a world that was already broken.

We who served – you can see the Great War in our eyes. But apart from the ones who are truly wrecked, we are who we have always been. The Great War is just the colour of our eyes as blue is, or brown. But it is true to wonder what would have happened to us all if it had never happened.

...

After the Great War my friend Barbara found herself in a series of London bed-sitting rooms: Madame Violette in her smart little dress-shop would only pay what Barbara's salesmanship was worth, which was not very much, and they always ended up sacking her. I remember giving her lunch one day in Cambridge, and she fell on the chicken and ham pie and baked potatoes which was all I'd had time to make. It was a week since she'd eaten meat, she confessed, and she spent the evenings in bed because then she had enough shillings to heat her room at the weekend. Then one day she got invited to a really smart dance, full of girls doing the Season. Without asking she borrowed a dress from Mme Violette's stockroom, and went to the ball. And when she arrived the ballroom was full of frocks; white and pink and green and blue, ribbons and beads, silk and satin and muslin. She was early: the gentlemen were still on their way from the port-and-cigars of dinner, or the office, or the House of Commons. She talked to a few girls she slightly knew, but there were still no gentlemen: no black tailcoats, no white ties, no pumps and waistcoats ... Then the frocks shifted and moved, and at the far end of the room she saw two, elderly, rather bent little men in tailcoats.

And that was it. There were no men. No men to dance with, no men to marry.

Only you can't even say that either, really, can you. You can't say, *she would have got married if there'd been enough men still alive to go round.* You can say something's true of a generation – of a nation – of a sex. You can add up the statistics. But that doesn't mean it's true of each member of that group. The closer-in you get, the less true the general statistic is.

One swallow doesn't make a summer, Gwen's brother Charles said once. He was arguing cheefully that women have a greater genetic investment in their children than men do, and were therefore the natural carers of the young. I'd quoted his own grandfather and namesake, who – Gwen said – had observed his own children every day for the first three years of life, scientifically, making notes... but if little Annie or even littler William started to cry, then the man of science became 'a most kind nurse', until they were happy again. I remember Uncle

William: a smiley old white-haired man with a stick, and Gwen's favourite of her uncles.

'The exception doesn't prove the rule,' said Charles to me, simultaneously admiring the clock one of his sons had dissected. 'And one swallow doesn't make a summer.'

And he was right, of course. Seeing a swallow in winter doesn't make it summer. But what you saw is still a swallow. And, maybe, a swallow that means more. What's true of a population may not be true in any real way at all of a particular person.

Not of Barbara. And not of me.

RUPERT BROOKE
1887–1915

9

Imogen

I've abandoned my desk and am striding round one of the standard, forty-minute loops of walk that my father would have called a constitutional,[72] and which I do every day. It's not just a basic health precaution for anyone who works at home, it's also because I do my best thinking when in motion.[73] Now I'm thinking wistfully, but also resentfully, how much, much easier it would be to write a novel about someone fictional. Not just easier – ease is never a good enough reason in itself for writing something a certain way – but also more fruitful, richer, more interesting, more creative than merely animating

---

[72] In which I suspect he was being a Cambridge child: the walk along the Cam to Granchester was a classic constitutional for generations of undergraduates.

[73] I'm not alone in this: Dorothea Brande in *Becoming a Writer* is eloquent on the uses of – for example – scrubbing the floor, as thinking time. Straightforward driving is another activity where the editing brain goes off duty and the creating brain can range free – not least because driving itself is a 'right-brain' activity.

biographies is ever going be. I'd be making something new and whole; something which never happened. How much more true it would be to what fiction really is and should be, than this hybrid thing I'm trying to conceive!

But I can't do that, my Inner Agent is arguing back. I can't build it on someone fictional, because then it's not about the family.

Then I get it: that gap-jumping spark – *the* creative moment when a connection is made. Like the little squeaks of radiation which are the echoes of the Big Bang, the spark is a tiny remnant of the invisible charge that blasts across the gap which Michaelangelo put between God's and Adam's fingers – and something new comes into being.

What if the central character *is* fictional – an outsider – and I insert them *into* the family?

Now we're getting somewhere.

So, who? It must be someone who isn't just an observer, but someone whose fate is bound up with the family. *The Great Gatsby* is not about narrator Nick Carraway, it's about Gatsby. But Gatsby matters painfully to Nick, so the arc of the Gatsby-Daisy story and the arc of Nick's telling of it are interdependent.

Who would want to join in with this big family? Who could I slide in, who would leave the mere factual chronologies and events fairly undisturbed, and yet still give me scope to do some real, proper imagining and creating?

My main characters often seem to be alone, cut off from family and other support networks in some way. When an interviewer pointed this out I was taken aback and had to think about it,[74] before I could explain that a novelist is in the business of knocking the props away from under the main character until the character reaches the crisis point: it helps if there weren't too many props there to start with. But it's also because I am a middle child embedded in the middle of a sprawling family on both sides. Just as brother-sister relationships intrigue me because I see them but haven't experienced them from the inside, I'm intrigued by lives lived – and viewed – without a family context.

---

[74] Which is one reason interviews can be fun: they make one think.

So, what if the centre of the novel is a fictional orphan, or near orphan? What if she – it seems to be a she, and I'll let that stand for now – what if she comes to feel that this group – three or four houses in the heart of University Cambridge – are the nearest thing she has to a family? What if they draw her in or, rather, are kind and welcoming and happy for her to tag along …

But that still doesn't get me away from the problem of – no, the *risk* of – of docu-drama literalism. If all I'm doing is animating *Period Piece* and *Gwen Raverat*, I know that's what it'll end up like, with Tremain's 'inert data' plopped onto the page. How do I make sure, for the sake of my sanity and in the cause of a novel worth reading, that I can get away from literalism?

All poets have had feedback which is too simplistically literal, I reflect, and then remember my cousin Ruth Padel's sequence *Darwin: a life in poems*. When I'm asked if I'd write a novel about The Ancestor, I sometimes say that it would be much more possible if I were a poet, but that Ruth has beaten me to it. Poems can be faithful to the particular stuff that they're working with but they are still allowed to stand alone: they may make literal sense, but they don't have to, and still less narrative sense. In fact, Ruth's are minutely faithful to the record – she even has marginal notes – but they still somehow take off from it, like the red balloon, and fly. A poem can be a journey – one of Ruth's best books about how poetry works is called *The Poem and the Journey* – but it doesn't have to be a story. Stories, because they need a literal chain of cause-and-effect, a plot of some sort, are so much harder to free from their tethers and make fly.

I'm thinking back to other ways I've tried to make things less ploddy. There was my idea of writing short stories on Emma's spaces, even if it did come to nothing, and I've been experimenting with snapshots of Tom's life – though he would have to have lived until the 1860s to connect that word with photography. They begin with his death and go backwards, so there's a double-consciousness: our knowledge of what's to come for him inflects his every moment.

And some of my favourite photographs involve frames, reflections, and reflexive references to things which used to be there or aren't there yet, and many of my favourite novels do too. What if my central character – what if she – what if Imogen … Yes, Imogen, of course. And she's a – she's a photographer. Of course. Her lens can be my lens, and she is powerfully – even irrationally – terrified of losing her negatives … She falls in love with the very earliest colour photography because it would give me something new to me and new to her century to grapple with … The maiden aunt who brought her up in Cambridge, who knew Sir George Darwin, and through whom she met Gwen and Frances and all the others … And years later Aunt Claudia is long dead, and Imogen has no anchors: no lover, no child. Everything is broken. Somewhere around *Job* she lost her 'family'; these friends, the Darwins who'd been the underpinning of her life, from *Comus* to *Job* …

* * *

from *Get Started in Writing Historical Fiction*

Write: objects hold stories

Think of an historical object which you've never seen, but know would have existed. It might be a toy your German grandfather left behind when he came to England on the Kindertransport, or the dagger that Brutus used to assassinate Julius Caesar. Don't look things up, and don't worry about being accurate for now. Bring the object to the front of your imagination and make notes to evoke its physical presence. Make sure you've checked in with all six senses including kinaesthesia (what's it like to pick up, hold, throw, sit on?).

Now start imagining outwards to one moment in its life, and keep jotting down notes. You probably first thought of the big moment – grandfather leaving the toy behind, Brutus holding the dagger – but our first thoughts are usually our default ideas: rather well worn or clichéd. So imagine further: where else might it have been? And where else again? Maybe your grandfather's toy had been his grandmother's. Maybe Brutus's dagger had been captured from a Phoenician slave-trader. Again, this is crazy first draft stuff: let your imagination run.

When you've found an atmospheric place, start making notes. Is the object here old, or new? What's around it? Again, go beyond your first thoughts to your second or third: are they more interesting? Who in this setting might have interacted with your object? Who else? Who loved it? Who hated it? Why? Pick one of those people. What did they do with this object? Hide it? Sell it? Buy another? Steal it? Destroy it? Give it away gladly? Give it away reluctantly? Who to?

Draft a story jumped off some of these ideas. Don't worry about it being historically accurate or polished. This is a crazy first draft: a rough-hewn story complete with a beginning, a middle and an end.

* * *

Since, as it happened, I needed to head north from London anyway, I emailed the National Media Museum at Bradford with the confidence I never had before I was published. I was researching a novel involving early Autochromes: might I come and look at some?

In the Museum's entrance hall, at 11am, it's full-on chaos of still-bouncy children and still-cheerily-in-control parents. I half-enjoy, am half-embarrassed at asking to queue-jump because I have an appointment in the archive and (I don't say) the need for coffee before then.

Photography is the on-again-off-again love of my life, my creative love long before writing became my marriage, and luckily a love which is content to be dropped and picked up again. I worship the work of Walker Evans and Henri Cartier Bresson as much as I do that of Henry James and Hilary Mantel, and I love the stuff of my craft. Besides, being a writer of fiction, I tell stories much of the time as photography does: through the physical bodies of *things* as they hold ideas. In Bradford, inside the Kodak Gallery of the history of photography, this stuff is profoundly satisfying. I know just enough of why the cameras are how they are, what each could do, what each couldn't; my mind's eye sees the cameras by the sea-side, in the high-street, on the battlefield; my mind's finger tips sting with the sharp, clean knurls on the brass wheels as I imagine racking out the lens; my mind's ear hears the crackle of the paper round a roll of film, the faint creak of the bellows' oil-cloth, the smooth slot of darkslides and the click-clack of reflex mirrors; my mind's nose smells the tarnish of blown magnesium powder, and the fish-and-chip vinegar of the fix in the 1930s bathroom set, with its open developing tank and an enlarger sitting on the lid of the loo.

At noon, in the wide, quiet, scentless, windowless Archive room is a smooth grey trolley where an archivist has set out what I asked to see in a couple of tidy stacks of all the traditional plate- and half-plate sizes, from matchbox to 8"x10". On the table is a light-box and a pair of cotton gloves, and I'm not to use pen, only pencil, for making any notes; at other tables sit another researcher or two, while the staff archivists gently come and go. Some of the plates are in original or modern passepartout boxes, some are wrapped crisply in brilliant white archival tissue, as perfect as Christmas presents, some have their own worn leather cases with a mirror in the base to reflect the light back up through the glass, because Autochromes are basically big, beautiful glass slides made in the camera.

A packet of ten Autochrome plates, with its Lumière & Cie. label, cost ten times the equivalent size with a monochrome emulsion, and the exposure is ten times as long, but the developing process is almost as simple because the chemistry is essentially the same. When the shutter opens, the light passes through millions and millions of tiny grains[75] of starch dyed red and green and blue, and darkens the light-sensitive emulsion behind them in direct proportion to the different colours. This makes a negative, and once the dark-and-light of the exposed emulsion is first reversed, by means of a careful sequence of chemicals and precise flashes of light to make a positive, and then fixed, you can view them

---

[75] The grains and suspended in the gelatin are potato starch, which somehow seems a delightfully French solution to the problem of finding a substance which is both tiny and consistent in size. But, being organic, this emulsion was a nightmare for the photographers of Empire and is still one for the archivists of today.

against a light source, or projected by a special, high-powered magic lantern.

I'm nervous in my cotton gloves, as if I've offered to wash Meissen porcelain and been given gardening gauntlets. Because the exposures for Autochrome were very long, the images tend to be static, brightly lit and brightly coloured: gardens full of geraniums or bougainvillea; still lifes of oriental silks and turkish vases; sunlit villages in Cornwall or Jaipur; patient, English Rose daughters in red capes; and Hungarian peasants willing to put on traditional dress and sit still in the sun. But because the grains of the emulsion are perceptible, Autochrome images have a physical presence that Kodachrome can never have, let alone a digital image on a screen: they have a visual, visible texture which to the eyes feels like an Impressionist or pointilliste painting. It's that physical presence which you're holding in your hand, made by the light of those few seconds, and preserved while the real people move and go on living and die, and the real trees grow and the real buildings crumble. But each direct positive such as an Autochrome is as unique and therefore as vulnerable as a negative. If the glass gets broken, if damp or mould or even insects get to the grains, if the plates are left in the special, ten-times-as-powerful magic lantern for a minute too long ... the image has gone. I had given orphan Imogen a terror of losing negatives for two very good reasons: it suited her psychology, and it suited my need to put her under pressure – and, of course, it was true to the medium.

It was also true to the history of the medium, and my family; Tom Wedgwood never did discover how to fix his 'sun-pictures'. Perhaps Gwen's kindly father, knowing Imogen's interest in photography, had a dig in the shelf of family books, and lent her a copy of his brother-in-law's *Life* of his great-uncle. Would Imogen not be rather thrilled to find this?:

An Account of a method of copying Paintings upon Glass, and of making Profiles, by the agency of Light upon Nitrate of Silver. Invented by T.WEDGWOOD, ESQ. With Observations by H. DAVY. Journals of the Royal Institution, Vol. 1, 1802

The alterations of colour take place more speedily in proportion as the light is more intense. In the direct beams of the sun, two or three minutes are sufficient to produce the full effect. In the shade, several hours are required, and light transmitted through different coloured glasses acts upon in with different degrees of intensity. Thus it is found that red rays, or the common sunbeams passed through red glass, have very little action upon it: Yellow and green are more efficacious, but blue and violet light produce the most decided and powerful effects.

And what would Imogen have photographed, back in 1907, when the miracle of colour photography came to Cambridge? What did she see in colour – and what would that mean for the writing of her? What would she be remembering, thirty years later, as she struggles to understand how she's ended up alone, belonging nowhere and fitting no-one's pattern of how lives are lived, and yet alive and still with a life to lead: a swallow in winter? Would that seem to be monochrome? Would colour seep back in, as she slowly, painfully re-makes her life?

* * *

In those days colour film was expensive and colour pictures were hard to sell. It also required a measure of good luck in exposure, as well as a great technical accuracy, that was beyond what even the experienced photographer in monochrome has to cope with. But for those who love the medium, it was worth all the expense and all the uncertainty. Imogen saved her colours for the moment when she saw something which spoke in colour, and so needed colour to speak.

She remembered on her first day off in Compiègne after arriving at the Red Cross post; the shop still had a few boxes of Autochrome plates. The Lumière factory wasn't making them now, said the shop owner; these were relics from before the War, but they should still be good, they had been carefully kept. She bought three boxes, which was all she could afford, and carried them back to her billet. Those boxes were as small and heavy as silver ingots; later the little rolls and canisters of Kodachrome lay in her palm like scrolls or neat phials, like jars of precious Rennaissance colours: the best and purest gold kept for halos, the best and richest lapis lazuli saved to clothe the Queen of Heaven.

A great cathedral window, from inside, blues and reds and greens making prayerful angels and demons and a purposeful-looking saint on a prancing horse; she'd had to calculate the exposure three times and still it wasn't perfect. A slab of blue sky, a wedge of inky, sun-sparked sea, a slice of yellow sand, and cutting across them all a black, crooked shape more like a jagged hole torn in the film than a living human hobbling home. A tiny shop in a village – *the* village? – toffee-coloured plaster and baskets of oranges and limes, big cabbages with leaves almost baroque in their elaborate curves and reticulated green, two open barrels with the dirty-silver curls of salt cod showing like surf, a crate of bottles with gaudy caps and neck-labels, and, as it happened, two figures in the doorway ... Was one of them him?

10

The White Space

The river side of Newnham Grange.

Writing a novel isn't just about getting the story you've imagined down on paper or screen. Knowing the *what* of the story tells you quite little, in itself, about the *how* of the business of telling it. Who's telling this story? Why are they telling it? Where are they telling it from, relative to these events? What do they know beyond these events? What other characters' experience do they have access to? What order should it be told in?

These aren't easy decisions to make, and you have to commit to them while the novel is still very cloudy – albeit a real and sparkly and profoundly exciting kind of cloudiness – in your mind. But such decisions are at the heart of my job, just as tackling the difficulties in deciding how to build a complex new machine is an engineer's job, and I love the days when my work is doing this kind of thinking.

The obvious answer to 'Who's telling this story?' was, of course, Imogen.

* * *

We moved to Cambridge because Aunt Claudia had been appointed Lecturer in French at Newnham College. She bought a little house in Hardwick Road for her retirement, but for now it was let out, and I went to board with the Baileys in Harvey Road.

I was fifteen. As a settling-in present Aunt Claudia gave me a camera. It was my father's camera, the one that was all he brought with him, almost, on the ship from Australia, and that's all Aunt Claudia knows about him, because he never said a word of what came before he emerged from the mists of Tilbury docks and married my mother six months later.

And, being Aunt Claudia, she also gave me a book about photography and how to do it, and a whole five pound note to do it with. I'm in my room at the Baileys, with my arms in the sleeves of the thick, silky changing bag, fumbling my first-ever exposed plates out of the magazine and into the developing tank. And Mrs Bailey comes in. I've taken some photographs of Barbara, she says, and she wants to see them. I only photographed Barbara because there wasn't much else to photograph: we're the same age, but we're not really friends, not yet. I try to explain that the plates are exposed – that they must stay in the dark. That they aren't anything she wouldn't like – nothing that any mother of any well-brought-up girl wouldn't like – and she can see them as soon as the plates are developed and fixed and dry. My hands are tied by the bag and I'm trying to get the plates into the tank and get the lid on straight so they're safe from the light. But it's all new and I'm clumsy and blind and the bag's hot and rubbery – my hands are all sweaty, and she – she grabs me, and pulls open the bag so hard that the buttons burst off and I'm crying, but the light has sent my pictures into the dark as surely as the fever sent my mother and father there: so completely, so utterly, that I can hardly remember them.

And the next day at my still-new school, in Prayers, I don't ask for anything. Usually, I'm asking for a good mark, or sausages for lunch, or please will I make some friends, even though I know perfectly well that's not what prayers are supposed to be for. Still, the Deity in charge of these things looks, I know, rather like my new not-school-friend Gwen's grandfather, and He has been known to oblige.

But instead, that morning at school, I made my mind feel deep down into the place in my own belly where the things which really matter lived – the real joys and the real hurts – and when I'd found it I planted a vow that I would never, ever let anyone destroy my photographs again, if I had to die stopping them. And the Deity, whoever He was, was my witness.

* * *

And then it slapped me round the face. Imogen would be an internal narrator, telling her own story, and so by the current conventions of mainstream fiction, I could only represent the Darwins to the extent that Imogen was there, and through her own voice and her physical and mental point-of-view. So however hard I tried to stitch her into the fabric of the family, when she wasn't there, my reader couldn't be either. Everything else would have to be conveyed second-hand.

On the other hand, if my narrator were outside the events of the story – the external, privileged, knowledgeable narrator often unhelpfully called omniscient – I could narrate Darwins whenever and wherever I wanted. The narrative could have as much context and perspective as it needed, inhabiting and conveying to the reader as many characters' consciousnesses and points-of-view as I chose.

* * *

'Gwen, my dear!' said Geoffrey, kissing her cheek. 'Margaret sends her love. Such luck to be coinciding in Paris. What are you looking at?'

She held them out: copies of *Manon Lescaut* and *Gil Blas*. 'Penguin are thinking of licensing some English translations.'

'And you to illustrate. So, which do you prefer: the bitter and beautiful path to tragedy, or the witty climb up life's long ladder to success?'

'I need to decide which will work best. And the Penguin printing's awful – did you see how dreadful *A Sentimental Journey* looks? Horrible paper and worse ink. I'll have to bear that in mind.'

'But you didn't sell them the rights to the Sterne images, did you?'

'No, no, only a licence. And *my* prints of the blocks sell quite well.'

'Good. I thought they were splendid – vigorous and earthy. Just right for Sterne. These will be different. Specially if you do *Manon Lescaut*.'

'Yes,' said Gwen. 'I thought I'd save some money by getting copies while I'm here. I... couldn't find them at home.'

She didn't say that these days she was mostly reminded of Jacques more by such absences than by any presence: gaps on the shelves of her life: the silence after she'd thought something and he should have been picking the thought up from her; a patch of sun by the back door where his climbing boots should have stood, covered in mud.

Though Geoffrey *might* have understood. He'd known Jacques before she did, after all: all young men together, grabbing at the life and art and ideas of the brand-new century, seizing and shaking them out and weaving them together. They were so sure that if they only grabbed and shook and wove hard enough, cleverly enough – and oh, they were clever enough – then everything would make sense and the world's grimnesses and griefs, as Rupert put it once... Surely, if they could only understand it well enough, it could be made better.

Yes, we used to think like that, Gwen thought, smoothing the cover of *Julie, ou la Nouvelle Heloïse* without really seeing it. Till we saw that sense and cleverness was no defence at all against governments who *wanted* a war. And later of course we thought we'd never let it happen again, that we were grown up, that we *wouldn't* let it happen again. But now? Look what even the people who think they're trying to make the world better will do to each other. Look at John Cornford.

Gwen shook herself. It must be the sharp, smoky air that made her think like this. The smell of Paris was like the light of the Fens: a slanting, captious clarity. It surprised you all the time by what it hid, and what it showed you more sharply than you'd ever seen.

'Who do you think I bumped into on the Night Ferry?' Geoffrey said when they'd found a café a few doors further along the rue de Rivoli, and he'd ordered. 'Nicholas Rowan.'

'Imogen's husband? How was he?'

'Oh, seemed very cheerful. I didn't gather what brought him to Paris. He's with Macmillan, apparently, so I assume it was business. They've separated, he said.'

'Who?'

'Nicholas and Imogen.'

'Yes, I knew that,' Gwen said, as behind them the coffee machine began to hiss, while the waiter set up a clink and clatter of cups on the zinc. These were the noises that made her feel she'd come home when she came to France – noises of ordinary life, and the smell of the cigarettes, the sceptical sounds of the waiter talking to the man who delivered the coffee beans, the fluting of those two women's voices over their *cafés-crèmes*. The shape of the panelling and the brass of the bar, too: the different proportions of pale to dark, straight to curved, the way the February light smeared as it fell through those tall windows and tipped the brim of a hat here, a nose there, a fork, a glass of *marc*, mollusc-like bowlers on chairs, the mackintoshes hanging on the wall like sea creatures waiting for the tide.

* * *

Gwen really did illustrate Sterne's *A Sentimental Journey*, but I hadn't only been reading books about the family. These Between-the-Wars folk seem so like us in so many ways, with their motor cars and telephones and visible legs, their democracy and vaccinations and film stars, but Philipp Blom's *The Vertigo Years* shows how so much that we think of as the texture and dynamics of the modern world was already there in 1910; *The Great Silence 1918-1920*, is Juliet Nicolson's exploration of the structure and texture of British society's post-War grieving; in *Singled Out* Virginia Nicholson tells the remarkable stories of the way women after 1918 dealt with losing all hope of being married. I'd also devoured Juliet Gardiner's magnificent *The Thirties*, Jane Robinson's *Bluestockings*,[76] Katie Roiphe's gorgeously gossipy but also informative *Uncommon Arrangements*, and dozens of others. I'd had a good excuse – not that I needed one – to go back to Dorothy L. Sayers, E. H. Young, Elizabeth Bowen and Graham Greene.

I knew that *Black Shadow and Bone* would be threaded with creative thinking crossing the boundaries we erect between making and analysing, between science and art, between poetry and engineering. And because the family's webbed together by science and art and always has been, I decided to book-end each chapter with Tom, discovering photography, thinking about vision, longing to see further.

And, in the same way that I write orphans to write about families, in *Black Shadow and Bone* I would use the not-having of children to write about having children. First, in the usual way – the way Imogen expects – the way that … *yes*!

Among the grandchildren Erasmus Darwin – always called Ras – was 33 in 1914; he'd been born, just, in his famous grandfather's lifetime. He made a steady climb from an excellent Engineering degree at Cambridge to the workshops of the big engineering firm Mather &

---

[76] And felt shame at Bernard Darwin's only fairly shamefaced admission, in *The World that Fred Made*, that he was one of the thousands of undergraduates who rioted against the idea of Cambridge's woman students being admitted as full members of the University and being awarded degrees.

Platt in Manchester, and thence up the professional ladder until he was Company Secretary of the iron- and steel-making company Bolckow & Vaughan in Middlesborough, which also owned collieries and salt works; he was, as well, a director of his father's Cambridge Instrument Company. I found him on a passenger list for a professional trip to the USA, and listed for the Army Territorials a couple of years before the War, all of which are mentioned in a surprisingly long obituary in *The Times*.

There's no sign of a wedding, a wife, a fiancée, or anything much except a taste for sociable walking and climbing, and a love for Cambridge May Week balls and boat races which brought him back to his parents' home almost every year. Was he in love with a married woman? Was it simply the family habit, in the men, at least, of finding satisfaction in work and friends, and not getting round to marrying till their forties? Or was he gay?

Having been in the Territorials for years, he was commissioned immediately as a Second Lieutenant in the Green Howards, was sent to France in April 1915, and died at Ypres. His men buried him in a shared grave with his colleague Captain John Nancarrow, although the grave was at some point before 1918 obliterated by the fighting, and he's now only a name on the Menin Gate.

I gaze at the photograph of Nancarrow on Wikipedia … Maybe … It wouldn't surprise me … Who knows?

I don't have to care. Imogen was only fifteen when they'd first have met, in 1908, but it's the way of teenagers to grow up faster than late-twenty-somethings.

Here, at last, was some white space: the First World War made it, and I can write on it.

* * *

She could pretty much understand the mathematics and geometry on one of Ras's blueprints but he could *read* them, to create in his mind the snorting, clanking, murmuring nature of the machine that didn't yet live.

But it was only at the last that Ras learnt to read, not just understand, what Imogen did.

An autumn day snatched from 1914, the flank of a Suffolk valley that Constable would have recognised: the trees on the turn to copper and brass, and a tangle of rosehips and mountain ash. The swallows are sitting on the telegraph wires and talking about flying south. In the sun-struck distance a stretch of stubble-gold is being rolled over, furrow by furrow, to chocolate brown, the horses planting their stately, feathery hoofs and the seagulls hovering like bridesmaids behind the plough. Ras is looking at her, his chin on his hand, because she's just declared that the pointillism of her colour photographs might be more true to a subject than the perfect detail, the precise record, of black and white. And to persuade him, she's told him not to move, reached for her camera, put in a colour plate, and taken the photograph.

And later that week she ducked out from her darkroom under the stairs at Hardwick St, to where he was sitting, smoking and reading *The Times*, and showed him what she meant. No, the exact forms weren't rendered so crisply – the detail and structure of the trees, the parts and joints of the plough, the bones and build of his face. No, they didn't show so well. But look how the colours were patterned across the plate – how they danced and glowed as they had that day, how copper played against chocolate, how the seagulls were made into lace and feathers by the grains of the emulsion. How because of the slow shutter the horses' great heads were blurred, nodding with the weight of everything they know. Didn't that, too, say something about the day?

A fine and ever-wakeful sense of beauty. Who said that? She couldn't remember, but it was written of Thomas Wedgwood, who was the first person to use light to make images on paper. Gwen's father showed Imogen a book about him once: Tom was his great-uncle. Good scientists – good engineers such as Ras – they knew that sometimes you don't reason, not for now. Sometimes you just stay awake to it ... sometimes you just watch.

Ras went on watching for a long time. At last he said, 'I think I see what you mean. At least, I don't understand it. But I think I do feel it.'

A colour plate is unique. It's all you have. If it gets broken or damaged it's gone forever.

The tears were harsh on Imogen's wind-sanded face and she put up her gloved hand to scratch them away.

* * *

So, through the summer of 1914, I decided, Imogen and Erasmus Darwin inched towards courtship, he teaching her to drive (handy for when she wants to drive ambulances) and she coaxing him towards understanding visual arts and poetry. And then the war broke out.

The real Ras turned down the offer of a senior job managing munitions in the safety of Britain: at that point in the war new junior officers had an average life expectancy of six weeks,[77] but he decided he couldn't let the men of his unit go to the Front without him. And nor, I decided, could my Ras bring himself to propose an engagement to Imogen: what if he were maimed, or broken in mind? She mustn't be tied to him. Did she persuade him that she wouldn't mind? That they shouldn't worry about the future, but do what they could to be happy today? That would be a scene I'd like to write.

Then when he was killed at Ypres in 1915 – shot dead on 24th April, which was not his sixth but only his first week at the front – Imogen lost her hope of become a real, married-in, legal part of her adopted family, and lost, too, her hope of a child of that family.

* * *

Nick didn't say that he'd climbed up the hill to Imogen's billet, the summer's heat already beginning, to bring her the news that was

---

[77] Junior officers had a far higher mortality rate on the Western Front than either other ranks or senior officers. By 1918, when my non-Darwin grandfather was delayed going to the Front by measles, average life expectancy for junior officers was down to three weeks. Before he recovered, the Armistice had been signed, or I might not be sitting here writing this.

all over Valetta: the news that Rupert Brooke had died. They'd been friends in Cambridge, he knew, although he rather thought it was a different chap she wrote to. But then, everyone had a brother or a cousin or even a father at sea or at the front whom they wrote to, out of love or friendship or simply duty. So when Nick heard at the ambulance station that Brooke had died of blood-poisoning before he even got to the Dardanelles it seemed wrong to let Imogen hear casually, as she went on duty.

He found her on the roof of her billet, sitting under the canvas that she'd stretched for shade between two chimney stacks: sitting stunned, half-blasted with shock, with a telegram pressed to her belly as if she could somehow bring something – anything – to life again.

DEEPLY REGRET ERASMUS KILLED 24TH APRIL YPRES LETTER FOLLOWS WHEN WE KNOW MORE MUCH LOVE NORA

There was no one else to read what she had read and know it, no one else hold her while she wept, so he did, awkwardly.

When at last he found the strength to tell her about Brooke – because it had to be done – she said, as if the words were wrung out of her, 'The day before … Oh God! Ras – my darling Ras … Now Rupert …' She wasn't looking at him, just staring out over the roofs to the horizon. 'It's never going to end, is it? It won't end till there's no one left alive to be killed.'

SECOND LIEUT. E. DARWIN.

GRANDSON OF THE SCIENTIST KILLED IN ACTION.

We regret to announce that Second Lieu-' tenant Erasmus Darwin, of the 4th Battalion Alexandra Princess of Wales's Own Yorkshire Regiment, was killed in action on April 23. He was the only son of Mr. and Mrs. Horace Darwin, of The Orchard, Cambridge; and a grandson of Charles Darwin.

11

John

So Ras was dead, but I still had nearly twenty years to cross before I reached *Job*. What else could forge Imogen's deep, emotional connection with the family – and what could then break it?

Could I make her have conceived Ras's child, out of wedlock, in 1914? It would involved changing or distorting *so* much of the real family history: another baby Darwin, an invented cousin for my own, real father, an element which would be present in every interaction with these real people. Could I do that? Yes, I decided, if I made Imogen run away and make a new life with the baby, if in the end I could, as it were, leave the future of the family unchanged. No, if I was going to keep her involved with the family. And for reasons of good storytelling (coinciding with commercial good sense) I *had* to keep her involved with the family in the present. Besides, knowing that such a baby would be an invention made a storyline of that kind feel like a cliché: a vulgar, bolt-on gravitas which courted the reader's tears as crudely as any plastic poppies and quick-mix Flanders mud.

When in doubt, go back to dates and ages. From 1914 to 1936 meant that Imogen would be forty or so ... The generation just old enough to have fought the First World War as adults would be bringing the next generation forth into a bitter, corrupted peace. And somewhere, on that theme, I remembered coming across a comparison between the Neo-pagans growing up and entering the First World War, and the next generation growing up and entering the Second.

Compare Rupert Brooke, the golden boy of golden summers before the War, the beautiful, brilliantly clever and conscientiously Fabian socialist poet who volunteered at the outbreak of war and died on a hospital ship moored off Skyros. Rupert died of septicaemia, of all unglamorous deaths, because he was already ill with dysentery when a mosquito bite went septic in those pre-Penicillin days; he died on his way from the siege of Antwerp to Gallipoli, and was glorified because a young (or at least young-ish) Winston Churchill, as First Lord of the Admiralty, was badly in need of a national hero.

* * *

'I think that I was made to be a soldier.' That was Rupert, stock-still at midnight outside the Auberge d'Aragon in Valetta in 1915. 'With soldiering you know what you want – what you're trying to get. Love – all the dirty little deceits – it drags everything else down to its own muddle. For men, anyway. For me... You women – I don't know. I've never known.'

* * *

Compare him with John Cornford: the young man with a face like a dark cliff, the equally brilliantly clever, fiercely and orthodoxly

Communist poet,[78] the precociously political teenager who looked around him at the grimness of the Thirties and saw that though everything seemed to have changed after 1918, actually nothing had; the veteran of the great hunger marches and the Battle of Cable St, who came to an embittered, embattled certainty that if Communism didn't win, then Fascism would.

* * *

'It doesn't matter if I'm wounded – or killed. As long as the cause is still alive – as long as the will of history is being fulfilled – what does an individual life matter?' That was John. 'All I'd regret would be that it wouldn't be me fighting any more.' He said it quite seriously, as an article of a faith which for him explained everything – made sense of everything.

* * *

John Cornford was the oldest son of Frances and Francis Cornford, so he was, you could say, the child of Comus and The Lady; he was named Rupert John for the Attendant Spirit, because he was born five months after Rupert's death. He was christened, to atheist Gwen's surprise, and one of his godfathers was Geoffrey Keynes – so why not slide Imogen in there alongside? Childless Imogen.

When war broke out it could be Imogen who went with Gwen and Jacques to France, as Jacques desperately tried to get the French Army to take him on as an interpreter. Imogen could take the chance to buy as many Autochrome plates as she could get her hands on before Lumière & Cie. ran out. And when, after Rupert's death and John's birth, Frances sank into another profound depression, in my novel it would be Imogen who came to the rescue. Working for the Red Cross and coming home on leave, she would help with baby John and his big sister Hilda, and support Francis when he came back from Catterick in Yorkshire where he was teaching marksmanship. She'd welcome Army

[78] From not needing any sleep to the bust of Marx in his school study, as he told me, Adrian Mitchell based Judd in *Another Country* on John Cornford.

surgeon Geoffrey back from France and share Margaret's joy at their engagement; she'd rejoice in Gwen's pregnancy; she'd write to Charles and Billy out in France with the Royal Artillery, and to RVW driving ambulances in Salonika. When the Armistice came, and everyone tried to put the pieces back together again after the deaths of Ras and Felix and Cecil Wedgwood, and more children were born and Jacques died, Imogen would be part of the web of cousins and friends, stitched into the life of the nearest thing she had to a family of her own.

Then John, going to Republican Spain in 1936 as a journalist to report on this brave new world of practical Communism, volunteered on the spur of the moment to join the militia established by POUM, the *Partido Obrero de Unificación Marxista*, which at the time was larger than the official Spanish Communist Party. I would give photographer Imogen just enough commissions to finance her following him – along with a side-order of anger that back in the UK the Spanish Republic was supported by neither the government, nor most of what wasn't yet called the media – and send her off with a Press Pass to Madrid.

John was killed on December 26th 1936, his twenty-first birthday, or on the 27th: no one's sure because no one found his body. Now, in 2016, as Spain has yet another try at confronting the legacy of the *Guerra Civil*, the pit of burnt bodies from the battle of Lopera – burnt for hygiene, not revenge, perhaps – may yet be dug up; but nothing is decided.

In 1937, I decided, Imogen escaped from the Spanish Civil War, northwards, and was wounded getting across the border into France. That was where the novel would start, and when, for some of Imogen's most exalted, distressed or simply concussed moments, I found myself slipping from the narrative's third person and past tense, into the contextless immediacy and transience of first person and present tense, I let it happen.

* * *

I open my eyes and the air is cold on them. The woman standing by me isn't Aunt Claudia, but the nurse – nun – nurse – nun.

There's something else. Something new.

But at the moment I can't think, only feel … because John is dead.

Yes, that's the new tears. My boy John, who isn't my son but was always my boy.

Now that I'm more awake the pain is becoming a sensible size. I lift my arm a little: it's bright. White: the weight is a plaster cast and it sends fire up into my shoulder again.

'*Il est cinq heures moins quart*,' she says. Quarter to five? She thinks I'm looking at a wristwatch. John would have laughed. Those last days in Madrid: how his poet's eye saw things aslant, and his newly-acquired soldier's eye saw them as unavoidable, so that he could laugh, and get you to laugh with him.

Oh God!

'You must lie quiet, Mlle Lefranc,' she says. She's talking French. 'You have a bad concussion and you have broken a bone in your wrist. The doctor comes from Luz tomorrow, in the afternoon. Then we will know more.'

'But where is this? Where am I?'

'This is the infirmary of the Convent of the Sisters of Mercy, Gavarnie, Hauts Pyrenees. Now, you must sleep.'

How can I, when John's dead? Horrible, urgent grief swells again, swells as if it never, really, went away: urgent because I must tell. I know he's dead, and no one else does. I try to sit up, but I don't seem to have any power left in my body at all. 'I must tell them about John. They need to know. His mother doesn't know – oh, God! Frances doesn't know!'

She presses me back down, her hands on my shoulders. 'They will be told. Don't worry, *le bon Dieu* will make all right. But you must sleep.'

I try to resist her – fight against her hands – but she's immensely strong, it seems: a sort of nightmare. It's like pushing against something more than human and it's hopeless; she forces me down against the pillows as if she hardly notices my resistance, and then my bad arm gives way and I collapse. I've lost. Tears start to squeeze out of my eyes.

'They will be told, *ma p'tite*.' She slides her hands under my shoulders, straightening pillows, and I can't even resist that. 'The man who brought you here assured us. You've nothing to do except sleep and pray to *notre Seigneur*.'

'How did I get here?'

She hesitates, then says, 'He didn't give his name.'

But I know it. He'll tell them and I don't have to. I don't have to push through five years of silence to find Frances and tell her about John. She will know that her child has been killed on the road to Lopera. Yes, the name comes to me. The Cordoba front. Boadilla. They lost Boadilla. I can remember that much, at least. Frances will know, and I won't have to coffin my own pain out of respect for hers, keep quiet and steady for her, because it was she, not I who conceived him, carried him, bore him ... because John wasn't flesh of my flesh.

No one is.

I can't claim John as my own, but he's gone from me, as everything goes, in light – heat – fire. *A crack of black lightning*, one man said in the Great War as we loaded him. In Salonica, that was, and by then it was all just a job, ordinary, leaving me sense enough to hear his words, and let them weave into my memory. *A crack of black lightning, and I knew I was done for*.

'*Not done for yet*,' my mind says, the way we always used to, however torn the body or the mind we said it to.

But I am done for.

12

1937

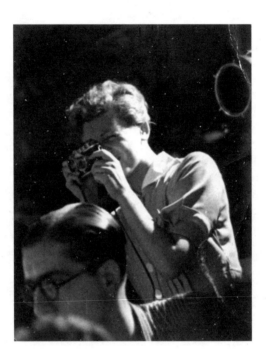

As Imogen gets better physically we learn how she came to have a place in this family which wasn't hers, how when war broke out she joined the Red Cross and was posted to Malta – Malta for the connection with Coleridge, though I don't know how I'll make it – and because I can raid *Testament of Youth* for local colour. But Imogen was an ambulance driver not, like Vera Brittain, a nurse, because that's more fun and more unusual to write, as is Salonika[79]. I wanted her to see

---

[79] Early 20th century spelling, of course, so no K in the novel's Salonika, I decided, apologising mentally to any future copy-editors, typesetters and proof-readers. I try not to be high-maintenance in these matters, but even when, as a writer, you've stopped chasing the chimera of 'authenticity',

more of Ralph Vaughan Williams, and luckily I never did find out if the Red Cross sent woman ambulance drivers to the Balkans or not, so I could put her there.

But what happened after Ras was killed? Was Imogen simply going to be the 'surplus woman' whose fate – for good, surprisingly often, but also for ill – Virginia Nicholson evokes and analyses so well in *Singled Out*? In 1919 what was left for so many women was a celibate spinsterhood: half a life by almost any of their contemporaries' standards, at best a second-best life. And besides, I wanted Imogen in 1937 to have more sexual experience, and a more complicated, contested sexual history than that. Nick was a pacifist ambulance-driver to contrast with Ras as the longstanding volunteer soldier, and he won a medal for courage under fire to contrast with how Ras never had a chance. Imogen married Nick because he was kind and decent and it was better than what else there was for her. Nick proposed to Imogen because what else there was for him was the love of men – which would echo Tom Wedgwood's sections – and so the frustrated, sad, frightened or sordid life that the law condemned them to. But of course Imogen and Nick's marriage didn't work sexually or emotionally, because for both of them their marriage could only be a half what it might have been. When in affection and friendship they knew that it must end, Nick agreed to do the decent thing, as Colonel Jos Wedgwood did. But then their landlady, believing that no man, not even a judge, should put asunder those whom God has joined together, betrayed their arrangement to the King's Proctor. Their divorce was thrown out, and Nick and Imogen remained tied to each other.

Hugely sympathetic to Imogen's miserable situation and the insecurity of the creative professions, I decided, Gwen would offer Imogen sanctuary in Vence, up in the hills behind Nice, where the real Gwen had moved with the invalid Jacques and their young daughters Elisabeth and Sophie. Here Imogen slipped into a different kind of half-a-life. While helping my Gwen with Jacques she met married Klaus,

---

period spellings are such a simple way to defamiliarise a narrative set in the past that they're impossible to resist.

whose wife is elsewhere, and had a long affair with him which was creatively and professionally fruitful, but which ended bitterly: he ended their relationship because he backed out of getting a divorce but, when Imogen's divorce fell through, he proposed they start their affair up again. And, I realised, there would be another, even more fundamental way that Imogen's is only half a life, lived second-hand: the Darwins are primary to her – her 'family' – but she is secondary to the Darwins, and when the breach came (*note to self: work it out*) it didn't change their lives by more than a Christmas card. The only Darwin she stayed in touch with was John, and it's the need to stay close to John – the nearest thing she has to her own child – which drives her to Spain.

This, then, was Imogen's back-story, as the film-makers have taught novelists to label it. And her front-story (which is not an official label, but should be) – what was that? As she convalesces and Europe inches closer to war, each of these lost parts of her life rise up again not just in her memory, but in her present: her estranged husband, her married ex-lover, and her old life as an adjunct to the Darwins. The novel would be the story of how, partly through these encounters but even more through the memories they bring to the surface, she learns to believe herself worth more than half a life, and to live at more than second-hand.

What is the 'more' that she's worth? It won't be hard to write her working to re-build her creative and professional self, but what of her emotional self, whose foundations are so much weaker and more damaged? Is there a new, tentative possibility of love? This must be a man for whom Imogen is primary, not secondary, but who's willing to stand back and help her to be herself. However, before you join me in a good feminist rage about defining Imogen's future in terms of men, it's worth saying something that doesn't get said often enough: lovers (and foetuses, and death, come to that) in fiction are as often the embodiments of the story's structure as they are the subject of the story. So, a story exploring the complexities of the human need for sexual and familial love will use actual and potential sexual partners to embody something about your main character's story. That *doesn't mean that love, sex or motherhood define her and her fate.* It just means, first, that fiction must embody ideas in things, and second, that most humans would rather try to establish familial and sexual partnerships than not try.[80]

In terms of hours, an astonishing amount of writing time gets spent on innumerable small problems found and solved, but for every tiresome detail which you discover you can't bend to your will, something surprising comes along for which you can do nothing but render thanks to whichever saint is in charge of historical novelists. I found that 1937 was the year that the Matrimonial Causes Act fought its way through to become law. It was initiated by the journalist and playwright A. P. Herbert[81] and passionately supported by Jos Wedgwood, whose own efforts in the previous decade to get reform through had come to nothing. Might Imogen see the news, remember Gwen and Ralph's MP cousin Jos, and get in touch, as part of building that full-time, first-hand life for herself? Tick another box for Darwin links if she did.

It was time to see what Catriona thought about how this novel was developing. I revised what I'd done: each chapter was topped and tailed with some of Tom Wedgwood, making 30,000 words altogether and so between a third and a quarter of my projected wordcount. I gave it a quick, fierce polish, called it *A Swallow in Winter*, and emailed it to her. What did she think? Did it look as if it was working? Kind friends

---

[80] Cheap fiction explores fundamental desires cheaply and simplistically, good fiction explores fundamental desires richly and sophisticatedly; to dismiss a book because its project is to explore sexual love and come to some kind of resolution is like dismissing *Macbeth* because it's built on the same ambitions as *Dallas*, or *Crime and Punishment* because it and *Robocop* both create stories from violence and redemption.

[81] Herbert had, to his surprise, been elected as one of the MPs for Oxford University, and then come high in the ballot for Private Members Bills, which gave him a chance of actually getting something into law. He chose divorce reform because in 1934 he'd published a novel, *Holy Deadlock*, inspired by the same nasty charade that Jos Wedgwood and my Nick Rowan went through. Herbert later published a delightful and rather moving little book, *The Ayes Have It*, about the process of getting the Bill through Parliament in the teeth of opposition from all sides but with support from unexpected quarters, including many clergy, and even bishops in the House of Lords. Among slews of letters was one which said, 'Please God, your Bill will pass unmutilated. I am a Roman Catholic, a happy wife and mother, but there are others in this world of ours who most grievously are not. With what anxiety they must be waiting the result of this truly great reform. We pray for you.' Herbert read that to the House of Commons at the crucial Second Reading, and the Bill passed by 12 Noes to 78 Ayes, although that was by no means the end of its journey to the final announcement of 'Le roy veult'.

said, 'Don't worry, I'm sure she'll love it.' Close friends knew that the previous novel hadn't worked out, this wasn't under contract, and I was doing something that I didn't—

No, it wasn't, by now, that I didn't want to do this project. I'd found a way that I did want to work with family stuff, a form which did play to my interests and, I hoped, to my strengths: something that would – touch wood! – sell, while still being true to me and my writing self.

And thus I joined the ever-changing company of writer friends who have work out there with agents and editors and are suffering the misery of Waiting To Hear, and got on with writing, teaching, blogging and parenting.

* * *

Thursday, December 15th, 1791: After a little snow overnight, the sun is brilliant and the view towards Burslem is soaked in light. By eight o'clock old Josiah has stumped off to the Works and Jos is riding into Stoke to catch the London Mail. At twenty-two he is already a shrewd businessman; there are sales contracts to see to, and the ambassador from St Petersburg wishes to discuss another commission.

Tom goes to the laboratory. It's cold, for he cannot have the light of a fire. He locks the door, just in case, closes the shutters and then the curtains, and lights a single candle. He moves about the dim room as easily as if it were the nursery – the pottery – the billiard room. He measures two gills of distilled water into a glass beaker, unseals the paper of silver nitrate which he brought home yesterday from the Works, and measures one ounce in the scales: it glitters craggy and white in the candlelight as the pan dips. When he tips it into the water its old name comes to him: *lunar caustic*. He stirs to dissolve it. What might a poet make of such a name? One answer comes immediately:

The sun to me is dark
And silent as the moon,
When she deserts the night

Hid in her vacant interlunar cave

That's *Samson Agonistes*, but he can't recall if Milton wrote it before, or after, he was blind.

The solution is made, but he holds it up to the candle to make sure it's completely clear. Then he takes six squares of fine white leather from a box, and opens a glass frame which the works carpenter made for him. Leather works better than paper, he has established: one day his sister caught him eyeing up one of her evening gloves. 'Stop it, Tom!' she cried. 'Buy your own, if you need more.'

He takes a square of leather, lies it on the workbench, brushes it evenly, steadily, with the silver nitrate solution, and sets it in the frame. He repeats this with the rest, and stands, watching the leather squares until the dampening has evened. Then he consults his notebook, and leaves the first leather empty. On the second he lays a small wooden block; he spent a happy half-hour in the old nursery upstairs, looking through their old building blocks. On the third he lays a cylinder he also found: he's slightly sanded it on one side so that it will not roll. On the fourth he sets a profile of his mother, copied in black ink on thin white paper half-an-inch narrower all round, and on the fifth the same but with the paper oiled to transparency. He recalls watching, entranced, how the artist who took the original profile drew her silhouette on a glass while his mother sat still, with the lamp beyond her head almost burning her ear. On the fifth he places a vineleaf from the greenhouse, and on the sixth a dragonfly which he took from the collection he made with Jos when they were boys. They found a grass snake by the front door once, and in the larder a spider bigger than the palm of Tom's hand. And once at Litchfield with Ras and Robert Darwin a great, black Devil's Coachman of a stag beetle, although Uncle Erasmus said their range is not thought to extend further north than Berkshire or thereabouts, and would not be not convinced until they showed him the creature.

Finally Tom closes the frame over all, and covers it with a black velvet cloth. He opens the curtains and the shutters so that sun and snow-light pours in. Then he opens the window; the air crackles with ice and behind him the candle dips and streams in the draught as if it's angry at being superseded. Tom sets the frame on the sill, takes his watch out of his pocket and opens it. Then with the other hand he whisks away the cloth.

Two minutes seems a lifetime, but the leather begins to tarnish: at first a faint, silvery-grey like the under-curve of a snowdrift, then the soft brown of his sisters' braids. The profiles and the dragonfly, which stood out so clearly against the white of the paper, appear to sink into the darkness as the leather they lie on turns to the irridescent almost-black of a starling's wing. Then he casts the cloth back over the frame, sets it back on the workbench and closes the window, the shutters, the curtains.

This moment where the dark stoops over him before his eyes have adjusted ... It's always a moment he dislikes: a moment of un-steadiness, of dis-orientation, of dis-ease. Milton might name it a shadow of the Divine, or of its opposite. One might instead conclude that the physical effort involved in the iris contracting draws in some way on the body's vital forces. Tom decides it is merely a moment – a fraction of a second – when perception is adjusting to material conditions. But even as he can see his way again he can't help but observe his stomach's queasiness and the shiver which travels from his upper arms and through his body.

Then he takes up his notebook and a pen, draws the candle close – for he has established by experiment that nitrate of silver in a concentration of 10:1 will not darken by candlelight in less than twelve hours – and opens the frame. He lifts off the objects and sets them aside. Then he studies the sun pictures, making notes on each one: colour, evenness, hue and image. The block has left a neat, white square but round the edges of the cylinder and the dragonfly's body the tarnishing is shaded: a kind of penumbra, he notes. The dragonfly's wings are perfect: in both it and the vineleaf the veins and more solid structures are delineated exactly by the sun. You might almost think you could raise the paper to your lips and blow the leaf away. And would the dragonfly take flight?

Most interesting of all are the two profiles. The plain paper of the first profile has blocked all light from reaching the nitrate of silver on the leather, so that it is all white, and only the blackened border reveals that it was ever exposed.

But on the other, where the oiled paper is half-transparent, the paper below is faintly tinged, a brownish dove-grey, and where his mother's profile was black, the profile on the leather is absolutely white. The image has been reversed.

He has known this would happen, but to see it! He sits quite still, observing: waiting to see anything that he has not yet seen, waiting for observation to become thought, waiting for thought to become idea.

13

On the Night Ferry

THE NEW TRAIN FERRY BOATS

SLEEPING CARS EVERY NIGHT between LONDON (VICTORIA) and PARIS | VIA DOVER-DUNKERQUE | FAST THROUGH SERVICES EVERY DAY for GOODS, CARS & PERISHABLE TRAFFIC

Full details of Services, Fares, Rates, etc. from
SOUTHERN RAILWAY CONTINENTAL DEPARTMENT, VICTORIA STATION, S.W.1.

Once you have an agent you know that your writing will be read when you send it. But that doesn't mean your agent will think it works, and Catriona didn't think my first three chapters were working.

'I made a note of each new name as I met it,' she says. 'And in that thirty thousand words there are sixty – *sixty* – of them. And mostly in the back-story. In fact most of everything's in the back-story sections.'

'But that's kind-of the idea,' I say, more because I'm staving off the inevitable realisation that she's right than from much conviction that, all those months ago, I did actually make the right decision about how to create this novel.

'But it's all in the past, and there's such a lot of it. And anyway, there isn't really a story there, just a chain of things which happen.'

I probably say something which signifies approximate agreement while not committing myself to what to do about it.

'The back story isn't the real story,' she goes on. 'I got someone else in the office to read it as well, and she felt the same. And the real story – the "now" story – isn't very interesting at all.'

We talk for a while longer, me scrawling notes about her thoughts without – yet – trying to work out what I might do about them. Catriona's no doubt hearing my voice getting steadily more disheartened, because she adds, 'She said how well-written it is.'

It's always good to hear that, especially from someone who's worked with so many wonderful writers. But I can't help thinking, 'I know it's well-written. That's my job. The day I can't turn in a well-written manuscript is the day I really *shall* throw in the towel. It's just …' and this was thinking that I only did after we'd finished the phone call and I was storming round the park '… it's just everything else. Everything *bloody* else.'

In his book *The Craftsman*, social philosopher Richard Sennet describes a crucial part of any craft – from 15th century goldsmithing to 21st century Linux programming – as problem *finding*: intuiting and then analysing what, exactly, it is which doesn't work. Solving the problem comes later. But throughout that big, baffled, stomping-round-the-pond, despairing, I-give-up, I'm-damned-if-I-give-up, red-or-white, where's-that-bloody-corkscrew day, though I could see what the problems were, and agreed with Catriona about them, I still couldn't find the *real* problem.

Problem: too many people? Then just cut some of them.

But my people were there because the whole point of the novel was to embody what the family was like: the arts-and-sciences, the connections, the overlaps and differences, the similarities. How could I reduce the size of the cast while staying true to what I was trying to bring alive in the novel? And to make the novel thick with family, I'd instinctively gone for lots of connections with Imogen, rather than one big one.

Mind you, that was my respectable reason for the big cast; my less admissible reason, which I only acknowledged weeks later, was that I'd been reluctant to inhabit a single family person's head and consciousness too closely, because that would either mean making up too much, or writing a biographical novel.

Problem: too much story in the back-story? Then just cut some of it.

But the back-story *was* the story, in the sense of being the story of the family. Without the back-story, this was no longer a novel about the family.

Anyone who's ever been in a writers' circle knows the sound of a writer explaining just exactly why they did the thing which the whole group is telling them doesn't work, and just exactly why it must stay as it is. With rare exceptions, that isn't because the writer's convinced that they are the next Proust, but because they're imagining the piece without the bit that isn't working, and seeing, rightly, that the story is much impoverished: it is just less than it was. It will take a completely different kind of imaginative work to put new, different things in the place of what's gone, and get the story back to its original richness – albeit made of different riches. Seeing beyond *what is* to *what might be, but isn't yet*, is the central challenge of the drafting and re-drafting cycle. I knew that, yet here I was, *but – but – butting* away with the best (or rather the worst) of those defensive writers

Problem: too little story in the frontstory? Then just put more in.

This, on the other hand, was relatively easy. I would make 'Now' – 1937 in France – the main story, the big story, and 'Then', from *Comus* to *Job* and Imogen's great estrangement from the family, just scraps and memories.

But with much less being told through the filter of Imogen's memories and so coloured by her voice, the voice of the narrative was losing its character. Voice, as Courttia Newland says, is the 'dark matter' of fiction: it's the human interface between the reader and the story-universe, and so it holds everything together. I needed the voice of *Black Shadow and Bone* to be one side of that human interface, to have a personality … but what kind?

I thought about storytelling and storytellers … Who might tell this story? Imogen wasn't the type to sneakily turn out be a narrator after all – she isn't a writer – and I didn't want it to be explicitly me. But a novelist? A mid-century novelist? I wasn't trying to pastiche Rose Macaulay, or (*per impossible*) Elizabeth Bowen: this entity wouldn't be named, nor even be a fully-realised character. But she would be writing from the war which the readers – though not the characters – know is coming.

* * *

Two days later *le train bleu* huffed and snorted its magnificent way into Nice-Ville with as much drama and ceremony as if it had come from Istanbul by way of Sofia and Venice, and not merely twenty miles along the beach from Menton. In those days the Blue Train took nearly twenty-four hours to get as far as Paris, loop round it, and reach Calais, and no doubt it will again, but that makes it no more tolerant of tardy passengers than any of the other great trains of Europe. The engine is huge, and, attached like an afterthought behind the last of the glossy blue *wagons-lits*, are the second- and third-class sleepers: boarding them feels rather like being a servant clambering into the dickie seat of a Bentley to spend the journey staring through the rear windscreen at the gentry inside. Or a child left outside a pub on a country walk, thought Imogen, while father goes in to buy bread and cheese and beer and orange squash. She heaved the lunch basket up the steps into their carriage: Mme Bouchard had the utmost scorn for the catering of the *Société national des chemins-de-fer*.

…

In those days, of course, there was no blast-tape on the windows of London, no posters and placards about sirens and shelters, no gaps smashed, no cascades of brick and stone and glass, no tarry, brutal baulks shoved into place to hold up what remains. And Paris? Those who know are those who will not, for the duration of the present emergency, tell what they know.

* * *

I had a structure and a narrator, so I had a form.

I had a story-journey which needed a much bigger and more dramatic plot-route.

I decided that the man who helped Imogen over the Pyrenees was Theo, my Czech photojournalist from *The Mathematics of Love*, who had been in the Spanish Civil War.[82] And I gave him a print journalist half-brother, Miko; when Theo arrives in London he has some of Imogen's photographs, and Miko falls in love with them.

I still needed a villain.

And I needed to go to France.

* * *

It wasn't busy in the restaurant car and Nick had a table to himself to spread the text-book manuscript out. The whisky and the sandwiches – even other human beings around him, strangers though they were – all did the trick. It was like being back in a more than usually amiable staff-room. Vaguely he noticed the change in the wind's note as they went through a station, and the rattle of the bar's shutters going up. 'Folkestone,' someone said. 'Not long now. Just Dover Priory, and then the docks.'

A hand clapped him on the shoulder. Nick jumped. 'Nicholas Rowan, my dear fellow!' said a voice. He blinked but couldn't place the bony, long-chinned face stooping above him, or the bright eye. It was faintly familiar but who the devil was he? 'How are you? And what's the news of Imogen? I haven't seen her since *Job*.'

Job was – oh, yes, that ballet she photographed. The name came to Nick: Geoffrey Keynes. Cambridge friend of Imogen's. A doctor, but something literary too – the ballet was his idea. 'Keynes! How nice to see you!'

---

[82] I love it when other writers' major characters from one novel turn up as minor characters in another (Mary Wesley does it very well), so I assume some other readers do. It's a metafictional joke if you care to read it as that, but even for the reader determined to stay inside the frame and reading as if this all happened, the second novel feels wider: part of a larger world than simply its own.

Keynes glanced at the bar. 'This carriage stays in England, and I've got some whisky in my compartment. Care for a nightcap?' Nick hesitated. 'I can usually sleep under any conditions, and what I didn't learn about sleeping on call at Barts I learnt in a field hospital cot. But even *I* am defeated by the racket they make on the Night Ferry.'

'Is it that bad?'

Keynes grinned. 'Well, first they couple up a shunting engine and shunt the coaches in batches onto the steamer. And then they chain down every single set of wheels, one by one. Chains. And *then* they jack up the coach bodies, one by one, to take the pressure off the springs. And then they slam the ship's engines into forward. And then the hooters go to make sure all the good citizens of Dover are also wide awake. And then we're off. And a couple of hours later they reverse the whole process at Dunkirk. And if you can sleep through that lot without morphia, you're a better man than I. You can get a good four or five hours before Paris, though.'

'Whisky sounds like a much better idea,' said Nick. 'Thank you.' The other inhabitant of Nick's compartment was probably asleep by now, so it wouldn't make much difference.

Clots of salty, rusty air buffeted them from the open stern as they clambered across the rails. There was no platform, of course, and only a rickety wooden step placed to help the passengers get up. The door of the carriage was at head-height. Nick was reminded violently of troop trains: of sidings and depots, names and places scrawled in chalk, the endless, helpless waiting, the stench of dirt and cold sweat and war.

'Are you in this one?' said Keynes. 'I'm next door, but we can go through from here.'

Nick reached to pull himself up into the coach, but the manuscript under his arm slipped. Keynes caught it before it fell. Then he climbed up too, and tucked it back under Nick's arm. Nick stood back to let him lead the way along the corridor and through to the first class coach.

'Sit down, sit down,' said Keynes, lifting an attaché case onto the washbasin, opening it, and taking out a bottle. Sitting down was easier because First Class, Nick realised, had the upper bunk folded flat against the wall; nothing to bump your head on, and no snoring stranger either. And they still gave you two glasses: one each for host and guest.

'So, how are you these days?' Keynes was saying. 'And Imogen?'

Better get it over with, thought Nick, sipping whisky. It *was* very good in a strange, harsh way. 'You know that we separated?'

'Oh, no, I didn't. Sorry to hear that. Are you still schoolmastering?'

'No, I work for a publisher – educational, textbooks, that kind of thing. Actually, I've your brother to thank for that.'

Keynes raised his eyebrows. 'Maynard?' Nick remembered Imogen saying something about Geoffrey resenting his astonishingly brilliant older brother. Perhaps it was that which put a – a *twist* into the way he said the name. 'He was helpful?'

'Yes, very. I was – well, looking for a way out of teaching, and Mrs Bell introduced me to him. It must be ten years ago, now. He put me in touch with Macmillan, and luckily they'd just had a junior editor leave.'

'Ah, yes, those Friday evenings. Vanessa the presiding deity. She was always particularly kind to my wife and me. And our boys, too; they've practically grown up with the Bell boys.' He sighed. 'Vanessa's terrified that Julian will go to Spain. And after poor John Cornford ... '

Nick made sympathetic noises about having seen the news about John – so sad.

Not that he'd ever really felt at ease among them all. It was all very well for Imogen. *She'd* practically grown up with them – or rather, she'd grown up in Cambridge, with Darwins even more than Keyneses. But he'd always felt leaden on those Friday evenings, not to mention stupid.

Imogen protested once that Vanessa and Virginia and the others never *showed* they thought you leaden or stupid. At least not in ways they could help.

No, he'd replied. *But still—*

Yes, you're right, she'd said, the way she did, suddenly finding words for him that said what he could only feel. He sipped his whisky. *If you aren't at your best, the talk edges you into a backwater, and the river of the evening streams past. Just out of reach.*

It was one of the nights that it was good to have her there, good to be rolled together by that wretched bed: companionable. But he wasn't going to tell Geoffrey why he was going to France.

On the other hand, he did have one thing – perhaps the most important thing – to thank those Friday evenings for. He sipped again. It must have been one of the first times he and Imogen went, and he couldn't remember what the joke had been, though it was Maynard who had made it. Everyone had laughed, and then a friend of Maynard's – a painter, a beautiful man – had leant forward and kissed him full on the mouth.

And no one had turned a hair, he remembered. Then the talk had started again, but Maynard and his friend … they'd stayed looking at each other. They neither spoke, nor moved, but as if Nick had been wired in parallel, he felt whatever was running between them run through his own skin and inwards, deeper, like a galvanic current, so that every molecule of him was changed. From then on he knew, with his mind as well as his body, that you could – you really *could* – love the same person with your body and your mind. And a few weeks later, at midnight, as Imogen and he walked back to Doughty St, he had asked if she would give him a divorce.

Keynes was looking at him, and then he started to ask Nick about medical textbooks.

Nick thought later that if he hadn't had a fair bit to drink already, and if Keynes hadn't been so intelligent about what so often was wrong with medical education, and if the coaches hadn't been shunting and banging about as they were hauled off the steamer, reassembled and hitched to a French locomotive, he would have been quicker on the uptake. Perhaps he'd even have read the signs much earlier, in the bar, and been more careful. Not mentioned Maynard, for one thing. But he hadn't had much practice at manouevres and evasions when it came to sex; not the sort of practice which he knew from Imogen most women who worked got, and from Alec that some men did: men who looked like Alec, at least. Nick had never been the kind of man who other men make passes at.

He settled the folder of manuscript more firmly on his lap. Keynes moved towards him to point at it, saying something about proof-reading marks, and reached across him to turn a page. His forearm was warm against Nick's chest.

Nick downed his whisky so fast it seemed to rasp his throat, and stood up away from Keynes, bumping his head on the wall after all. 'Thank you so much – just what I needed. But I've just remembered that – that – there's another chap in my compartment. I think I'd better go back and go to – get myself sorted out while all this noise is still going on. Otherwise I'll be disturbing him just as it's gone quiet.'

Keynes stood up too, undisconcerted as far as Nick could tell. 'Of course. And do give my best to Imogen when you see her.' Nick had his hand on the door. 'Actually, Rowan, if she has any letters from Rupert – Brooke, I mean – I'd be most grateful for sight of them for the *Collected Letters*. The Brooke family have asked me to do it. *Most* grateful. Fully acknowledged, of course. *I* certainly don't cherish any ill-will.'

'Any ill will?' Nick said, wondering madly if his own polite, if clumsy, evasion could merit ill-will, even from someone like Keynes.

'Towards Imogen. For all the furore over that article. It was my wife who was so upset. And Gwen, of course. Those Darwins, bless them – so straightforward! And of all of them Frances had the most cause to be upset, but she may have forgotten. She's ill again, as you may know.' Nick hadn't known. 'God knows what poor John's death is doing to her … But you know as well as I do that one shouldn't let family matters spoil a scholarly project. In fact, I'll write to Imogen myself, but if you see her first —' He got up, fishing a card out of his waistcoat pocket, and held it out to Nick.

'I'll tell her when I see her,' said Nick, backing out of the compartment. 'Good night. I hope you have a successful conference. And thank you for the drink.'

'Not at all. As well as the letters – you will keep in touch, won't you? The Royal College of Surgeons will always find me.'

14

In the Mountains

None of that, I suppose I should emphasise, ever happened. It's fiction. Nick Rowan is fictional, and my 'Geoffrey Keynes' is not the Geoffrey Keynes of the record – although mine is consistent with the record. 'Get over it,' I say robustly to students who are fretting about whether they're 'allowed' to do this kind of thing: 'Your book, your rules.'

My Keynes's villainy is in how he tries to damage Imogen, and keep her away from the Darwins, but the disadvantage of borrowing a real person to be a villain was that one of his sons was still alive, and so were slews of his grandchildren. And what about John Cornford's son James, come to that? James's mother was Rachel (always Ray) Peters:

she and John met in the London Communist Party when he was seventeen and she a few years older. They were together for two years, she living in Cambridge while John was up at Trinity College, and a few months after they split up she gave birth to their son in January 1925. James Cornford died in 2011, and to judge by his obituaries, he was an exceptionally nice man, a social scientist who also worked for left-wing social charities, causes and think-tanks. But how would his widow and children feel about his existence being hijacked and fictionalised by a third cousin they probably don't know exists? Could I take the easy route and just pretend James didn't happen? Or would that be even more of an insult?

That was one more uneasy, nagging worry on a long list. Worry-lists are in the nature of the job, at least if you want to write anything which is complex enough to be worth writing and worth reading. But even though most such worries are minor, if there are enough of them the cumulative effect is to destabilise everything, and trying to write onwards is like trying to walk on deep, loose sand. So, after declaring 'Your book, your rules', I usually suggest that what *is* a good idea is to make some rules of your own, for your own book. That way, you don't keep having to make each decision *ab initio* and you create for your story a consistency, underlying its relationship to the record, which I think readers sense.

So I made myself some rules for the new version of *Black Shadow and Bone.*

1) I wouldn't mention anyone living. Then I couldn't be guilty of libelling or even annoying that person, whether or not I knew them, whether or not they were family.[83]

2) I would restrict myself to printed sources, rather than risk making public something which had up to now been private. This was the first moment that I was grateful for the sheer volume of writing about my family: printed sources would – touch wood – give me enough to build on.

---

[83] It wasn't long after a case in which a crime writer had been successfully sued because, by sheer accident, his fictional nasty, failed big-band singer shared a name with a real, nice, former big-band singer.

3) I wouldn't ask anyone in the family for information.

I'll admit that the origins of Rule 3 were visceral – it's not only poetry which originates in the gut but only flowers in the head – and it probably sounds completely mad to you, especially if you're a journalist. Why deny myself the chance of talking to people who had actually been there? My Aunt Cecily, for example – my father's older sister – would have been eleven in my fictional 1937, and she is still alive as I write, as is Horace Barlow, Ruth's youngest son, who was born in 1921.

Yes, Rule 3 meant that I wouldn't risk making something public that my interviewee wanted to keep private, but I could perfectly well have coped with checking such things. My real reason was that with an interview notebook next to my keyboard I knew I'd struggle, as I so often do when I have a history book there, to fight free of what it said. Even if no one objected as a matter of emotional principle, they could still tell me I'd got it 'wrong', made 'mistakes', or 'left things out'. And I do mean those scare-quotes, because when it comes to fiction how can the writer be 'wrong'? This is *fiction*. And yet everyone – including me – feels able to say that something in a novel is wrong.

One reason for writing fiction, not plays or film scripts, is that the writer of novels relies on no one else for any part of the storytelling: each of us is the sovereign ruler of our kingdom. Even an editor who has bought the book can only be the Grand Vizier. She or he can help, negotiate, advise, warn (or, I'm told, even bully) the writer, but it's your name on the book: you have sole responsibility for, but also power over, the words inside it. But if I spoke to people who had more knowledge and closer kinship to the real-life originals of my characters than I did, then they would, in most people's minds, have a stake in my novel which it would be difficult for me to deny. My source would have more authority in what was 'true', and by extension 'right', than I had, and a legitimate voice in what counted as 'honest and responsible' in my contract with my reader.

Maybe that, too, sounds mad to you, or maybe you just think I was hopelessly weak-kneed. But when I was growing up, there were three real, routine family crimes: being horrible to your sisters, taking the last biscuit without giving everyone else the chance to bid for a share, and arguing badly. 'He can't argue' was almost as much of a black mark against a new acquaintance as snobbery, prejudice or bad manners, because the crime of arguing badly included not only inarticulacy and bad logic, but bad evidence: my father's family had a whole category of 'dining room books', which were those books – encyclopaedias, dictionaries, text-books, reference books – which had the authority to settle supper-table arguments. But it was also bad arguing to refuse to acknowledge and give way when someone else's position was based on better logic, more information, more accurate definitions or greater understanding. If, in family argument, someone refused to withdraw their bad position voluntarily the discussion continued, *forte*, till the other side had, unarguably, won.

I knew I would find it incredibly difficult to reject, creatively speaking, what my interviewees said about the real people I had taken for my characters, even when what I wanted to do instead was emotionally and creatively valid. I couldn't – I *wouldn't* – give anyone else such power over my empire.

So my Rule 3 had its origins in the family itself but, ever since, I've worried that it was a cowardly mistake. Might one or other of the interviews I didn't do have given me the key to a novel which actually worked? Then, quite recently, in a Facebook conversation about this book, a hugely experienced and award-winning journalist friend, who also writes fiction, said this:

> I think your decision made sense. The minute you interview people you enter both an explicit contract – they talk and you use selectively but accurately and with context – and also a murkier, ill-defined contract, in which interviewees often feel they have rights over the form of the final work. You are also more inclined to self-edit, particularly with people you know and like, because you will try to protect them even as you try to honour the integrity of your novel. I think you were smart to stick to what was in your head, and the printed

sources; it was a hard enough project without you allowing lots of other emotive streams to rush in and confuse your sense of purpose and integrity. You were trying to work out the appropriate route map for your research and that's freighted with pros and cons. If it had been a straightforward non-fiction book on the family I would probably say: 'Use as many sources as you can and where there is disparity, note it.' But it wasn't. Writing a novel based on your family was a complex and overwhelming task, and it called into question all those lines between objectivity and subjectivity, fact and fiction (because everyone's sense of family is half-fiction), and a thousand other questions about the relative roles of writer and subject. The tangle is in the topic. So I think you needed to keep your sources as tangle-free as possible, otherwise you'd have ended up with a big mess.

This book is not titled *The Tangle is in the Topic*. But it certainly could have been.

The next step was to go to the kind of sources I *did* need and want to find. I'd sent Nick to France on the Night Ferry because the whole setup has such a wonderfully Between-the-Wars atmosphere. It was still just about going in the 1970s, and my father sometimes travelled to Strasbourg by that route. To a child who liked trains and engineering, the thought of a *whole train* being put onto a ferry and sailed across to France was at once absurd – I thought he was joking when he first told me about it – and delicious. I imagined the whole train trundling on, curling round and round like a snake in its basket until it was all safely tucked in and the ship could sail, and as an adult writer I'd been trying for years to get it into a story. So I was just a little disappointed, when I got in touch with the National Railway Museum and found the inevitable and blessed railway enthusiasts' websites, to realise that in fact the Night Ferry's coaches all had to be uncoupled and shunted onto the ferry in instalments. But the saint in charge of historical novelists had evidently bestirred him- or herself again: the service had started in 1936 as the *de luxe* competition for the bone-shakingly primitive aeroplanes which were becoming the fast-and-expensive way to Paris. As with the Matrimonial Causes Act, the sense of affirmation that this kind of coincidence gives you is a lovely little reward for your imaginative courage, and to feel rewarded isn't entirely irrational, since it confirms that your imagination is, as it were, working on the same wavelengths as the real history.

The Night Ferry, which itself was never cheap, had survived more and cheaper air travel but given way – in both senses of the phrase – to the Eurostar. Sadly, going by train was going to take me too long and cost too much, and my whole itinerary was more strenuous and organised than would have been pleasant for a holiday, but my sister Sophy was nonetheless amused to come with me. We would fly to Toulouse, pick up a hire car, and drive into the Pyrenees. There, at Gavarnie, I'd already decided from Google Earth, Street-View *and* Maps, and the distant memory of one of Mary Stewart's weaker thrillers,[84] Imogen had been smuggled over the border from the Aragon front at Huesca.

But John's day-to-day life in Spain is pretty tightly documented, not least because he wrote a long diary-letter to his lover Margot Heinemann which ended only a day or two before he was killed at Lopera, east of Cordoba, in late December. That's a good five hundred miles away from the French border, and I had a nasty feeling that anyone who knows more about mountains than me (which includes a lot of people) would just *know* that Imogen couldn't be trying to escape through the highest of the High Pyrenees at the end of December.

No, Imogen would have to hear of John's death at Lopera in Barcelona or Madrid and, poleaxed by grief, drop out of the business of chasing stories. Then, in perhaps February, and desperately short of money, she decides that her best hope of saleable pictures is be in the north on the under-reported Aragon front, for which all I'd have to do would be re-read Orwell's *Homage to Catalonia* and add snow. Not being by nature a war photographer, in escaping during a flare-up of the fighting Imogen would stumble across the border into France,

---

[84] *Thunder on the Right*, since you ask.

picking up a mule-bolt or crevasse-fall injury on the way. In early April, Sophy and I would be following her trail only about six weeks behind her in the calendar year, or perhaps eight weeks if I factored in climate change.

But if John's death wasn't utterly new and raw, where was the emotional charge going to come from? How could I put Imogen under pressure *in the present*? I had Imogen's obsession with never losing negatives, and a recent news story of the 'Mexican suitcase': a caseful of negatives of the Spanish Civil War by Gerda Taro, Robert Capa and Chim (David Seymour), lost in 1939 and found in 2007. So, Imogen lost her last photographs of John in the dark and the snow of the mountains, when the mules bolted. The way that her ex-lover Klaus begins to worm his way back into favour is by helping her to retrieve her negatives.

Oh, and yes, of course, it was a story of the Darwin family, let's not forget. Pity that was making things so awkward.

The honest answer to the perennial question, 'When do you do the research?' is 'When you have the time'.[85] Sophy and I were travelling in our only shared window of time for months either way, so the fact that I hadn't yet worked out quite a lot of plot was just too bad. I did know that Imogen, commissioned by Miko to take photographs for a feature, would work her way from Gavarnie to Vence, where, out of gratitude, she has agreed to see Klaus again – and Miko would go with her. So Sophy and I would do the same: make for the Mediterranean somewhere north of Perpignan, and run all the way up and round the coast, past Nîmes and then Aix. Then we'd cut away from the *autoroute* that nowadays swoops down to skim the north edge of Marseille and, on the grounds that the old coast road was ravishing but over-photographed and ridiculously indirect, we'd run through the less-known hills and forests behind St Tropez and Cap Ferrat, towards Vence.

---

[85] The other honest answer is 'when you have the money'. Years before, when I mentioned to Sophy that my MPhil workshop, discussing what wasn't yet *The Mathematics of Love*, had said that Suffolk was fully realised and Brussels was also convincing, but the north coast of Spain was dead on the page, she sent me a cheque for the air fare to Bilbao.

We booked the flights and most of the hotels, because one of the reasons I'll never be a travel writer is that I can't concentrate, let alone enjoy myself, if I don't know where I'm going to sleep tonight; we rounded up maps and guidebooks, which was easy since I'd been using them for months; and we packed thermal vests and sun cream.

I made one more important decision before I set off on the new version: to cut Tom Wedgwood's sections. It helped with the over-grown cast-list, and with the fact that to have two full-scale, separate narrative strands in a novel may be counted a misfortune, but having three looks like carelessness, or *Cloud Atlas*. And in *Cloud Atlas*, wonderful as it is, David Mitchell has the good sense to keep the individual threads short and simple, in basic story-telling terms at least. Mine were neither. I got out the knife, murdered that particular set of darlings, and set off for Gatwick.

It was the week after an early Easter; the Lourdes pilgrims had all gone home, and in the High Pyrenees those hotels which were still open were almost empty. The roads and passes were clear, however, and stringy, light-starved grass was visible in the bowl-shaped meadows. Each peak had a thick cap and upper slopes of snow, while crusts and curls of it lingered further down in sheltered and north-facing spots. It was the lowest of low seasons, we discovered, with no longer enough snow for skiing, but the terrain too unstable and prone to avalanches for the walkers and climbers to have arrived. Everywhere was sodden with snow-melt, the pine-trees inky against the iron-grey granite and roofs of wet black slate. Even in Luz-St-Sauveur, where we stayed, the watering-place gaiety of pastel-coloured houses and lacy wrought iron seemed dimmed to near-monochrome, and streams fat with meltwater poured through culverts and under bridges; when the sun did reach down into the town, it had the rinsed-clean clarity that comes in the wake of a storm.

We bought a large-scaled, small-folded, close-detailed walkers' map in the supermarket – more for my armchair research than serious hiking – along with the bread-ham-cheese-apples of picnic lunches, and drove up a Napoleonically solid and tenacious road that clung to the side of the gorge. With so much closed, Gavarnie was a ghost-village, almost, and we left the car and walked past the small, plain, locked Romanesque church – the last stop on the Via Francigena before you entered Moorish Spain on your pilgrimage to Compostela – and along level, well-worn paths that skirted one or two tough little smallholdings, towards the Cirque du Gavarnie.

The flattish plain gave way to ground which to our inexpert[86] eyes bore out the signs on a barrier which said 'Risk of Avalanche. No Entry'. We stopped, and looked up and up and up and … up.

It was astounding; the sense of it is bigger in my memory than any photograph could be. Was it glaciation or volcanoes – ice, or fire – which formed this great, grey, granite amphitheatre? High above, clouds rolled up and slid away, sun came and went, and one or two big birds of prey cruised across from cliff to cliff. The only, and partial, breach in the wall was formed by Roland, with his sword, after the battle of Roncevalles. There was a small, sharp wind, but we turned away from the No Entry sign onto an un-barred path up one side of the valley, and after a while we were warm enough to be down to tee-shirts. The path led through copses of pine trees and across open meadows patched with marsh and threaded with stony, melt-water streams, and headed for a little alp which jutted up and out into the space held by the great curve of rock wall.

Yes: however much fun it was to play with the ideas of this border between France and Spain, Moors and Christendom, pilgrimage and war, Imogen and Theo could not have got through the Brèche de Roland within a couple of weeks of John's death. But with the scent and sense, now, that I had of the terrain, which neither maps nor Google Earth can really give you, I *would* be able to guess and fudge a route for them through the pass in the next valley in early March.

---

[86] At least, mine are inexpert. My sister has lived in Canada, and has more experience than me, but this wasn't a walking holiday, we didn't have proper clothes or kit, and we weren't so foolish as to stretch ourselves beyond our experience or equipment.

* * *

And as if some great bird of prey has dropped a piece of memory onto my chest where I'm lying here in bed, I can see one of those last photographs: the Philosophy building of the University, a couple of weeks after the bombing raid that nearly caught me; after they lost the University city to the fascists, and then took it back again. John's head is bandaged and he's wearing no helmet, sitting on the floor of a billet which was a classroom not so long since, holding his Complete Shakespeare so he can read it in the light that creeps through the space left between barricades of books stacked for want of sandbags.

His head-wound bled like a pig, he said, hence the bandage, but it wasn't serious. And – would you believe – it was from their own anti-aircraft shrapnel? How he'd roared with laughter when he discovered that.

'No laughing matter, though,' I said, laughing in my turn because it was that or give away how sick I felt. 'How could they be so stupid?'

'There seems to be no stupidity someone isn't capable of, in war. Ah well. We're learning. I'm learning. Ironic, after refusing to go near the OTC at Stowe. Did I tell you my father gave me his old service revolver?'

'No, I didn't know that. Must be good to have,' I said, and remembering that makes me wonder where my father's camera is. Did I bring it to Spain? I can't remember.

I hate not being able to remember.

John nodded, and I couldn't have told you why I knew it had hurt his head, because his own consciousness didn't seem to notice the pain. 'I just wish I could have inherited his skill as well. If I ever do kill a fascist it'll be a miracle. But at least this is a good billet and now we're a proper Brigade the Madrileños think we might actually save the day. As much German Romantic philosophy and Indian metaphysics as you could wish for, and everyone knows the words to "When this Bloody War is Over".' He grinned. 'I've written a Marxist version.

'No more bourgeois lackeys bawling,
"Pick it up" and "Put it down"!
If I meet the ugly bastards
I'll kick their arse all over town.'

So then of course I had to get him to sing the whole thing, and a couple of his fellows heard us and came along to join in, and I remembered how Ralph Vaughan Williams used to bang out the original on the Red Cross mess piano in Salonica. It had a missing middle C and cigarette burns on the ivory.

But not long after that I had to leave John because we were nearly at curfew-time, and 'Good bye and good luck' rang in my ears all the way back to my lodgings. And a couple of days later I got a hasty note at my hotel: they were off to the front at Boadilla, and he'd hope to see me when he got back.

Where's that note now? And where are the negatives?

I didn't know I'd never see him again.

15

Camp Vernet

I put the scene of John in the Civil War together from a letter of his to Margot Heinemann, his known taste for bawling out music-hall songs with the comrades, and my own Marxist makeover of 'When This Bloody War is Over', which is itself a First World War makeover of 'What a Friend We Have in Jesus'. The image of a machine-gun port made of books came from the letter too, but him reading Shakespeare in the light of it was mine, and I made it one of the recurring photographs in the story, from Miko falling in love with it – and by extension with Imogen – to Frances finding a little ease as she weeps over it at the end.

But once the lost negatives were rescued, they were rescued. End of story, 100,000 words too early. I needed something else which Imogen would be desperate to find and not to lose, as she's lost so much else.

What could be urgent and important *now*, for these people?

I looked back at (Rupert) John Cornford being named to commemorate his mother's great friend, the dead Rupert Brooke, and then being killed in his turn. I remembered hearing Anne Karpf interviewed about her book, *The War after Living*, which is about the children of Holocaust survivors, including herself: she spoke of the burden of being the one thing that in some way redeemed your parents' suffering: that you were what made their personal past bearable. Children in fiction, structurally speaking, embody renewal and the future – hope – even if that hope is denied or destroyed. But what if such children are asked to bear more burden of hope than they can stand? Part of Imogen's problem in 1937, I decided, was that her hope of a real child had come from a marriage made by the War To End Wars and had, inevitably, died in a late, dangerous miscarriage. Then her quasi-child John has been killed by the first, inevitable, battle between State Communism and the Peace of Versailles. Now her life and her age are reducing by the day her hope of a new child of her own, as the world hurtles towards a new war which is really the old war re-ignited. With Imogen's hope for herself so fragile, so likely not to come to fruition, how could I embody the next generation in character-in-action? How could I make *that* be the drive?

It was one of those moments when it's so obviously right it hardly counts as a decision.

* * *

from *The Mathematics of Love*

'So how did you meet?' asked Crispin.

'In Spain,' said Eva. 'I had my first big commission.' She smiled. 'It was a piece about a nunnery. It had been an artillery barracks after the dissolution of the religious orders, but they were turning it into the municipal museum.'

'I was working on a story about the effect of martial law in the Basque country,' said Theo. 'We argued till the café closed about what should be done with buildings that have lost their purpose. The Party's attitude was very utilitarian in those days – how you would have disapproved, Crispin! – but Eva saw it in terms of architecture.'

'When I went back to Madrid I found the man I'd been living with had moved in with someone else,' said Eva, reaching forward to fill everyone's wine glass again. 'Theo turned up on the doorstep two days later. He offered to console me.'

'Successfully, it appears,' said Crispin.

Eva laughed. 'Most of the time. We swear undying love, and pick a country where we can live together. Then we have a row, and Theo flies off to Berlin, or Havana, and falls for some pretty little interpreter. And I decide to move out.'

Theo said, 'Or the *Paris Review* invites Eva to New York to shoot some literary *grande dame* who has just published a muck-raking memoir of her affair with Hemingway, and Eva and she end up in bed together and *I* have to get rid of the flat.'

'It wasn't Hemingway!' said Eva. 'It was Picasso!' and everyone laughed.

* * *

So why shouldn't Imogen, having known of Eva as 'Theo's girl' in Spain, meet her in France? Eva and Theo's strand of *The Mathematics of Love* was set in 1976; I did the maths and decided that in 1937 Eva could be seventeen and Theo about twenty-seven, while Miko is thirty-seven to Imogen's nearly-forty.

I had been fascinated by books like Eugen Weber's *The Hollow Years*, which in describing how France's Between-the-Wars was both parallel with and startlingly different from Britain's, gave me so much delectable material. By early 1937 the fascist paramilitary groups in France did have far more power and success than Mosely could even dream of, but France still had the texture and smell of ordinariness, of un-preparedness. There was, as yet, only a trickle of refugees over the Pyrenees, as north-western Spain was squeezed and cut off from the main Republic by Nationalist forces; the horrors of refugee camps like Argèles-sur-Mer were yet to come. It's only our hindsight, our knowledge of names and places and later events, which invests that ordinariness with a delicate, persistent foreboding, a small sting and crackle for readers. So while it was important that each *character* mustn't exhibit more foresight than would be natural to him or her, I hoped some readers would look up from that 1937 and see the ordinariness of 2014, and think, 'What might I be seeing in the street or on the news which seems very nearly ordinary to me, but not quite? What small thing is the seed of an unimaginable awfulness yet to come?' And as I finish this book in 2017, it seems even more important to get people to look up, and ask those questions.

Only a few miles off our road from Gavarnie to Vence was the small, old village of le Vernet-en-l'Ariège, and half a mile north of it, where the Foix-Toulouse railway line and the Toulouse road run side-by-side, Camp Vernet was marked. I googled, and found a – well, an *enthusiast's* website isn't quite the right phrase in this context, but a website maintained for the human value of historical knowledge, not for profit or as part of a scholarly institution. The camp had been built by the Army, at the beginning of the First World War, to hold colonial troops (African? Asian? Caribbean?), and for a while was used to hold prisoners of war, before reverting to normal military duty in the 1920s. In 1938, as Republican Spain fell, it was one of the places that was used to house the torrent of refugees, and although gradually many found permanent asylum in France or abroad, after 1939 the Vichy government continued to hold undesirables there – including those Spanish refugees who they counted as such. As the German dominance of France developed, a station was built on the railway line, and le Vernet became a holding camp for those destined for Auschwitz, Ravensbruck and other concentration camps. Arthur Koestler wrote about Camp Vernet in *Scum of the Earth*, and other notable inmates included the Spanish artist Miguel Garcia Vivancos, and the German

Jewish writer Kurt Julius Goldstein. In 1944 the camp was emptied, and the 'ghost train' took the last families to Dachau.

I could hope that the name Camp Vernet would send a shiver through at least some of my readers, but for my characters it was just an ordinary, small, dull army camp and depot. Yes, it was still only 1937, but if a group of refugees *had* got over the mountains – few enough to be likely, many enough to need a proper effort to house them – surely somewhere like this would have been the natural place? If a photojournalist and an editor were looking for stories, and heard about a bunch of refugees from Spain, they'd try to find out more, wouldn't they? And if one of those refugees was John's age – had John's politics – had been saved as John hadn't – might she not seem to fill just a little of the void in Imogen's heart?

* * *

As they drove east and north the landscape became slowly more ordinary, at least to Imogen's Cambridge-bred eye, and the weather gentler too – a bit of sun, a mild wind. She wondered how it looked to Miko. Vincent the driver was off his own ground by now and knew no more than they did, but with Imogen reading the map le Vernet proved easy enough to find, sitting in open country in the skirts of a last, small rib of Pyrenees. Just before the village limits a vineyard tractor trundled out of an *allée* on the right, almost under their bonnet (Vincent swore under his breath) and with the confidence of having asserted its legal priority, proceeded like a leggy snail down the road in front of them at a speed which gave Imogen leisure to look about her.

The centre of the village was almost a parody – certainly a paradigm – of its kind: square, flat-faced houses of varying ages but much the same shape, a small cemetery, plane trees reduced as only the French can to neat lollipops that Le Nôtre wouldn't have scorned to install at Versailles, and a red-brick, vaguely Italianate church spire. They saw a farmhand leading a cow into a yard, but other than that the only creatures visible were one black-clad widow and a ginger cat.

'Where do we go now?' said Miko. 'I wonder if there's anyone in the Mairie.'

'I bet it's only open till lunchtime. And you know how it is. They get twitchy about letting journalists loose in their patch. Specially if there's an election due. Better to go for what we want, and apologise afterwards.'

...

The camp was in truth little more than a biggish compound of sturdy huts surrounded by a high, wire fence with a token couple of strands of barbs at the top, and the gate was just a barrier guarded by a couple of soldiers with rifles. The two groups of soldiers they passed on their way through the camp might have served for a Before and After item, Miko murmured to Imogen: the first marching sharply out of the gate and wheeling to the left as if Napoleon himself were inspecting them, the second slouching home from the opposite direction covered in mud, with faces dark with fatigue as much as camouflage paint.

The CO's name was Captain Vidal and he was a small, moustachioed man who had obviously been happily sitting out his last few years' service in his spotless little office-hut, when a hundred Spanish refugees of dubious political colour and worse health were foisted onto his nice, tidy camp.

He inspected Imogen's and Miko's passports and press cards, and Miko explained that Mlle Lefranc was a journalist accredited to several English papers, with perfect French and fluent Spanish, as well as recent experience of Spain, and would be happy to offer her assistance as an interpreter, if Captain Vidal could make use of it.

'We're pretty full at the moment because of ... Well, that's operational,' said Captain Vidal, catching himself in time. 'We've just about managed to give the poor blighters a roof over their heads, but it's pretty cramped,' he explained, raising his voice as the the teletype machine in the corner began to chatter. A clerk trotted into the office, rolled up the page, ripped it off and went out again. 'They're all suffering from malnutrition, the quack says, but I don't get the budget to give them Army rations, of course, just the minimum, and one of the huts has got a stomach germ already. Lost one of the babies yesterday. Offered to fetch the padre up from the village – we don't keep one here – but they said no, they were atheists. It was too late anyway. And the cooks resent the extra work, but I can't use the refugees for labour in the cookhouse or anywhere else because I don't want the men going down with anything – the quack says TB's a possibility, as well as this vomiting germ and the Spanish flu – Spanish – get it?' Miko and Imogen laughed dutifully. 'The soldiers we've got in now are about to ...' He slid a blank sheet of paper over the pile of lists and teleprints in front of him. 'Never mind. Toulouse has sent through a stack of forms that have to be filled in, and I've got hold of the Red Cross but they say they're short staffed, and of course the department and the commune are arguing with my DHQ about who's responsible for paying for it all. What I really need is to get all the names and details, so at least I can put in the proper requisitions. But no pictures.'

* * *

Nowadays, the building in the village square where I put a café is a museum of Camp Vernet, and has a sign saying that the key is held in the *mairie*. But the door turned out to be open nonetheless: the museum had the builders in, and the mayor was helping move things. We shook hands all round (I rather think one of the builders was the mayor's brother-in-law), and I explained my project: I was writing a novel about John Cornford, who was the first Englishman to be killed on the Republican side, a poet and – I knew that 'radical' had rather different connotations in 1930s France[87] – a Communist. The mayor himself was

---

[87] By 1937 the French Radical party, once the guardians of all things post-Revolutionary and Republican had, apart from a die-hard anti-monarchism and anti-Catholicism, become as sclerotically part of the conservative establishment as any British Tory could ask for. 'Communist', on the other hand, doesn't have a different meaning in France, but it does tend to have very different connotations.

Spanish, said the mayor. His grandparents had been Republicans and died in Spain; his father had come to France alone in 1938, as a refugee child of eight. He hoped one day to find which mass grave his grandparents were buried in, now that there was more willingness in Spain to dig up the past. But he had to get on; would we just pop our heads into the *mairie* and let him know when we'd finished, so he could lock up?

There were photographs, timelines, identity cards, letters, accounts and registers, postcards of false cheer, and drawings in chalk and black ink, some modern, some I think contemporary: men in bunks, men eating from tin cups, men talking, smoking, sleeping. The sure-handed curves of the drawings, the confident filling of the page's space, were those of someone who knows his craft, and must use his art: not just a way to pass the time or simply a record of this existence at this time and place in history, but as a way of staying alive.

In the two rooms most of the display was, inevitably, about the camp after 1938, as France, having its own considerable economic and social problems, while also increasingly right-wing and decreasingly pacifist, interned the fleeing soldiers of the Republican army and the International Brigades. There wasn't much about the camp before 1938 but that was a good thing: I had freedom to conjure what I wanted: that delicate moment when a normal, flawed, but essentially humane system for helping those in trouble is about to cease being able to cope.

We drove the kilometre or so up the Toulouse road to the site itself. There's little to see now except for a plaque and two brick gateposts; beside them stands the camp's original water-tower: old, cast concrete, shabby, but with the purity of form that follows a simple function. The farms in the foothills of the Pyrenees don't normally suffer from lack of water, and the tower had been left there with some sure instinct, I felt, for the chill that runs through you to see the normal, everyday ingenuity of humans put to the service of evil.

We got back into the car and headed across the river-plain into the dark, razor-edged Cathar hills, skirting Carcassonne and making for the Mediterranean. Later, my military-history-mad son helped with likely ranks and probable duties, while English Wikipedia proved to have strength-in-depth when it came to comparitive ranks in the world's armies. What's more, although my French could only roughly keep up with that of a brisk Languedoc mayor and his builder brother-in-law, it's good enough for French Wikipedia, which often has far more substantial entries on French subjects.

Fortunately, Imogen's French is much better than mine: for convenience's sake I'd made her guardian Aunt Claudia bring her up virtually bilingual so that Imogen could cope easily with living (which meant my coping easily with telling the story of her living) for quite a bit of each year in France, first in Vence with Gwen and Jacques (who *was* French) and then with Klaus. This is also true to the period, of course, still shackled to the idea of languages as a prime accomplishment for middle- and upper-class girls; French governesses were standard equipment, and every girls' school had its 'French table' for meals, where no English might be spoken. Some – for example The Study, where Gwen Raverat was sent when she begged to go away to school as a means of escaping the claustrophobia of home – operated entirely in French.[88]

But I was also trying to pin down something that it's easy to forget in the British Isles, though not in Continental Europe: how porous – even fluid – national boundaries and identities are. As Eurocrat children in 1973 my sisters and I realised it vividly: Dover had notices about Colorado beetle and rabies and £25 being all you could take out of the country, and proper customs officers opening suitcases. How different it was crossing the border between Belgium and Holland! The road ran onwards, marked only with a normal, triangular traffic-sign which declared '*Douane*' with about as much drama as one announcing a slight and brief narrowing of the road. But in human if not legislative or geological terms, the British Isles are just as porous. I look and sound

---

[88] My Irish granny, born in 1901, who went as a teenager to Queen Alexandra College in Dublin, used to say how inconvenient it was if you were on the French table when you needed permission to leave college early to meet a cousin; you had to choose between telling an outright lie in saying 'ma cousine', or admitting to the racy 'mon cousin', and perhaps being forbidden. Of course, in the tiny world of Dublin's Anglo-Irish professional classes, no friend, ever, wasn't also a cousin.

quintessentially English, and yet both my Irish LeFanu granny, and my American great-grandmother, Maud Darwin, *née* du Puy, were part of the Huguenot diaspora, while my maternal grandfather's ancestors were Episcopalian Scots who fled south of the border so as to be allowed to practice their religion in peace. And I was reluctant, too, to shrink my characters to fit our self-stereotype of Britons as a monoglot race, insular in the figurative as well as the literal sense. During the First World War Margaret Darwin, standing on the Gog Magog hills just outside Cambridge, heard the guns of the Western Front, and in most kinds of daylight you can actually *see* France from England across the Straits of Dover, while in most genealogies you can find people who arrived on ships and stayed, or left on ships and became 'My cousin in Calgary'. Dig down two generations, or twenty, and there will still be incomers and outgoers, marrying in or moving out. As forceful Aunt Etty says to Gwen at one point in *Period Piece*,

> '*Don't tell me*,' (I wasn't telling her), 'that all those Roman soldiers lived all that time in England and didn't leave a lot of Roman babies behind them. And a very good thing too, I dare say.'

But, apart from Maud, William Darwin's American wife Sara Sedgwick and the splendid Sismondi, the Darwin-Wedgwoods are remarkably English, albeit with an admixture of Welsh. So it was the fictional, imagined characters in *Black Shadow and Bone* who embodied what I wanted to explore: the mixtures and overlaps, the possibilities and probabilities of how language and nation form our identities: neither nothing nor everything, just as all the other ways we define ourselves are only parts, potentialities, elements in the whole.

* * *

'You said you were an orphan,' said Miko.

'Aunt Claudia wasn't really an aunt – just my mother's best friend. My parents died when I was three.'

'I'm sorry. That sounds so inadequate, but – you know. My

mother died when I was born, but my father had married again by the time I was one. Maminka – Theo's mother – *is* my mother, in every sense that matters.'

Imogen ran her open hand through a big, straggling rosemary bush, then held her palm out. 'Smell.'

He dipped his head and breathed in: the warmth of her palm softened the astringency of the scent, and he was reminded of the great incense-burner in St Vitus' Cathedral when he was a boy, swinging out clouds of frankincense and myrrh to clean the air of all the things he'd messed up and got wrong, so he could start again.

'Did you speak Czech at home?' Imogen said after a moment.

'Mostly. My father was a civil servant, so in Prague he worked in German as much as Czech, and of course he spoke Hungarian when he was growing up. Maminka was Czech, but she wanted me to learn English, for the sake of my English grandparents. She grew up in Yiddish, but they decided three languages was quite enough for me. Theo speaks Yiddish a bit, for the sake of *his* grandparents.'

'And Theo's – what?'

'Ten years younger.'

'A big gap,' said Imogen. By now they were out of the town proper and the *quai* was just a narrow road running along the grass banks of the river, with fishing boats and launches lying passive in the slow, strong flow of the water.

* * *

Even Imogen's long-dead father is Australian, but his surname Lefranc is French and possibly Huguenot – I'd originally used it for Imogen for the implications of 'franc' as 'free' – while the implications of her mother's background are a mixture which was inspired by Edmund de Waal's *The Hare with Amber Eyes*, although the names came from *The Merchant of Venice*.

* * *

Jessica Lock ran from her rich and clever home which had been built on trading in furs, and banking, and now collected paintings and composers. She wanted to marry Laurence Lefranc, who wasn't a painting or a composer but only a jobbing journalist from Sydney, and she did so on the day after her twenty-first birthday. Her family refused to see her ever again, said Aunt Claudia, and when her father died the following year she wasn't invited to the funeral. Eventually, along with admitting that Jessica had been her favourite pupil, Aunt Claudia admitted that the Locks had also refused to acknowledged Imogen's existence.

Laurence, on the other hand, might as well have materialised out of the mists of the Blackwall Dock where the ships from Australia tie up, for all he ever said, or Imogen ever knew. All they had was the three of them, and wasn't that enough, he'd ask, swinging her up into the air till her pinafore billowed and she was shrieking with delicious terror.

* * *

All the important fictional characters in *Black Shadow and Bone*, in other words, belong partly somewhere else, and even the somewhere-elses have mostly been some*thing* else. And this – I realised suddenly – was one of the things which was helping me to claim the project as my creative territory, not one more Darwin thing. These characters might be all-fictional, but in their mixedness, their part-otherness, they were all mine.

So, equipped by the complexities of their origins, Imogen and Miko could talk their way into the camp and Imogen could offer to help out with translating as the refugees were counted and identified, their papers inspected and their stories recorded.

* * *

Miko knew these things – had seen the photographs – even written captions for them. He'd sub-edited the articles if they were short-staffed, and after a late night on Press day, he'd bought the early editions of *The Times* or the *Daily Mail* on the way home, still damp from the presses, and seen more again. You only had to look about you, only had to go to a street in the Rondda Valley, or Toxteth, or Smíchov, to find a hundred people who were cold and hungry and in pain, and without much hope of relief. And refugees ... if it wasn't Bulgaria it was Palestine or Guadelajara, and soon, Maminka wrote, it would be the Sudentenland. Theo spoke of it too: the stories tumbling out of him in a scalding rush until he stopped equally abruptly, as if words would never be enough.

And these things were going to happen more. No one could possibly think otherwise.

The group in the space between the huts was getting bigger, and there were only the last few men in the queue to register: they were nearly done. In the windows of the women's hut he could see heads gathering: they were next. He lit another cigarette and turned back, and there, in one of those windows, was a face he knew. Absolutely knew.

But who? Where?

It was a photograph, he thought – that was how he knew her.

Young – barely out of her teens, and beautiful, or would have been if she hadn't looked so gaunt. Big black eyes like pits, cheeks hollow, hair scraped back, a coat clutched tight around her as if she were cold. She looked full at him and for a split second her face opened as if she were about to smile. And then like a shutter it closed, and she turned away.

Theo's girl.

16

Vence

It was Eva, of course, alone, shunned and in poor health, and now Imogen must break the silence of years, while the whole family is still raw with the death of John, and ask the Darwins for help. And not help for herself, but for a total stranger, a radical in political trouble, a sexually experienced near-child, who has survived, as their child John has not, and now needs housing, feeding and supporting for an indefinite period. Will Nora take her? Or Gwen?

And that meant, of course, that I could no longer dodge working out what caused the silence in the first place. It must be rooted in the real history of the Darwins, in tandem with some of the themes of the novel, it must be adequately true to the material facts and, most difficult of all, it must be true to the personalities involved.

* * *

Imogen rubbed her forehead. 'I went over and over it, trying to work out what happened, and I still don't really understand.'

'What *do* you know?' Nick said, suddenly the kindly Physics master again, the Nick of Malta, of those early months in England. 'What you do know is always a good place to start.'

'I suppose so.' But the story was ready and waiting, if not the understanding. 'It was a few weeks after the première of *Job* – do you remember? At Sadler's Wells. It was Geoffrey's idea, basing it on the Blake illustrations. He wrote the scenario and Frances helped him. Gwen designed it – sets and costumes. And Ralph did the music. Mme de Valois was the only one who wasn't family. So Geoffrey's idea was that I should make a record of it, in photographs.'

'When Alec decided to have *The Lark Ascending* in his recital, I told him I used to know Dr Vaughan Williams. He was very envious.'

She smiled back at him, and somehow acknowledging that Alec didn't exist for Nick then, but did now – that Alec also fitted in the scheme of their once conjoint and mostly disjoint lives … somehow it made it easier for her to go on.

'I got some wonderful shots backstage. And some of Gwen in the cellars of the Old Vic, painting backcloths, and of course I always ended up helping. It was serious – a major event, the first British-born ballet. But it was fun, too, just like the old days in Cambridge, before the Great War – putting on plays and everyone mucking in.'

She felt a tiny crack – not even a crack, really, just a single tremor in her throat.

Quietly, Nick re-filled their glasses.

'And in among it all, the *New Statesman* asked me for an interview – Maynard was on the board, though goodness knows why it was me they wanted to talk to. But that wasn't the problem.' She stopped.

'What was the problem?' said Nick, after a moment.

'There was some muddle. The journalist wasn't really prepared – no idea what questions to ask. So I just chattered on – ended up saying everything I could think of – about how we'd all known each other since before the Great War, and so on. I think I mentioned Rupert, because of those Cambridge plays, but I really don't remember.'

Nick smiled.

'And the piece came out and it was all right. Quite short, but a couple of my photographs so I got paid for those too. Everyone was pleased. But then the journalist – he didn't tell me – I could never prove it was him, but there was no other way he could have got that particular collection of memories ... He wrote another piece, under a pseudonym, for the *Daily Worker*. And it was quite different. All about how the Arts were the playthings of the establishment and the bourgeois élite, and they didn't care about the working man, or what he – always he, of course – wanted to see, just having jobs for themselves and shows for their friends to go to. How they – we'd – all fallen for Rupert Brooke's magical spell of dilettantism and pre-War romanticism.' She found herself spitting the words out. 'And how they only let me in because I didn't mind being a dogsbody for their schemes. That's what it said I'd said.'

'That must have been very unpleasant. But did it matter? Who reads the *Daily Worker*? Who that you care about, I mean.'

'Plenty of Gwen's friends – Ralph's too, I should think. And John, of course, though he was only fifteen. He had a subscription – he used to sell copies to his friends at Stowe ...'

Would she ever be able to think of John without the pain flaring up, like a bonfire you've poured more petrol on? Would she ever want to? 'That wouldn't have mattered. But it was picked up by the *Daily Express*, and they ran a piece. You know the kind of thing: *Our War Hero was 'abandoned by his friends', by one who knew him*. They made it sound as if we all scorned Rupert, and he volunteered when the Great War started because no one took him seriously – made it sound as if everyone in Cambridge had turned on him because he was so glamorous – so beautiful. Geoffrey was specially furious – he could never bear anyone to imply that Rupert was—' She caught herself up and tried not to look self-consciously at Nick.

He seemed unperturbed. 'But Brooke – well, he's a long time ago – more than twenty years. Surely they're not ones to bear grudges? And you gave the interview in good faith.'

She sighed. 'It wasn't really that. They hated it, but they knew that I was – that what I said was … Well, misrepresented. No, it was that they stopped talking to me.'

'They sent you to Coventry?'

'N— no. No, not really. But … Whenever I saw them, after that piece came out, I knew they – it was as if I was an acquaintance. Telling me tid-bits of news, trivia, nothing which mattered. As if they wouldn't say anything worth saying, in case I ran chattering to the gutter press! I – I … It's difficult to explain. They didn't *trust* me. They were my *friends*, Nick – my closest friends, since I was fifteen. They're the nearest thing I have to a family. The only thing, after Aunt Claudia died, apart from …'

'Apart from me,' he said, hoping his voice didn't sound as hollow to her as it did to himself.

But she was too wound up to notice. 'Yes. It was years after Klaus and I … Apart from you, they were all I had. No one said anything, but I could tell … In the end I couldn't bear it. I stopped going round – stopped writing letters to Frances when she was in the nursing home – stopped sending postcards when I was away on a job – stopped being in touch.' She was crying now. 'They were all I had. And I'm not sure they even noticed.'

'Oh, Immie,' said Nick, putting his hand over hers. 'Oh, my dear …'

He didn't know what to say; he'd never really known. Gwen and the others always seemed to have ideas and reasons – they'd discuss the problem, think about it, work out the logic, add any facts they knew, any experiences they had which might shed light on the matter, sympathise, come up with things that could be done, and offer help to do it.

All he could do was be there.

* * *

I based Klaus's house and village very precisely on the little town of Tourrettes -sur-Loup, inland from the Côte d'Azur between Nice and Cagnes, and a few miles east of Vence. It's one of the most perfect *villages perchés* in an area with plenty of competition, and I was thrilled, when Sophy and I went there, to find that there was even a house where Villa Per Gynt could be, perfectly placed on the next little spur along. It had a spectacular view of the village, the spur formed a big garden and orchard for encounters deliberate and accidental, and there were some nice steep cliffs and paths if I needed anyone to break an ankle or get soaked in a storm. There was even a disused narrow-gauge railway line a little further down the valley which had been well-used in 1937, before it was blown up by the Germans as they retreated in 1944. There wouldn't be many who would know that, but still, it was another little shiver of things to come for anyone who did. I tested the name of Tourrettes on a friend or two, and with howls of laughter we agreed the village should be renamed. That, of course, meant I also had a bit more freedom to stretch the train journey from Vence, fiddle with the details and generally bend the material facts to my storytelling purposes. I called it Mirageon-sur-Loup, because what had felt like home to Imogen is actually a mirage. And, of course, national borders being the transient things they are in mainland Europe, the oldest inhabitants would remind the younger ones every now and then that not so long ago it was Miraggione, in the Kingdom of Savoy.

Eva has become the quasi-child that Imogen *can* save, as she couldn't save John. And Miko wants to save her because she's his little brother's love. However, there is only so much drama you can (I can) extract from scenes of will-the-telegram-come, and will-the-paperwork-be-stamped, especially when kind and sensible people have set about the business in a kind and sensible way, in countries that do have systems, however inadequate and sometimes faulty, for coping with refugees. I badly needed to raise the stakes.

'The answer to the question *what's at stake?*', I say to students, 'is made up of two different things. What the main character hopes for and is fighting for, and what she most fears and is trying to escape or defeat.'

What could make the hopes not just bigger, but harder to make come true? What could make the fears not just bigger but more likely to happen? It would help if what threatened Eva wasn't an ill-disposed consul or a beaurocratic muddle but something bodily – physical ... What could threaten Eva so badly, when everyone wants her to be safe?

... if she was poorly ... the cough she caught in the camp hasn't improved... and the doctor realises she's pregnant, and secretly tells Imogen ...

... if she didn't want to be pregnant ...

Theo's child? No, too easy for Miko to adopt it if Theo won't. But Eva *is* pregnant ...

... if she wanted to get rid of it ...

... if it's the child of rape ...

... because *anyone* would sympathise with her wanting to get rid of it, even childless, child-wanting Imogen. But maybe ...?

* * *

When I came back to Cambridge on leave from Malta Ras had been dead a year, and John was seven months old, black-eyed and plump and strong. He was lying on the nursery hearthrug shaking a bear to and fro and giggling, and when I gathered him up in my arms he didn't seem to mind at all, but butted his head into my breast, still laughing, and then leant back to see what I thought. So I kissed him. His cheek was cool and firm under my nose, and he smelled of powder and soap but the back of his neck had the sweet, animal smell of babies, and the weight of him in my arms felt like the weight of a lover that I'd never had – the weight of everything I'd lost in losing Ras – the weight that told me I was still alive because I could feel this creature who'd been born, it almost seemed, just as Ras had died.

I sat down in the chair his nanny had just left, and we played pattacake until suddenly he stopped playing and turned on my knee to stare at the cat where it was sitting on the hearthrug, washing. He watched every careful, methodical stage of the cat's toilet so intently that when he turned back to me it seemed entirely likely that he would tell me something profoundly interesting and important about cats, and people, and the relationship between the two. And then he put out a hand to the cat as if thinking about it had made him want to stroke it, and laughed again.

After that I spent most of my leave playing with him, and when I was posted to Salonica, I went with the weight of John still aching in my arms.

* * *

Could Imogen adopt this second-hand, equivocal baby, this child conceived in violence and born of war and between-the-wars, the child who no one wants, the child which Imogen – the woman that no one wanted enough – can therefore have?

That would raise the hopes side of the stakes equation, but what about the fears?

Eva is ill … really ill. In the 1930s pneumonia is a death-sentence as often as not, and the child that may be Imogen's best hope will die too.

I raided Vita Sackville-West's *Family History* for the pneumonia scenes, and decided that Nora has agreed to have Eva, so Imogen must telegraph her about the delay.

The biologist granddaughter of Charles Darwin still does genetics in her garden and lab, in between having six children, and this was another moment when the saint in charge of historical novelists took a benign hand in things. The earliest of the first antibiotics – the sulphonamide drugs – were discovered in the late 1930s and gained publicity, and acceptance by doctors, after President Roosevelt's son

THIS IS NOT A BOOK ABOUT CHARLES DARWIN

was treated with it in 1936.[89] Nora keeps up with the scientific news in *Nature* and she knows about this new 'anti-biotic', this miraculous medicine, this Prontosil. Surely she can do something, even from England, to help this girl Imogen's trying to save. Does Geoffrey Keynes, the senior surgeon, know anyone who's got Prontosil? And Geoffrey does, of course, because Geoffrey enjoys knowing everyone and helping everyone,[90] even Imogen, and especially if it gives him a reason to be back in touch with Nick.

Will the trains and the planes and the meeting-of-strangers at the Gare du Nord happen in time? Miko's flight is four hours – Cannes – Marseilles – Lyon – Paris Le Bourget – and no luxury or heady sense of modernity can soften the crudity of air travel in those days: coffee and tea in thermos jugs, and the roar and shake like travelling inside a raging wasp. Nick hands over the precious, carefully-packed parcel of phials of Prontosil, to be kept as cool as possible. Thus the stakes have just been raised a bit more: the hope of the antibiotic is on its way, the fear is that now Eva is dying.

---

[89] The archetypal antibiotic, penicillin, was only discovered during the Second World War.

[90] The real Geoffrey Keynes helped to save Virginia Woolf's life after her first suicide attempt in 1913: he and Leonard Woolf caught a taxi to Bart's Hospital, leaning out of the windows to shout 'Emergency! Emergency!'; Geoffrey got hold of a stomach pump and they rushed back to Brunswick Sq. He was also – in the opinion of others as well as himself – a pioneer of the conservative treatment of breast cancer, and of blood transfusion as a routine procedure. He may be an anti-Darwin, but he does represent the interacting of art and science to a remarkable degree.

17

The Verdict on Version Two

The 1937 present was now the bulk of the novel, but the Darwins were still disastrously absent from the actual story, *and* I still had to build Imogen's reconciliation with them. Then, when I was googling archives for letters I found not an image, but a formal description, in the archive of the Rare Book and Manuscript Library at the University of Illinois:

> 1034: RAVERAT, Gwen. Black and white lino cut design, depicting peasant family with donkey fleeing bombers and burning town. Reminiscent of treatments of the flight of the Holy Family. Produced for the Cambridge branch of Medical Aid for Spain. 34 x 39 cm. (Apparently unrecorded). Nice.

I emailed the library and they kindly sent me a scan for my research.

* * *

This friend of Imogen's was perhaps ten years older: square, brown hair greying, with a broad, strong face and thick spectacles, and clothes that looked as if she didn't worry about them from one year to the next. Her voice and her handshake were solid, clear, firm, like a plain oak table or a good loaf of bread: honest stuff, the same all the way through. 'Come in out of the damp,' she was saying. 'If you want the taxi to wait he'll want a cup of tea. Go on through to the drawing room – you know the way – and I'll take him to the kitchen and get some tea for ourselves. And turn my worklamp out, would you, Imogen?' Imogen went to turn the lamp out, but Miko strolled over with her and stayed her hand so he could look at the work.

'She wouldn't mind?' he said.

'No, not at all,' Imogen said. 'She likes working with people around. Her father was the same – always had his study door open. She puts away anything she feels private about.'

In the hard, white light that the engraver's globe gathered and poured down he saw that half the block had a pencil design on the fine dark surface, neat and clear, and the other half was already engraved, with chalk rubbed white into the lines to make them show: a row of trees, and between their massive trunks the glimpse of a river. Pencilled on the paper sketch which lay beside it were the words 'Horse Chestnuts at Granchester',[91] and below it '(for Gareth Pryor / Solmani Press)'.

'Look at this,' said Imogen.

It was another, bigger drawing: getting on for a foot square, squared-up and ready, and lying next to it was a piece of linoleum. The lines were bolder – broader – better for the different medium.

---

[91] This, too, is a real Gwen engraving of 1937, although the Solmani Press was invented by me for *A Secret Alchemy*, in which Una knew and collected the work of Gwen Raverat; this was a reciprocal nod to the fine Press which forms the heart of that novel's modern strand. Because why not? It might amuse someone who read both books.

For a moment Miko thought it was the Flight Into Egypt, only there were more figures: a woman riding on a donkey with a small child; a man trudging beside them with a goat on a string; a boy like Bru, with a sack. Then he saw that the burning town behind them had sloping roofs and a church tower: it wasn't Judaea but Spain. And in the air was a squadron of bombers.

There was lettering outside the boundaries of the picture: *HELP THE BASQUE PEOPLE* and further down, *Cambridge Committee for Medical Aid for Spain.*

* * *

So, taking Eva in would come naturally to Gwen. And the estrangement? The row, the silence and the hoped-for, difficult reconciliation?

But my characters were so sensible, so practical, so reasonable. In her biography of Gwen, Frances Spalding describes how underlying the family debates lay 'the assumption that family characteristics, such as persistence, intelligence and common sense, would inevitably arrive at an authoritative truth,' and that had also shaped my Nick's experience of them. Spalding quotes Virginia Woolf, too. Virginia had known the Darwins all her life[92] and although she was sometimes no more charitable about them than she was about anyone else, she did write that, 'The best of these Darwins is that they are cut out of rock – three taps, and one is convinced of their solidarity.' Whether Woolf really meant 'solidarity' – as in fellowship and loyalty – or 'solidity', as in unshakeability, unbreakability, it wasn't a helpful quality as far as spinning stories was concerned.

That persistence, intelligence and common sense seemed to infect my fictional characters too:

---

[92] As well as being connected by marriage through two of Virginia's mother's sisters, Virginia's historian father Leslie Stephen, editor of the *Dictionary of National Biography*, was a great friend of George Darwin. Virginia was not always kind to or about plain, forthright, unconfident Gwen, but years later, when Jacques was ill, she took to writing long, thoughtful letters to him. The letters were mediated through Gwen since she had to write and read for Jacques, and the correspondence became one of the few real pleasures for Jacques during the ghastly years of his dying. It has been edited and published by Gwen's grandson William Pryor as *Virginia Woolf & the Raverats: a different sort of friendship.*

For three weeks, Imogen thinks she's lost all her negatives of John forever ... and then she gets them back.

For a tense moment it looks as if Geoffrey won't send the life-saving antibiotic to Eva, since it's for Imogen, but ... then he does.

For a chapter or two Imogen says she must be reconciled to and forgiven by the Darwins before she can commit to Miko ... and then she does commit to Miko.

For a moment the grieving Frances hates Imogen for having been with John in Spain, but then ... she forgives Imogen's place in John's life, and is comforted by her photographs.

So where's the story? Catriona's voice should have echoed in my head, months before it did echo on the phone. She went on, 'There's not enough at stake.' By two-thirds of the way through the novel, Eva was going to live, and after that the stakes not only didn't rise, they positively sank: one character's problem after another was resolved and the few fears and dreads left got smaller and smaller.

Where was the story indeed? And why wasn't it with the Darwins?

Somewhere in the middle of my working on *Black Shadow & Bone*, I was invited to the memorial lunch for Andrew Huxley. Both my sisters went to Cambridge and had benefitted from Andrew and Richenda's old-school University hospitality: their table was always full of students, as Gwen's had been when she was widowed and moved back from France.[93] I couldn't have been a more peripheral cousin, but the couple of times I'd happened to be visiting a sister, the Huxleys had instantly scooped me into the party too.

I'd decided not to tell anyone what I was writing, but I was on the alert, in case it suddenly made sense that I should break Rule 3 and ask for information. There were plenty of family and there was a lot of 'When did we last meet?' followed by quite a few possible answers:

---

[93] Given her politics and her nephew John Cornford's, at one time or another most of the Burgess and Maclean generation were habitués of Gwen's lunch-table. Inevitably, one wonders which way John would have gone, as the years passed and it required an ever larger, more willed, and arguably criminal self-delusion to go on believing that the Soviet Union was on track to become a proletarian paradise.

Nora Barlow's 90th birthday, when I was a child? Someone's wedding? The opening of Erasmus Darwin House in Litchfield, when my sister Carola, who is a professional singer, performed a song written by Erasmus and arranged by our cousin Jeremy Barlow?[94] The Josiah Wedgwood Bicentenary? The smaller Charles Darwin Bicentenary dinner in 2009? The year Andrew and Chenda held four big parties at Trinity College, Cambridge, where he was Master, for the four branches of their joint family?[95]

Then Carola, at my elbow, said, 'Come and meet Horace Barlow.'

* * *

'I'm used to living like that: being with Klaus, but working and having my own life,' Imogen had said to Nora one breakfast-time a couple of months later, after the children had got down.

'And Klaus knows you'd want to go on working?' asked Nora, starting to stack the dishes on the trolley.

Imogen stooped to retrieve Horace's bib and assorted bits of egg and toast soldiers from under the high chair. 'He'd be horrified if I didn't. The last thing he wants is a tidy little wifey with nothing to think about except what next to embroider. That was – well, never mind. And I couldn't bear not to have my own income. And when it's all settled, we'll start trying for a baby.'

'That all sounds splendid,' Nora said. 'I do think it's important to keep up something for your mind – something which isn't domestic. It's so easy to let that slip. Specially if those around you don't think it matters.'

'Of course,' Imogen said. 'Once at Newnham I heard someone crying in their room – one of the first years. The door was open so I knocked and asked if she was all right – I thought she might be ill or something.'

---

[94] If you're thinking that there are a lot of Barlows in this story, you wouldn't be the first: at the family's Darwin Bicentenary dinner, I made a rough guess that nearly half of The Ancestor's total living descendants were the product of Ruth and Alan Barlow's marriage, while the other half came from all the other grandchildren combined.

[95] My Uncle George and Aunt Angela (née Huxley) were invited to two of them.

'But not?'

'No, she was crying with happiness.' Imogen started stacking plates. 'At home she shared a bedroom with her three sisters – four of them in two beds. She did her studying in the attic on some boards across the joists. And sometimes, to avoid being called down to do the mending or mind the baby, she'd climb out of the skylight and down the drainpipe. She even asked me if I'd take a photograph of her room.'

'To send home?' Nora put the last few things – toast rack, butter dish, milk jug – on the trolley and pushed it towards the door.

'No, for herself. She said that whatever happened when she left – whether she got married or became a teacher or she just had to go home to look after her parents when they got old … Whatever happened, she'd have this to remember. It was a pokey little room, just like everyone else's: dreary green curtains and Tottenham Court Road furniture. But it was her paradise.'

'I wonder if she did get married,' Nora said, putting the last of the breakfast things on the trolley.

'I don't know. It must have been 1913.'

Nora said nothing, and the photographer in Imogen thought how pretty she was in the soft light coming in from the garden, and then that new grief blurs a face, and happiness transforms it, but it's old grief – so many years of grief for Ras – that shows you the real form of a human. Carefully, Imogen lined the marmalade, jam and honey jars up on the sideboard. 'You don't … You *really* don't regret only being able to do scientific work in bits?'

'No, I don't regret it at all,' said Nora with that quiet, stubborn truthfulness of hers. 'Although when I read *Nature* or hear from someone I knew in William Bateson's lab, and get excited by what he's working on, I feel a little wistful. And it has been worth it, to have the children. I couldn't have been a full-time researcher *and* had children – Joan especially – *and* been married to someone with a job like Alan's. It's not like Gwen's work, or Frances's.'

'It's not easy for them, either,' Imogen said indignantly.

'No, of course not.' Nora went to the french windows and opened them. It was April: the air was sharp and clean, the sunlight the colour of primroses. 'And goodness knows I'm not complaining. I've started growing trimorphic flowers again, now we're not in London. Hybridising them is fun, and I should get another paper out of it soon. So I'm not neglecting genetics, any more than you'll neglect your work when you marry Klaus. Come out with me, and see how they're getting on. And there's editing the *Beagle* diary, though that always seems to get pushed to the back of the queue in favour of sewing on name tapes and packing trunks.'

'Only two things certain in life, Aunt Claudia used to say: death, and the Autumn term,' said Imogen, and Nora laughed.

* * *

It was as if the novel had flooded out from its usual cupboard in my mind, and filled my mouth. I gazed at Carola, dumbfounded. I knew I ought to be pleased to meet Horace. He is a distinguished neuroscientist, he was in his nineties, and the oldest of the great-grandchildren still living: his name was the only reference I'd made in the novel to a person who *was* still living. Much more importantly, perhaps, he was 'my' Ras's, admittedly posthumous, nephew, and his mother was *there*, on so many of my pages.

But I couldn't, I just couldn't, meet my second cousin one removed – the one whose toast-soldiers and eggy bib Imogen had just picked up – and hope to embark on yet another lunch-party conversation: 'I'm Henry and Jane's middle one – I'm a writer – no, novels – what a lovely day – Andrew would have loved it – which of your part of the family are here? – oh yes, I think we met – can I get you another cup of tea? – let me move that chair for you—'

I would be trying to say all that, and I knew that instead my mouth would say, 'I'm writing a novel about John Cornford, and you're in it, but I don't want to talk about it in front of all these people.'

And if we had talked about it at some point, what then? The

questions I'd really want to ask were the ones I couldn't find out from the books and the websites – which meant personal, private things. And the more personal and private the answers were, and the more unarguably straight-from-the-horse's mouth, the less I could toss what I learnt up into the anarchic, gift-conjuring place that Rose Tremain so exactly describes. It wouldn't be my story, it would be Horace's – Nora's – Ras's. I would be ceding some of my sovereignty.

I shook my head, and Carola, who knew about the novel, nodded silently and moved away.

This moment, like my inhibitions about RVW's life all those months earlier – a year or more, by now – should have been a warning that my rules for this book full of real people were inconveniently contaminated by my rules for a life full of real people: behaving decently; having good manners and a certain amount of self-restraint; respecting other people's privacy and other people's point of view; and not declaring opinions I can't back up with facts, logic and emotional intelligence. It should have been a warning, but it wasn't.

Not that ethical rules of some kind are anything unusual for a writer. I was in the audience on the South Bank when the late Helen Dunmore said of writing her novel *The Siege* that she felt she must be faithful to the memories of Leningrad siege survivors that she had actually met and talked to:

> They have a right to it. I don't believe we have the right to say, 'I will do what I like with this material'.

Toni Morrison, interviewed by *The Paris Review*, agrees that these things are not simple:

> Making a little life for oneself by scavenging other people's lives is a big question, and it does have moral and ethical implications.

She goes on to the creative implications:

> In fiction I feel the most intelligent, and the most free, and the most excited, when my characters are fully invented

people. If they're based on somebody else, in a funny way it's an infringement of a copyright. That person owns his life, has a patent on it. It shouldn't be available for fiction.

At heart this was the Daemon/Prig fight starting up again, albeit with a Prig who has the right to censor the writer for her ethical rather than her grammatical or socio-political decisions. Yes, there was the rub: in some strange way I *did* feel that these things still belonged to their owners, and while I might borrow them, and reproduce them, they were not mine to mess with. And when I was trying not to mess with them I, though I'm no Toni Morrison, also felt stupid, shackled and, in the writerly sense, bored.

But as well as those inconvenient but at least – I hope – honourable inhibitions, as I talked it over with Catriona I had to face up to the fact that I'd pulled my punches too often elsewhere. Looked at coldly, there was so much that I had fudged, skimped, or avoided altogether.

There was the complex, embroiled, overwhelming, resisted love between Frances and John, and the tensions of family, politics and class brought about by his relationship with Ray Peters, which ended before James was born. There was the agony of bereavement which put Frances in a mental hospital for months. There was how Ray's only hope of earning a living was to go into service and board James out: not an uncommon arrangement in those days, but meaning he was all but lost to his Darwin grandparents for some years.

There was Nora's oldest child, Joan, who was born with a learning disability; Nora insisted on bringing her up at home, in the teeth of most advice of the period – including that of her persistent, intelligent and commonsensical family – that if such children must be born at all, they were best sent to experts to bring up in expert settings.

There was Billy Darwin's falling in love with Babette Giroux, the young Northern Irish woman whom Gwen first employed to help look after her daughters but who, over the years of Jacques's illness, had become a willing model and much-loved friend. Not long after Jacques died, Billy and Babette got engaged despite a few raised family eyebrows, since Babette came from a considerably lower social stratum than Billy's. Babette was not daunted, cheerfully pointing out that their timing was good, since Billy and Gwen's brother Charles was doing all the suitable-marrying that their widowed mother – by then Lady Darwin – could possibly want: Charles's fiancée, the mathematician Katharine Pember, was the daughter of the Warden of All Souls College, Oxford. Although it was all tricky – and made more so because Babette by then was pregnant – Gwen was wholly delighted by the engagement, and no one else was so over-dramatic or so unkind as to do worse than try to make the best of things. With the wedding planned, Babette travelled home to Northern Ireland to see her family, but was suddenly struck down with some kind of intestinal problem: a first operation was conservative in the hope of saving the baby, but after a second, more radical one, she died, with Billy and Gwen at her bedside.

I'd been a little braver in the matter of Jacques and Gwen's artist friend Jean Marchand. Drawing yet again on Frances Spalding's *Gwen Raverat*, I *had* slipped in that during the years of Jacques's dying Gwen and Marchand had fallen passionately in love. To this day, as with Tom Wedgwood, I feel that there must be a novel *somewhere* in that, albeit not one that I can write, but when I came to Jacques's death, I took refuge in flashback.

***

Jacques was dying day by day and nerve by nerve – unable by then to move, to eat – everything gone except pain and terrror and still the last shards of his intelligence; that, it seemed, no disease could quite paralyse. Gwen could do nothing but look after him with as much patience as possible, which sometimes very little because sometimes he was so horrible.

It was perverted, somehow – an inversion of everything human – to say that the best hope was that Jacques wouldn't live much longer. But it was true, and so Nora said it because she was incapable of not stating a truth. And Imogen had to agree.

Gwen had said it too, and more, after one particularly dreadful day when Jacques was ill and in the kind of agony that only the paralysed know, and begging to be allowed – helped – to die. 'What purpose is served by allowing him to live, when his life is like this and he doesn't want it?' Gwen said. 'Why shouldn't we be allowed to die when we chose? And why can't I help him? He can do nothing for anyone – least of all himself. You wouldn't let a dog suffer like this. It can't come soon enough, if you think sensibly about it.'

After that illness Jacques had clawed back some peace and pleasure, for a little while: being read to, and thinking, and dictating letters to friends. But not for long.

And in a way they'd done years of mourning already, Imogen thought now, inspecting her autumn-leaf dress. She'd come back from Copenhagen and was hiding in Cambridge, stunned and miserable at losing Klaus, but she hurried back to Vence and Jacques … Jacques died a week later. After that nightmare … after the days she could hardly think of without feeling suffocated – choking – drowning … after that, Gwen was quite calm and the girls too. Jacques had died long ago, their demeanour seemed to say. His physical death was just the coda – the full stop – the endpiece.

But you could still weep for what had been lost a long time ago, Imogen found as Jacques's funeral approached. You could still cry for the cruelty, and for each good thing you saw – a yellow puppy chasing a pigeon from sheer exuberance, a pair of lovers wrapped in happy quiet under the silver and green shimmer of an olive tree, the way the wintry sun made the red roofs glow, and slanted down steep alleyways till the old stone and patchy plaster seem alive and warm and friendly … you could still hurt, when you saw good things, because of everything that wasn't good.

* * *

What I'm perfectly willing to Tell here, but couldn't bring myself to Show in a fully dramatised scene, was what Gwen later confessed to Margaret: that when their useless doctor took one look at Jacques and ran away, Gwen seized a pillow and ended the horror.

222

Years before, when I first read Spalding, I'd promptly put euthanasia-by-pillow into the novel I was working on at the time in its full physical and emotional glory – or, rather, hideousness. Why in *this* novel had I not been willing to draw on such things, the sort that normally make me rub my writerly hands with glee?

I reviewed all the apparently good decisions that had added up to a novel which so manifestly didn't work. There were so many places where, when the question 'What should happen next?' had come up, I had looked for the interesting, subtle, likely and original path. But storytelling, fundamentally, isn't a subtle business, nor is it about originality. A story can only afford to have those virtues when they don't undermine the storyteller's true and vulgar business: earning food and a place by the fire by understanding the hearer's emotional and intellectual being, and constructing an imagined reality that the hearer positively wants to be gripped by, and not be let go. My argument to myself that certain paths were subtle, interesting, likely or original, was usually true, but it was also a rationalisation. It *was* partly that somehow writing about Ralph Vaughan Williams having sex, or my great-aunt killing her husband, seemed prurient, sensationalist, and vulgar.

Yet it was also about me. After the way *Novel Three* had not worked out, life inside my writing was short on confidence and long on self-doubt, while for various reasons life outside my writing was also being complicated and at times painful. Working on *Black Shadow and Bone* was in many ways a refuge from both, but the act of trying to write well will always force your writing self into connecting with the rest of your emotional circuitry, and my circuits were very tired and a bit broken. In making decisions about the novel I had, unconsciously but consistently, chosen the emotionally easier paths. In other words, if one necessary form of writerly courage is being willing to kill your darlings, then another is being willing to give birth to monsters.

Time and again my courage had failed me.

* * *

'Maybe you need to forgive yourself,' Miko said, almost casually.

'I have,' Imogen said, which was true. 'It wasn't my fault that those ... Well, I've even forgiven the journalist involved. Sort of.'

'That isn't what I meant – though of course it wasn't your fault. I meant that maybe you need to forgive yourself for running away.'

It was like being dropped into an icy lake; she was deprived of speech or even thought by the shock of it.

'Courage isn't an infinite resource,' he said. 'You know that as well as I do. Sometimes the bravest men – men who fought for years at the Front, won medals, saved friends' lives or tried and failed to save them, seized guns, held the line ... sometimes, in the end, they simply ran out of courage. Some were allowed to have shell-shock. Some weren't. But what they really needed was time. And forgiveness. And the chance for their courage to grow back ... Your parents – your husband – your aunt – your lover ...' He hoped his voice and hands hadn't betrayed him. 'Each time you've stood the loss, and started again. Then the people you call your family – your chief support – suddenly became mere acquaintances, and you can't see how to put that right – you think you can't face trying to put it right ... But maybe you'd just run out of courage.'

Under his hands he felt her sway, as if she were giddy. She blinked, and then shivered: the kind of shudder that passes through a river when the tide has reached its peak and is turning. And then she blinked again, and met his gaze, and he wondered if he'd ever recover from loving her.

'I'm sorry,' he said. 'I shouldn't have said it. I just hope – I just hope you'll forgive me some day. It didn't – I didn't mean to be quite so brutal. Or so impertinent.'

'You weren't impertinent,' she said, and she took his hand and held the back of it to her cheek for a moment. Now it was his turn to be silenced. 'You weren't impertinent at all. You were right ... And you've got ten minutes to catch that train, and it's half a kilometre down the hill, so you'd better get moving,' she went on, releasing his hand and pointing. 'That way. Now, go!'

He went, fleeing down the street, dodging the shoppers and the idlers, the waiters setting out tables for lunch and the stray dogs sniffing at dustbins, and caught the train to Nice with seconds to spare. And Imogen sat in the most sheltered, sun-struck corner of the café's terrace and looked at the ash tree that Gwen had loved, which was planted when Good Queen Bess was three and her great Protestant cousin Henri IV wasn't even born; which was middle-aged when the Bastille fell; which was elderly when Germany invaded France for the first time, let alone the second; and which still stands now, watching the third invasion. And she thought about courage, and time, and Aunt Claudia, and Ras, and John … and about what happens when protecting yourself from pain means running away from what you most want to keep.

18

Rebuilding

The only way to write is to exist in a state of hope. You have to think that what you want to say is worth saying, and the way you say it deserves hearing: that the whole project, however minor, is, as it were, 'the real thing'. And you have to believe that it will be heard, because it's the hope of being read which creates a bubble inside which you can keep going, and keep trying to make the piece better.[96] The essential difference between an innocent beginner writer and a battle-hardened, experienced writer is that the beginner's *only* perception of their work

---

[96] Of course a finished project is always compromised, imperfect, a failure at the very least in that, by writing *this* book, you haven't produced all the other kinds of book this project might have become.

is from inside the bubble, where the work is the real thing.[97] The experienced writer, on the other hand, deliberately enters that state of hope while equally deliberately ignoring their parallel knowledge that outside the bubble this may not turn out to be the real thing at all, not what they were trying for, not good enough, not saleable enough, not even a little bit of what they hoped it might become. That's why feedback that the writing has failed is a visceral, sometimes excruciating shock: that hope has been assaulted. Feedback which is a version of 'No one will buy this,' is the most explicit destruction of hope that you can have:

No, no one will listen.

No, you can't speak.

No, you will not be heard.

Then, running into the void where your hope once was, come the chattering white mice that Anne Lamott describes in *Bird by Bird*, squeaking relentlessly that you – all right, I – have spent too long on this book already, or have got the wrong project, or should start something else (preferably the next *Wolf Hall*, *Cloud Atlas* or *Fingersmith*), or are a very bad writer, or are very stupid. And since there is always an objective possibility that the mice (for which read your Inner Critic) are right – that you *have* made a misjudgement and should cut your losses – at this stage it's very hard to do as Lamott suggests: pick each imagined mouse gently up, put it back in the imagined soundproof jar on your desk, and put the imaginary lid on.

Should I give up, I wondered as I applied my first anaesthetic by storming up the hill for a long walk, and came home armed with the next two anaesthetics – chocolate and alcohol. Clearly, the 'Darwin thing' wasn't trivial in the least, and if I couldn't get through it *Black Shadow and Bone* wasn't going to be published at all, let alone to take me anywhere, or provide me with cash for the fourth anaesthetic, which is shopping.

---

[97] That's why part of the early stages of learning for most writers must lead to what I call 'learning to be bad': in learning to understand what's possible in writing, you also learn to recognise just how little of what's possible you're actually doing. It's also the reason for the common observation by teachers that the worst students at any subject are the ones who least know it.

So what? Who cared? Face it, half my brain argued, if you never wrote more than a shopping list before you died, even the lovely readers who still email to ask if there will be a sequel to *The Mathematics of Love* will not have their lives altered by more than the single day they didn't spend reading that non-existent sequel.

I cared, of course, and by extension my agent did. But writing is what I do, in the sense of what I am, far more than I am an accident of surname and genes.

So what? Who cared?

I cared because I teach creative writing and mentor writers and, like a sailing instructor, I have to keep my own feedback loops open and live by continuing to get out on the water, year after year. I must keep on re-learning and re-calibrating the relationship of intuition and reason, and the interaction of imagination, craft and technique, as the industry weather changes; as the writerly equivalent of the sand-bars shift; as the kit gets worn or is replaced; as the students want to try new things; as the world warms up.

I cared because I *am* a writer. With each story I create a fictional empire, and in telling a story about that world, and building and peopling it so that my story makes sense and seems real, I make sense of our existence in this world. Without something to write I have no means of making that sense.

I cared, and I was damned if I was going to let this project defeat me.

When the anaesthetics wear off, your first job after a rejection is to re-build the bubble. You must re-find your sense of your own and your writing's worth, the conviction that both deserve to matter and so does this project, and the certainty that you *will* go on.

So I set about rebuilding the bubble.

First I took it as a given, albeit only for now, that I was not very stupid and not a very bad writer, nor a vulgar money-grubber, a shameless show-off, a physician who could not heal herself, a teacher who knew nothing, or a failure. If all that was so, then my decisions along the way which seemed right, but led to a bad result, must have been based on something wrong. I reconsidered the two sides of the story's DNA. Some of my creative DNA comes from my family, and the creative DNA in the family was actually what I was trying to write about, but that same DNA was making it impossible to write. In other words, *the impossibility was built into the project*: the tangle was indeed in the topic. So I wasn't – in this case, at least – just a bad, stupid writer, and a teacher who knew nothing. It was fair enough that I had got it wrong. I could forgive myself. That was the equivalent of getting myself out of the dressing-room and onto the course. I still had to get back on that horse.

The strange thing is that although the bubble depends on hope, which has just been destroyed, the only way to start re-building it is to ignore your battered heart's honest conviction that this project is dead, and make a cold-blooded, unbelieving decision to act as if it's still alive. Back on the horse – with apologies for mixing my metaphors – all *I* needed to do was to find a new plot for the second half which had drive, momentum and thematic coherence. It also needed to demand a darned sight more action from my characters-in-action; their problems needed to be urgent and immediate and their efforts to solve their problems needed to make sure that, as the story continued, more and more, and eventually *everything* that they had or were was at stake.

Also, of course, it needed to be full of Darwins.

Easier said than done, though. Provence is not an earthquake zone, it was the wrong season for forest fires, and although a storm or landslip might do, they were in thematic terms a mere bacillus; in a form of storytelling whose unique quality is access to minds and souls, a purely impersonal, external pressure of that sort will never be as rich as one which is also formed by a character's own psyche. And not only were the Darwins back in England, their minds and souls were real and even discoverable, and so were prescribed – circumscribed – even proscribed.

Still, I had to try.

There was nothing closer to Imogen's soul than photography: how could photographs create danger? What would make a breach between Imogen and the Darwins which which only she can mend, and mend only with a supreme effort? How could I meet the central challenge in writing historical fiction, which is to make a story both absolutely true and evocative to its specific time and place, *and* true and evocative of the nature of human mind, heart and soul, and everything in between? In other words, how could photographs create conflict in a way that grew naturally out of the nature of France and England in 1937?

* * *

Eva swore mildly under her breath, which was hardly surprising given *Je suis partout*'s political position considerably to the right of the *Daily Mail*. She lowered the paper a little to get more of the car's interior light onto a photograph on the page. Imogen looked across, and the image echoed something she knew, in the way a face at a party looks familiar though you're sure you don't know the person, and then they turn out to be, say, the sibling of a friend. The headline was '*Espagne: atrocité infâme au prêtre et aux religieuses*' and the figure in the foreground, laughing, was … John?

'May I see that?' said Imogen through the nausea in her throat.

'The Army probably caught the priests smuggling guns to the fascists,' said Eva cheerfully. 'Pity there was a photographer there. It won't do the Cause much good abroad.' She handed the paper over. Imogen was trembling and clumsy; she tried to switch on her own light and managed to drop the paper, bent to retrieve it, straightened the pages, and took a deep breath.

It wasn't very big, and the printing was even worse than usual, but it was all clear enough: three soldiers in typically hotch-potch Republican uniforms kicking a black-cassocked figure who lay on the ground doubled-up and writhing. The soldiers were laughing, as was John, standing slightly to one side but not, also clearly, doing anything to stop it. To one side, against a church in the background was a line of nuns and not so clear, but clear enough, were the rifles in the hands of the soldiers guarding them.

And clear, too, was the credit: Imperial Photo Agency / Imogen Lefranc.

The car swayed and rushed through the night, and there seemed to be a lump of sickness trying to push up from her stomach into her mouth.

SPAIN: VILE ATROCITY TO PRIESTS AND NUNS

A single photograph from Talavera del Tajo confirms the earlier reports from the Nationalist saviours of Spain, of multiple atrocities carried out by the Jewish-Bolshevik-Masonic conspiracy against holy men and women whose only crime is to wish victory to the forces of righteousness. The priest is not identifiable from the photograph, but is thought to have been Fr Iago Machado, who has not been seen since the incident. The nuns were reported as having been raped the following day, although this has not been confirmed. Our correspondant in Madrid telegraphs that discipline in the Republican army is non-existent, compared to that commanded by Generalísimo Franco, and its aetheist and anti-clerical propaganda is well-known, but if there are other photographs, it would appear that the Communist forces of Republican Spain have successfully suppressed them.

Imogen opened her mouth, and had to clap her hand over it, stomach heaving.

'*Alto!*' called Eva to Miko. 'Stop! Imogen's ill.'

Miko stamped on the brake, the car bucked, swayed, and lurched sideways onto gravel, Imogen grabbed the door handle and dived out, almost fell flat, saved herself at the cost of a jag through her bad wrist, scrabbled herself onto her knees and caught *that* damage, and then was very, very sick into the ditch.

* * *

Googling and reading *Je suis partout* left me feeling soiled, while Paul Preston's magisterial, definitive *The Spanish Holocaust* left me shattered. But Preston did supply me with the reality of the much-referred-to anti-clerical violence, and enough evidence of Nationalist faking of atrocities and faking of the photographs of those atrocities. My idea was not absurd, and nor was my idea that John would not have cared that one of his men had stolen a cassock and dressed up for an exercise in clearing a building. From *John Cornford: a memorial volume* which was put together after his death, and *Towards the Frontier*, Abraham and Stansky's joint biography of John and Julian Bell, I knew that John was born a practical, forceful, energetic man. He was ideologically driven to embrace mainstream, USSR-dominated 1930s Communism with all the ruthlessness of the very young, but he was also a realist about human beings.

Then a furious telegram from Geoffrey: the photograph is in the pro-Blackshirt *Daily Mail*, John's name is in the caption as a notorious revolutionary, the photo credit is Imogen's, and all the Darwins have seen it. Frances is almost destroyed, Gwen and Margaret are on the warpath, Nora is outraged.

If it was *Miko*'s fault that, back in London, Imogen's original photograph went astray and has been used to fake this travesty, this lie which slanders John; if it was Miko's fault that Imogen's reconciliation with the Darwins has just been wrecked ...

Miko, with Imogen lost to him forever, must leave for London and fight to put things right.

* * *

'Pryce,' said the man, picking his tea up and blowing on it. 'Cheers.'

'Michaels. Cheers,' said Miko, doing the same though without the blowing. 'Mind you,' he went on, putting his cup down, 'sometimes I do know exactly what I'm looking for. Wanted a pic of a priest being assaulted. You know: there's so much rumour, but nothing you can prove. And could I find one?'

Pryce shook his head. 'Not so easy. Seems like there's never a snapper there when it happens.'

'If it happens.'

'Oh, it happens. At least, we've got some of them being held at gunpoint. Nuns and stuff.'

'But not the assault? Not a priest?' said Miko, closing himself down into bland, blank stillness.

Pryce hesitated and Miko held his breath. 'Not as such. Not with guns. Not in – well – not in the same photo. But soldiers get to messing about. Dressing up in clothes they find.'

'You mean a composite?'

'It's been known. I wouldn't say any more than that.'

'No, of course not. What your customers do with the prints you supply is their business.'

'I reckon,' said Pryce.

Behind Miko, from a long way back in the café, came the clatter of a chair being pushed back. Pryce appeared to catch the eye of someone, and then Miko felt the someone coming past them: a thin back view, an ordinary, dark, rather worn suit, nothing remarkable except that his boots were military, and so was his walk. As he reached for the door-handle Miko reached for his paper, knocked his cup of tea over and swore. The man whipped round, with his hand on the door; Miko registered the face – narrow too, with bad-tempered muscles round the mouth – then saw that under the jacket the man was wearing a black shirt, military cut, and tie.

'So, if you were to supply me with a couple of prints?' said Miko, tutting busily at his own carelessness. He pulled a fistful of paper napkins from the holder and dropped them onto the puddle of tea.

'The nuns is the agency's. I can withdraw it for you, but you'd need to get that at the counter. And you'd need to credit someone else. Not the agency – it's more than my job's worth. The other one, that'd be a special arrangement.'

'Right you are,' said Miko, taking out his wallet and looking round for the waitress. 'And what's the best way to do that? Make the special arrangement?'

'I take over the counter at one o'clock, while the others have their dinner. Old Tortoise doesn't always go out, but he wouldn't know what's happening if Charlie Chaplin turned up and did a tap dance. Come in then.'

'And these two – they make a good composite?' Miko glanced at the bill and put half a crown down on it; the waitress was going to have to clean up the tea-sodden napkins, after all. Then he put a ten shilling note on the table a little further towards Pryce. 'As if that might be the first half?' He began to fold up his newspaper.

'Oh, yes,' said Pryce, getting up, and palming the note as he did so. 'They go together lovely. I've seen it. They're both very good prints, the originals. You'd never know, once it's been screened and printed.'

19

Finishing

By now it was June 2013, and although of course I'd long given up the idea of this novel being about the First World War, the 2016 anniversary of the Spanish Civil War was nicely timed, if I could just get the damn novel right and – touch wood – sold. By now the third complete re-build and re-write of *Black Shadow and Bone* was fighting for its space in the lumpy mixture of one-off and recurring paid work that freelance writers know so well. Unless it's under contract – and sometimes when it is – our real writing falls so easily and disastrously into the category of 'important but not quite as urgent as the stuff which needs to be returned tomorrow.'

My freelance diary was bulging. I was teaching for the Open University from October to June, which, as with all universities' hourly-paid teaching and lecturing contracts, meant a workless and payless three months over the summer. Payless, but not carefree: those months were routinely enlivened by legally necessary emails warning us that they might not have a job for us come October. So I never dared pass up other work when it came along, and even that didn't add up to quite enough, so I was thrilled to be offered a Royal Literary Fund Fellowship, spending two days a week up the road at Goldsmiths in New Cross. RLF Fellows work one-to-one on academic writing with students and staff in all disciplines, at all levels. It was heaven: all those glorious subjects; all that satisfying, crunchy thinking about how to think and how to communicate; all those worried students whose problems you can usually so easily help with. But it was a big bite out of my working week.

On the domestic front I had one child graduating from university and embarking on the hunt for his first proper job, and the other child about to go up to university and embark on her first living away from home. I also had a nasty and growing suspicion that my house had serious subsidence; I used to lie in bed at night, trying not to look at the crack in the ceiling, and trying not to think about how I'd manage if, come October, the Open University didn't have enough students to employ me.

Still, as for all the many writers who teach, the summer was the time when I could, rather more, call my soul and my time my own, and of course I used the time on the thing closest to my soul, which was finishing *Black Shadow and Bone*. I was due at the Arvon Foundation's Lumb Bank centre on 5th August, to join Manda Scott in teaching a residential course on Writing Historical Fiction, and when I got back I was going to be up to my neck in preparation for the madness that is September and the writing conference season. I was determined see the novel through all the normal stages before I went north, and get it off my desk and onto Catriona's.

What needed doing wasn't so different from any novel, not really ...

just, because of the uneasy relationship between the real people and the characters, worse. The Still-To-Do list had seventeen entries on it: everything from 'finish dissassemble-and-reconstruct' to 'check all driving times for 1937 roads/cars' and 'get in touch with Society of Authors re John's work epigraphs – ?out of copyright.'

Was each sentence fulfiling at least two jobs in this story? Did it contribute not just to the setting-out of the 'causally related chain of events' but to character, theme, ideas and story? Was that contribution made by sound, as well as sense? If not, should it be cut, or replaced, or changed and enriched? Did every paragraph, scene and chapter say the right thing in the right way? Right for the voice, the moment, the theme, the structure, the period? Was it expressive, elegant, punchy or gentle, according to need? Was it neither clichéd, nor awkward, nor incorrect – unless it was meant to be? Did it move the story forward without short-changing the moment?

This micro-scrutiny must all happen without you losing your sense of the macro needs of the story, even when the immersion in this scene, paragraph, sentence, sometimes feels more like drowning. It's not easy, but it's the business-as-usual of turning the novel you *thought* you'd written into the novel that will actually work on the reader as you want it to. But this novel was different. Here I was not only the director, playwright and stage-manager of this act of storytelling; putting the family out there was frighteningly close to being out there on stage myself. For the first time ever I really understood – at the unconscious, intuitive level – how Julia Wedgwood must have felt. If all revising is like immersion, revising *Black Shadow and Bone* was like being immersed in some substance with a different viscosity: not just the pressure, but the colour and transmission of light were different, swimming was infinitely harder work, and none of my usual intuitions and judgements could really be trusted.

Julia had chosen to be published anonymously. But with this project, of all projects, how could I hide?

And, of course, in this 'final draft' mode, I was (re)reading and (re)writing by the light of the imagined future: the book being read and sold and reviewed. That light is always harsh, but it's also very slanted, and now it showed up everything I felt most insecure about. Where I'd filled in between the facts, would it convince those who knew more than I did about the real equivalents? Where I'd departed from the facts, could I justify doing so? Had I been too vulgar? Too un-historical? Too trivial about the science, too solemn about the art? Too rose-coloured, too modern, too sentimental, too archaic, too anachronistic, too gloomy? Would readers judge the family in judging my novel? Would the family feel judged by me, or by the readers? Was I letting historical truth down in picking my way through the available period prejudices so that my likeable characters tended to have the more likeable ones? Was I letting the egalitarian side down because most of the major characters were officers and employers, not other ranks, servants and workers? Had I let in anything which would compromise my non-aligned status in the wars of science vs religion, or give the fundamentalist Christians or the fundamentalist atheists ammunition?

Time and again I had said to my RLF students that the basic skill of a scholar, an academic, a lawyer, a diplomat or a teacher is to assemble facts into a chain of logic which is also a chain of reason and reasoning, and which will persuade others that your conclusion is true. Fiction is trying to do much the same: assembling imagined events and characters in a way which persuades the reader to read *as if* it's true. At heart, the skill of any writing is *to persuade*: to win the argument.

Had I told this story in a way which would persuade the reader to let what John Gardner calls the 'fictional dream' take them over? Would it make enough magic, cast enough of a spell, that any reader's experience would refute, absolutely, the charge that I'd only written this because it would sell?

I didn't know – I couldn't tell.

On and on I sat, push-push-pushing to get it done, with only the obligatory stop for the daily walk and the minimum necessary housekeeping. I ached from sitting, day after hour after week, holding my self open to the flap of a slack sentence, the twinge of not-quite-right, the lurch and clunk and creak of plot or character, the cold updraught from a crack opening in the plot ... I felt each alarm signal, and tried each time to discern if it was a good and healthy twinge to be examined and acted on, or merely the neurotic jumping-at-shadows of a writer who can no longer differentiate reality from neuropathy.

Like someone floating in a life-raft in the Pacific, I could still tell night from day and up from down, but had lost all sense of the shape and structure of normal life, of normal storytelling, of how this would read to someone who'd never read it before. All I knew was that I seemed to have run out of To-Do lists, and all I could do was call it finished, and send it to Catriona.

BLACK SHADOW AND BONE

Emma Darwin

... when the next crisis that will shake the whole system explodes, whether it is war crisis, economic crisis, or political crisis, the relatively quiet and petty developments of these pre-war, pre-crisis years will emerge in their real significance.

– John Cornford, 'Communism in the Universities'

But when they shelled the other end of the village
And the streets were choked with dust
Women came screaming out of the crumbling houses,
Clutched under one arm the naked rump of an infant.
I thought: how ugly fear is.

– John Cornford, 'A Letter from Aragon'

19T   20-11-14   1

20

The End

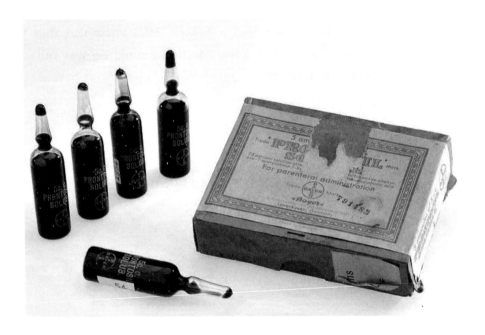

Catriona emailed: it had arrived safely, but no fewer than ten of her authors had chosen the last few weeks to send in manuscripts.[98] She'd get to mine as soon as she could, but it might be a little time.

You always think you want an answer as quickly as possible, but in a funny way this kind of delay is a relief. The Waiting To Hear is hell when every email, every phone-call, in the old days every post, might bring news of … well just possibly triumph, perhaps hope renewed, very possibly disaster … or, quite often, 'Just warning you that, sorry, so-and-so hasn't got back to me yet.' It's a lesser hell, merely Purgatory, to have a *terminus post quem*: to know that you won't hear until after

---

[98] What did I say about writers using the summer to finish their book?

a certain or even approximate date. Then half of your mind – half your heart, let's be honest – is a bit easier. It's possible to get on with other things, and the busier the better. In my case those other things were one bestselling author-friend, one visiting author and sixteen aspiring writers, all eating, drinking, talking, writing and probably sleeping historical fiction in a handsome old house in West Yorkshire that once belonged to Ted Hughes.

On an Arvon course the sixteen-hour days are stuffed full: the morning is a round-table workshop, the afternoon is packed with intense one-to-one sessions with writers whose hearts and minds are stapled to *their* pages, the evenings are full of readings, and even the meals are fun but never off duty, because as a tutor you're listening, talking, being interested, being informative, being encouraging, being realistic, being useful. When you're finally back in the tutor's cottage (at Lumb Bank, deliciously, it's the far side of a door-in-the-garden-wall straight out of any number of your favourite children's classics) you're simultaneously exhausted and wide awake, and a glass of wine will help you sleep. Two, if I'm honest.

I'm telling stories.

The course is over, and I arrive home late on Saturday evening, having broken the five-hour drive with a floating, spaced-out afternoon at the very beautiful Hepworth gallery in Wakefield. I want nothing except a long, hot bath and a long, deep sleep … but find that my otherwise perfectly civilised neighbours are having one of their not-rare-enough parties: thumping music through every possible wall, karaoke, and a storm of shrieky chatter in the garden just below my bedroom window.

I stay up as late as I can bear, trying not to think that Catriona might just possibly be reading the novel.

'No of course not, you idiot,' I say firmly to myself.

But the writer's hope of Hearing Something is like one of those blow-up plastic clowns with a round, weighted bottom: after every punch from common sense, it bobs back up and says, 'But maybe she's changed her schedule. Didn't she say she usually does her reading on

Fridays? Maybe everything else she has on her desk has gone up in flames. Maybe she'll email about *Black Shadow and Bone* on Monday.'

At 1am I go next door and ask them to turn the music down. Whoever answers the door says they will. I go to bed and lie there, trying not to think that *Black Shadow and Bone* might sell a million, or might not sell to a publisher at all.

At 2am I go next door again and ask them to turn the music down. Whoever answers the door fetches my neighbour herself, who says they will. I go back to bed and lie there, trying to not to think that most of my future rests on whether Catriona thinks she can sell *Black Shadow and Bone*.

At 2.30am I start trying to work out if sleep is more likely to come if I go on lying there breathing and blank-minding, or if I get up, put on a dressing gown, and go out into the cold night to bang on next door's door again.

At 3am the music stops, though the shrieky chatter doesn't. At some point I do fall asleep, wake late, and spend Sunday very, very slowly doing the wash, unwinding, talking to the children (who aren't children these days), and trying to forget all over again that Catriona's reading *Black Shadow and Bone*. Especially since of course she certainly isn't, not yet. No, she isn't.

I spend Monday wading through post, email and overdue admin, and prepping what I need to do for the big York Festival of Writing in three weeks' time (one mini-course, three workshops, two panels, two evening events, probably a last-minute chairing of something, eighteen ten-minute one-to-ones at 3,000 words apiece for me to read beforehand ...) . The Open University still can't confirm whether there will be a job for me in six week's time so I'm also trawling for other part-time teaching contracts which aren't so far away or so appallingly paid that, effectively, I am paying them to work there. And all the while I'm trying not to think that Catriona is ...

I get up from my desk and feel a pain in the exact, deep middle of my chest. It's no worse than the usual dyspeptic result of a week of too much adrenalin plus too much coffee, alcohol and rich food, but it isn't, in some indefinable way, quite the same.

My father and grandfather both died of heart attacks in their early sixties. I am forty-nine. I know (from where? Years of *Cosmopolitan* and Woman's Hour and *Good Housekeeping*, probably) that heart attacks in women usually present more diffusely, less painfully, more missably, than they usually do in men. And I know that although before the menopause heart attacks are less common in women than in men, they are very, very definitely not rare.

I do some googling. Considered on a scale of one to childbirth the pain is still trivial, but it is sharper. I feel a bit sick, a bit faint, a bit unpleasantly short of breath. It does fit. Unless of course I'm just noticing because now I'm noticing.

There's a new pain in my arms: the triceps and biceps. The parts where you ache when you miss your baby. Everything fits.

A long way ahead, at the far end of this rising curve, is dying.

I go carefully downstairs, ask my daughter to phone an ambulance, and sit down on the foot of the stairs to wait.

* * *

Eva was lying, eyes closed, her face slack, colourless, oily with sweat, her breathing shallow and hoarse. On the table was an open cardboard box, full of smaller boxes. One small box was open and Dr Dufay had an ampoule in his hand, turning it in the light to check what was written, holding it as carefully as if he were a priest holding a crystal reliquary. Nurse Becquerel swabbed the outside of Eva's arm. It was like a dream, it seemed, as it hadn't been for all the hundreds of times – perhaps thousands of times – in the Great War that Imogen had seen the quick, grave little ceremony: the pool of yellow light, the fitting of the needle, the snap of the glass at the ampoule neck. Then Dr Dufay drew up the drug, and it was as thick and dark-red and generous as if it were indeed some medieval charlatan's True Blood of Christ. Everything was quiet; the black silence of the night outside was muffling the life in here so that the lights were like weak candles at Tenebrae ... Dr Dufay sent a drop up into the air, in science to get rid of any bubbles but also a libation to a god – not Morpheus, this time ... they were all some celluloid dream, mere light and sound, flickering in the darkened hall, and somewhere flew a sparrow – a lark – an eagle ... and Eva's arm was so thin, the veins inky scribbles on old paper. Then Dr Dufay slid the needle in under the skin, and began to press the plunger.

...

Most creatures die in the early hours of the morning, slipping away into the cold and the quiet. Imogen knew it: had seen it happen often and often in the War. Aunt Claudia, too, had finally left her just as daylight began to creep into the room. Miko knew it too, and after the first joy of recognition – the first homecoming – the first words to each other as lovers though they'd done no more, yet, than kiss ... after that, it would have been wrong to go on claiming their happiness. It was just there, within them and between them: no more but no less absolute than Eva's dying. Imogen fetched another chair, and she and Miko sat side by side, holding Eva's hand, not talking much, doing almost nothing, Imogen even crying a little, once or twice.

But at a quarter to four Eva was still breathing.

* * *

God bless the National Health Service and all who sail in her. But it helps them to help you, as they say, if you arrange to suffer your serious cardiac event at half-past four on a Monday afternoon, three miles from a major teaching hospital. The car-borne paramedics arrived in six minutes, the ambulance in eight, and I was trundled straight past A&E and into the cardiac catheter lab for a good look.

Somewhere along the way it stopped hurting; I remember thinking that if the GTN spray which made the pain go away like magic and made you feel agreeably spacey with it, was glyceryl-trinitrate, was that the same as toughs in cowboy thrillers chewing cordite?

The good look was done by a good-looking Australian consultant; by six-thirty he was saying, 'It's not unknown, but it is very rare.'

I had suffered a spontaneous coronary artery dissection: the inner lining of one of my coronary arteries had, at some point in the previous few days, acquired a tear, which in trying to mend itself had formed a swelling, which got big enough to start blocking the artery. No one's quite sure what makes it happen, but 80% of cases happen in women, mostly my age or younger, and it often happens in combination with high blood pressure: mine had been at the 'keep an eye on it' level for some time. The treatment for a SCAD is usually to leave it alone, thin your blood, lower your blood pressure, steady your heart-rate, get you off anything remotely resembling HRT,[99] park you in a High Dependency Cardiac Ward with half a dozen wires monitoring every vital sign for a few days' observation, and let the body get on with healing itself.

I wasn't allowed to drive for a month, but other than that it was no worse – better, in some ways – than getting over a major operation, although it helped that the thrice-blessed NHS had a really good, joined-up programme of cardiac rehabilitation and support. That was a strange club to find myself belonging to, but I daresay the man no older than me who ran marathons before his quadruple bypass, and had every intention of running more now he'd had it, felt the same. He was interesting to talk to, and rather fanciable in that lean, runner's way, but everyone in a big hospital is a ship which is passing in the night. Gradually, I got my physical confidence back, and within a month I had, very slowly, set off on the steepest of my repertoire of constitutionals, and got home to tell the tale.

Not that I did tell the tale, beyond family and close friends, to anyone I could help. I had to pull out of the York Festival of Writing, and took up the Open University's offer of a year's unpaid leave for anyone who wanted it, but still I didn't tell anyone I didn't have to. For a start there was the self-employed person's insecurity: who would book me to teach a workshop if they thought I might collapse on them?

But it went deeper than that, I think. Winnicot is right, dammit, about the tensions that drive artists: on the one hand I'm a story-teller,

---

[99] Including 'natural' remedies like red clover, which I had been taking.

an ex-wannabe-actress, a teacher and a performer, and I'm by no means immune to the egotistical thrill of telling a story – and not even lies – that makes them gasp and stretch their eyes. But I write novels, not scripts for a collaborative medium, because I need to be in control of my story and to control, as far as is possible, my audience's reactions to it. I didn't – *oh*! how I didn't – want to see myself labelled by people's minds, which is to say, by my own mind, as a member of 'that' club: a somehow compromised life.

It got better as I had tests and MRI scans, and it was clear that I'd got away – most unusually – with absolutely no damage, and there were no signs of any other bits of me being likely to spring another such excitement. What's more, the older I get, the less likely it is to happen again. In other words I wasn't, actually, a member of 'that' club at all.

It got better to the point where I'm writing this book.

It was a couple of months later that Catriona said she didn't think she could sell the novel. 'It's better, but it still isn't working,' she went on. 'I think the problem is that it's had such a complicated genesis. I've read it so often, but I gave it to a colleague to read as well, and they agreed.'

I never look at my own writing just to read it: I only open the file when I'm planning to do some work. And if possible I set it aside completely when I'm waiting for feedback or a verdict, so that when I get it I'm coming back to the text with as fresh an eye as I can, ready to triage the feedback into the basic categories: *accept, adapt, or ignore.* So it was nearly four very peculiar months since I'd last looked at *Black Shadow and Bone.*

Now I did, though it's not easy to evoke what Catriona and I both recognised. With this latest version I had set out to solve the problems of the previous versions, and almost all of my solutions still looked as if I had made the right choice about what to keep, and what to change. Yet it added up to something profoundly unsatisfactory.

Explaining *how* it got like that is easier, not least because for this Idea I happen to have the perfect Thing. Some years ago I had to re-do my kitchen. The new units were all going to be on the other side of the room, the floor tiles were to go, and the bare floorboards would be sanded and sealed. Then the builder came to me. 'The thing is,' he said, 'I've got those tiles up and it's a mess under there. It's always been the kitchen, since Victorian times. They've had the floor up goodness knows how often, with the water and the drain, and the gas and the electricity. There's hardly a whole floorboard in the room, and some have been cut in four places. We'll need at least three new boards which won't match, and it's going to be like a jigsaw puzzle. Take us all day, so it'll cost you a fortune in our time, and it'll still look rubbish at the end. I wouldn't take any pride in it.' I saw what he meant, too, and horribly well. 'Whereas if you can give me £200,' he went on, 'I can nip down the builder's merchants, get you a room's-worth of brand new floorboards, have them down in a couple of hours, and it'll look great.' And I did, he did, and it did.

I'd done with the novel what the builder had known he must not do with my kitchen floor. Yes, thanks to my cutting, patching, mending and reworking, things fitted together adequately, the tensions were just about enough, each event lead to the next with basic logic, the stakes rose nicely, and the final crisis was, at last, a proper crisis. But none of it happened with a true, real, exciting unfolding and increasing, a great, coherent forward sweep, the arc of a story which had been conceived in one piece from the beginning to the end.

It had cost me a fortune in time, not to mention health, and I couldn't take any pride in it.

I asked a writer-editor friend I trusted to read it and tell me what she thought, and paid her as author friends have paid me to do the same for them, because we know better than anyone the value of a knowledgeable, professional reader. Then we met, and talked through her list of comments and what I might do about them. Could I make John be killed helping Imogen escape? No – the geography didn't fit. Could I make Eva be having John's baby? No – the history didn't fit. Could I make Imogen younger, and in love with John? No – the generations didn't fit.

No. None of it was possible without distorting the family's real story beyond the point of absurdity.

I was back, creatively speaking, at the beginning. I could *either* keep to the real historical facts and sell the novel as a novel of my family, *or* I could defy the real historical facts and the principle of dealing 'honestly and responsibly' with the reader, and lose all pretence that this was really about my family except in that oh-so-saleable name. And, even if I did brazen out the shame of being thought to have cashed in, wouldn't I just be wrenching out the nails yet again, ignoring the holes, sawing through yet more floorboards, and getting the floor up for the fourth time?

And yet there *were* riches there, my friend said: themes, characters, settings, ideas. It was as if somewhere, in some kind of novelistic parallel universe, there was a story which had the same smell and feel as this one but *did* work.

I went home and let things stew until I thought I could sense a new story. I imagined the big, crucial scenes; I worked out the new plot; I thought about what research it might need. And, as night follows day, I started to come up, yet again, against the things which I couldn't bloody do. Again, and *again*, and <u>*again*</u>.

So, exactly three years after I'd started *Black Shadow and Bone*, I opened a brand-new project in Scrivener and, as if I were starting a new novel, began to plan the entirely fictional story of a photographer who has lost everything. I gave nothing from the old novel an automatic job in the new one, let alone any special status. Every place, real or invented, every character, every event made-up or taken from life, had to audition for its right to rise into Tremain's 'anarchic, gift-conjuring' zone in my creative mind, where 'reimagining implies a measure of forgetting'.

Black Shadow and Bone had become pure fiction.

I had won back my sovereign land.

* * *

PART ONE
Philip

… when the next crisis that will shake the whole system explodes,
whether it is war crisis, economic crisis, or political crisis, the
relatively quiet and petty developments of these pre-war, pre-
crisis years will emerge in their real significance.

— John Cornford, 'Communism in the Universities'

But when they shelled the other end of the village
And the streets were choked with dust
Women came screaming out of the crumbling houses,
Clutched under one arm the naked rump of an infant.
I thought: how ugly fear is.

— John Cornford, 'A Letter from Aragon'

In those days you could lie on hot sand, wherever you liked, whenever you liked, and hear nothing but the sea slipping in and out ten yards beyond your bare toes. In those days you could prop yourself up on your elbows and see nothing but the oval sky fitting over the sea and the mountains, the edge of infinity precision-milled where it meets the earth. In those days you could have eaten your fill of little tarts sweet with buttery onions and gruyère and curls of that fine, soft ham that English grocers do not sell, and now be leaning back and listening to tales of the new world which had just begun: the new world beyond the mountains on your right hand, in which real, ordinary people had taken control of factories, mines, farms, governments, armies … taken control of everything which once controlled them.

In those days, before the present emergency, we had lost the habit of dreading what would happen to our young men.

AFTERWORD

A year or so later, I sold a book before I'd even written it, when I was commissioned by John Murray Learning to write *Get Started in Writing Historical Fiction* for their Teach Yourself imprint. Round about the same time, the Royal Literary Fund offered me a one-year contract to set up a new Fellowship at the Royal College of Music, and with that much work in prospect I resigned from the Open University and set up my own editing and mentoring service, the Itch of Writing Studio.

However, although I'd made my peace with my failure to write a novel about my family, my desire to write about the family in some form was by no means laid to rest. That, I realised looking back, was one of the things which had so confused my normal creative common-sense that I kept going for much longer than was wise: the stuffs of the family are genuinely interesting to anyone who wants, as I did, to evoke and explore human creativity. So every time I'd wondered whether to throw the family out of the novel, my reluctance hadn't just been because it would make it harder to sell, it was a genuine creative reluctance too: I was hating trying to write a novel about them, but I wasn't hating writing about them. In fact, I *wanted* to write about them.

But I am a novelist.

And yet, I realised as I circled round my situation yet again, so many of my problems with *Black Shadow and Bone* had been caused by the fact that a novel *is* fiction. None of what a novel describes actually happened (if everything did, then it's not a novel), but though readers know that, they want to read *as if* it all did, so the novelist's craft lies in keeping at least fifty percent of the reader's consciousness inside the frame and willing, for now, to read the story for true. To do that we use all sorts of writerly conjuring tricks, sleight-of-hand and smoke-and-mirrors: indeed, I'd started the Itch of Writing Studio to help other writers become better conjurers. But for *Black Shadow and Bone*, a vast amount of my material was intractably 'real': corporeal and non-negotiable. If a novel is a conjuring trick, then there were weeks and months when writing this novel had been like trying to saw the pretty lady in half without being allowed to build a magic box to put her in, nor to employ assistants to distract the audience's eye with whirling capes and thunder-flashes. All I seemed to be allowed to use, to create my illusion, was a saw and a pretty lady, while the audience waited restively to be astonished.

Drawing on my memories of my original Drama degree, I tried a radio play and then a stage play, but within twenty pages or so I was frustrated by my own lack of experience and skill in stagecraft, as a swimmer will find if she takes to a boat: the water and currents may be the same, but it's not her spine and limbs which she works with now, but a rudder and sails. I'd spent years learning to write novels, and I still did it – still do it – so badly so much of the time; I had everything to learn about dramatic writing and, given how tangled I was in the topic, this story was not the stuff to start learning it on.

Thanks to the Open University, I'd had to teach and therefore think a lot about life-writing, as a relatively new sub-species of what now gets called creative non-fiction. Life-writing inhabits the liminal zone between history-writing, (auto)biography, (auto)biographical fiction, and pure fiction, so switching to it from fiction is more like switching from swimming on the surface to, say, scuba-diving. What's more, as species do in liminal zones, life-writing has evolved fast since books like Richard Holmes's *Footsteps* were first published: it's still evolving and some of the books I'd most enjoyed recently were that kind of book. Maybe what I should have been writing all along was *A History of My Family in 100 Objects*. Or how about *The Plate with Wedgwood Eyes*? Or *The Suspicions of Mrs Darwin*?

But a project of that sort would take in half a dozen or more disciplines, almost none of them mine and not a few whose specialists were my own cousins. In fiction, the goal of research – 'free-search' – is to get the right stuffs, and enough of them, to write the best version of your novel. As long as the process results in that best version, what and how you gather the stuffs is up to you. In non-fiction, I wouldn't have the novelist's sovereignty over how she works in her world, but only the historian's *permis de séjour* and *permis de travail* in each one of those half-dozen fields; break their rules and they're free to deport you. My research would need to be bomb-proof and so would the marshalling, analysing and writing of it, if I were to win the damn argument with each and every one of those specialists. I doubted whether I could do research to that depth, and write it up to that impregnability, even if I'd wanted to. And, despite my own PhD and my abiding interest in scholarship and academic writing, I really, really didn't want to.

Books do sometimes get written about writing books, of course: non-fiction about fiction. Umberto Eco wrote a fascinating essay called 'Reflections on *The Name of the Rose*', which I'd used in my PhD, but the reflecting I'd be doing was that of a broken mirror. There was Kate Grenville's *Searching for the Secret River* but mine would be more like *Falling Out Of the Public Family Tree*. There was Geoff Dyer's *Out of Sheer Rage*, which is, ostensibly, about failing to write about D. H. Lawrence, but mine would be more like *Out of Sheer Embarrassment*. And there was Nicholson Baker's *U & I*, about failing to write about

John Updike, but mine was a case of *So Many of Them & What about Me?*

Things began to coalesce.

I've been known to say that I started writing fiction because it was the only respectable excuse I could find for ignoring the washing up. So, one afternoon when I should have been doing something else – very possibly the washing up – I got in the car and drove out through the south-eastern dribbles of London towards Kent: Crystal Palace, Penge, Beckenham, Hayes, Keston, make for Biggin Hill but turn left before you go past the Spitfires, and instead take the lane which scoops and dips and rises again towards the village of Downe. Past the *Queen's Head* and the *George & Dragon*, right at St Mary Magdalene where Emma is tucked in among the other graves along with Charles' brother Erasmus, until you're running out of the village on the Luxted Road towards Down House.

It was a weekday in June: softly sunny, and very warm, and the house had enough visitors to sound and feel inhabited, but not so many as to seem invaded. The man at the ticket desk noticed the name on my English Heritage membership card and asked me; I smiled and said, 'Yes, actually'.

I bought coffee and cake in the little tea-room that was once the kitchen, and sat outside in the sun to eat it.

I pottered through the house, looking at the pictures, the memorabilia, the billiard table, the china and the books, and remembered the summer that Down House mounted an exhibition about Emma herself; how the photographer undid the barrier so he could sit me at Emma's piano; how the exhibition's curator helped me to put on a bracelet made of Emma's hair; how the archivist took me upstairs to the archive to show me some of the photographs, books and letters in their cream-coloured, archival, acid-free, made-to-measure boxes.

I strolled round the Sandwalk, and paused for a moment in Charles' sentry-box at the far end, where he could sit out of the winds that blow cold across this chalky downland.

I wandered slowly round the walled garden, the potting sheds and the greenhouses, making photographs because photographs are my way of really noticing things: my way of being a scientist and a poet, when I am neither.

I walked back and stood on the lawn in the sun, looking at the famous view of the house which, appropriately it always seems to me, is the back of it. What the world knows of Down isn't the front, the façade for show, which can be seen from a car or a carriage or the back of a horse. It's the private, family face: the face which watches over a garden which was both the laboratory of a genius, and the playground of his children and grandchildren. And I asked if he'd mind if this particular one of his great-great-grandchildren wrote a book about his family, seen through the lens of her failure to write a novel about them.

He didn't seem to.

I think

Case must be that one generation then should be as many living as now. To do this & to have many species in same genus (as is) requires extinction.

Thus between A & B. immens[e] gap of relation. C & B. the finest gradation, B & D rather greater distinction. Thus genera would be formed. — bearing relation

ACKNOWLEDGEMENTS

To owe *two* books-worth of thanks and acknowledgements might look like carelessness, except that it's a pleasure finally to be able to thank so many people who have helped me along this particularly convoluted road to the bookshop shelf and e-reader menu.

My agent Joanna Swainson and my publisher Robert Peett at Holland House Books are the ones without whom *This is Not a Book About Charles Darwin* would not be a book at all. Francis Spufford, Andrew Wille, Jenn Ashworth, Maura Dooley and Blake Morrison gave golden advice, encouragement, feedback and support, while Francis Cleverdon did so from the bookseller's angle and Hannah Corbett from the publicist's.

I might never have started exploring creative thinking in my family without invitations to lecture from Professor Mark Pallen of the University of Birmingham, Professor Antonio Lazcano of UNAM, Dr Leonor Perez-Martinez of the Instituto de Biotecnologia UNAM, and Gabrielle Gale for the National Trust at Leith Hill Place, so very many thanks to them, and to Writers' Workshop, now Jericho Writers, for asking me to give workshops on Life Writing, which allowed me to work many things out that I needed to understand.

In the family, my sisters Carola and Sophy Darwin, and my cousin Andrew Darwin, seemed to think it was all right to write about the family, Sophy and Carola read the final draft to confirm it was still all right, Nicola LeFanu gave thoughtful suggestions, Antony Wedgwood helped with Julia, and William Pryor gave permission to use crucial pictures. Lucy Lead at the Wedgwood Museum, and Johanna Ward at the Cambridge University Library, went to great trouble to help with many of the illustrations.

Writer friends Debi Alper, Jenn Ashworth, Sarah Bakewell, Linda

✗ Buckley-Archer, Julie Cohen, Jill Dawson, Essie Fox, Elizabeth Fremantle, Caroline Green, Kellie Jackson, Roger Morris, Leila Rasheed, Susannah Rickards, Imogen Robertson and Ruth Warburton, as well as all the other Book Frisbees and Loungers, have for years been a source of both shrewd advice and endless, patient support, while Louise Cole made healing sense of my Rule Three.

My sister Sophy, Judith Murray, Gillian Stern, Clare Alexander, the Daily Breaders and the WriteWorders did their best to help me make *Black Shadow and Bone* work, and it's not their fault it didn't. The National Media Museum (as it then was) was efficient and helpful with Autochromes, and the National Railway Museum steered me towards the Night Ferry.

I owe a continuing professional debt to the Society of Authors and the London Library, and it is entirely possible that neither book would have happened at all without the support that the Royal Literary Fund gives so superbly to working writers as well as those fallen on hard times.

And, as always, thank you to Hugh Blackstaffe and Lucie Blackstaffe for being there, for putting up with my not being there, and for agreeing that it is quite fun, on the whole, to owe a small percentage of one's genome to Charles and Emma Darwin.

and the Ego edited by Clare Boylan; Picador for 'Yonder' in *A Plea for Eros* by Siri Hustvedt; *Publishing News*; *Punch;* the Virginia Woolf Estate and Random House Group for *The Letters of Virginia Woolf.*

List of illustrations:

Raverat (© The Raverat Archive); Erasmus Darwin obituary notice from The Times

ELEVEN: John - Rupert John Cornford (World History Archive / Alamy Stock Photo); Partido Obrero de Unificación Marxista poster, 1936

TWELVE: 1937 Gerda Taro (public domain); Cover of The Ayes Have It, by A. P. Herbert (author's collection).

THIRTEEN: On the Night Ferry – The New Train Ferry poster c.1938; Geoffrey Keynes, by G. Shaw (Wellcome Images)

FOURTEEN: In the Mountains - Cirque du Gavarnie, Hautes-Pyrénées, France (photograph author's own); la Brèche de Roland, Hautes-Pyrénées, France, 19th century engraving (Artokoloro Quint Lox Limited / Alamy Stock Photo)

FIFTEEN: Camp Vernet – Photograph of entrance to the camp; Republican soldiers rest for food, during the Spanish Civil War (World History Archive / Alamy Stock Photo)

SIXTEEN: Vence – Tourrettes-sur-Loup, Alpes-Maritime, France (photograph author's own); Air France timetable, 1937

SEVENTEEN: The Verdict on Version Two – Refugees, a linocut by Gwen Raverat; le frêne de Vence, postcard

EIGHTEEN: Rebuilding – Map of French Riviera from Fréjus to Menton, 1913; Je Suis Partout, newspaper masthead

NINETEEN: Finishing – Author's note to Black Shadow and Bone; manuscript title page, Black Shadow and Bone

TWENTY: The End – Box of five ampoules of Prontosil, Germany, 1936-1940 (Wellcome Image)

AFTERWORD – Exterior of Down House (© Historic England Archive)